Praise for John Hailman and *Thomas Jefferson on Wine*

"A fascinating look at our third president and the evolution of his life-long love of wine."
　Dorothy Gaiter and John Brecher
　Wall Street Journal

"Hailman has done an exhaustive study and provided a valuable window into who Jefferson really was."
　Mitch Frank
　Wine Spectator

"Hailman certainly knows his wines."
　Jay McInerney
　New York Times Book Review

"If you like both Jefferson and wine, you should read this book twice."
　Washington Times

"With abundant wit and erudition, Hailman illuminates an indispensable ingredient to the making of Jefferson the public and private man. It should delight all who are interested in Jefferson and all who are interested in wine."
　Annette Gordon-Reed
　Author of *Thomas Jefferson and Sally Hemings* and Pulitzer Prize Winner for *The Hemingses of Monticello*

"Dazzling . . . Hailman brings Jefferson to life for modern Americans through the unique prism of wine. A must-have for every wine lover."
　Robin Kelley O'Connor, Bordeaux Wine Bureau
　President, Society of Wine Educators

"John Hailman's biography tells our third president's life story through his adventures as oenophile and gastronome . . ."
　Bon Appetit

"Hailman delves deep into the gastronomic passions of one of our country's most important historical figures and presents a side of Jefferson's personality rarely explored."
    Cooking Light

"A fascinating exploration of the early days of the modern global wine trade . . . Hailman has produced an admirable work portraying Jefferson in vivid complexity while also illuminating the joys and frustrations of the eighteenth-century wine lover."
    Mathew Reid
    Gastronomica: The Journal of Food and Culture

"[An] eighteenth-century gastronomic tour with wine as a central theme . . . If your idea of a good evening is sitting down with a Simon Schama history programme on BBC with a bottle of claret, this is the book for you."
    Decanter Magazine, London

"Fascinating . . . exhaustively researched and entertaining."
    Steven Malanga
    City Journal

"John Hailman . . . brings out the most epicurean side of one of the most celebrated of francophiles."
    David Ross
    Le Figaro International, Paris

The Search for Good Wine

THE SEARCH FOR
Good
Wine

From the Founding Fathers
to the Modern Table

John Hailman

UNIVERSITY PRESS OF MISSISSIPPI   JACKSON

www.upress.state.ms.us

The University Press of Mississippi is a member
of the Association of American University Presses.

Copyright © 2014 by University Press of Mississippi
Manufactured in the United States of America

First printing 2014

Library of Congress Cataloging-in-Publication Data

Hailman, John R., 1942– author.
 The search for good wine : from the founding fathers to the modern table / John
Hailman.
    pages cm
  Includes bibliographical references and index.
  ISBN 978-1-62846-136-7 (cloth : alk. paper)—ISBN 978-1-62846-137-4 (ebook)
  1. Wine and wine making—History. I. Title.
  TP549.H35 2014
  663.2—dc23

                              2014013975

British Library Cataloging-in-Publication Data available

This book is dedicated to the women in my life:
My wife, Regan, and my daughters,
Dr. Allison Hailman Doyle and Lydia Hailman King,
And our beautiful granddaughter, Abbey McGrew Doyle.
And to my male descendant and ally,
Wide-eyed Leland Alexander King, born March 12, 2014.

Contents

Chapter Two. Going Places with Wine

CONTENTS

Chapter Three. Tips for Enjoying Good Wine

Chapter Four. Finding the Humor in Wine

The Search for Good Wine

Introduction

This is a book about wine for regular people. For casual wine-drinkers it should be a painless introduction to a potentially joyful subject. For the wine aficionado, it explores interesting byways like the wine-drinking habits of Ben Franklin and Sherlock Holmes and suggests what to drink and where to drink it if you find yourself in places like New Orleans, Paris, or Yosemite National Park. Like good wine, it is not meant to be too heavy. It does not subject wines to a numerical grading system like recalcitrant schoolboys. Wine jargon exists here mainly to be made fun of. Readers seeking in-depth answers to questions raised here can always refer to *The Oxford Companion to Wine* by Jancis Robinson and *The Winemaker's Answer Book* by Alison Crowe.

These essays are grouped into four sections: People Who Love Good Wine, since interesting people tend to find interesting wines; Going Places with Wine; Tips for Enjoying Good Wine; and Finding the Humor in Wine. The essays can be read in any order. Personally, I've always liked skipping around when reading essays, following titles I like the sound of.

This book is meant to be sipped, not drunk. The essays can be appetizers or desserts. Some are well aged, but all are modern five-minute reads suitable for the night table or airport. All are taken from columns written over my career as a syndicated columnist to over one hundred daily newspapers. Each is dated at the end to show when it first appeared, either in Gannett or the *Washington Post*. Some have short updates in italics at the end to explain anything unusual that's happened to the people or places or wines since it was first written.

Wine tends to be ever-changing, with a new harvest each year. Some once-great wine enterprises sink without a trace like torpedoed battleships. Yet wine is also highly traditional and consistent: most of the wines drunk and discussed by Thomas Jefferson two hundred years ago are still around under the same names and made from the same grapes.

Some are even produced by direct descendants of winemakers Jefferson knew.

Memoirs of a life with wine are nothing new. English wine-writer Hugh Johnson published a wonderful one in 2005 entitled *A Life Uncorked.* The genre goes back to 1933 and the inimitable French professor George Saintsbury and his *Notes on a Cellar-Book*, and even farther back to the medieval Italian physician Arnauldus who told of his life with wine, even recommending a white wine to treat depression which he described as "eyebright, colder than crystal, green as buffalo horn, strong as a monastery, subtle as Paris logic, and going down impetuously like thunder." Where is that wine now when we need it?

Nor are compilations of wine columns new. Some are classics like *Times* columnist Frank Prial's *Decantations*, *Gourmet* columnist Gerald Asher's *Pleasures of Wine* and *House & Garden* columnist Jay McInerney's *Hedonist in the Cellar*. This book combines the genres as a simple introduction to an endlessly fascinating subject which can be as complex or as simple as a reader desires. We sample together both sides of the menu as it were, taking wine as lightly as possible and only as seriously as is necessary to enjoy it.

The Making of a Wine Columnist

A recent Internet posting listed what American twenty-somethings think are the top twenty ideal jobs. Not far below rock star and professional athlete were, surprisingly to me, restaurant reviewer, wine critic, and travel writer. It seems the young generation hankers to enjoy their work. And who can blame them? Getting paid to have a good time is hard to beat. But is it as easy as it's cracked up to be? Frankly, it probably is. Despite a few bad days tasting harsh wines from moldy barrels and eating the occasional bad snail or mushroom, tasting your way from vineyard to table is not half bad. How do you land such a gig? Here is how I did it.

Drinking and eating for pleasure seem to have been in my DNA. In his old age my father told me, while my mother blushed, that I was conceived in a fancy bed in a fancy room in the fancy Palmer House Hotel in Chicago after a long, lazy Cubs game and an especially fine dinner. My first memories all relate to food and drink. The very first memory of my life relates to intense gustatory pleasure. I see myself sitting beside a little dark-haired girl with my head fully inserted in and surrounded by a glass bowl coated heavily on the inside with chocolate icing from a cake my mother had just baked. The eating pleasure was intense. My mother told me this incident happened on my third birthday.

My second memory is different, yet similar. I'm at the top of a long flight of carpeted stairs at my grandmother's house when I miss the first step and go tumbling end over end. It didn't hurt at all and was more exciting than scary. My reaction: "I broke my tookie," I allegedly said, referring to fistfuls of cookies greedily crushed in both hands as I tried to descend the stairs without holding on. The date of that event: my fourth birthday.

The first drinks I recall were a glass of fresh lemonade made by my grandmother from her own lemons, and a jug of fresh apple cider made by her from apples I had just picked from a tree in her backyard. I was five that year.

My parents were stone teetotalers until I corrupted them late in life with an Anjou rosé, a good beginner's wine. The first alcohol to pass my lips was an ice-cold beer sipped secretly at age sixteen on the back of my uncle Walter's hay wagon after I'd spent all afternoon baling his hay. It was delicious. I was an even slower starter on wine. It was not until my freshman year in college that I tasted my first wine, a beautiful late-harvest Mosel from Berncastel bootlegged into my freshman dorm room by upperclassmen just back from Germany. It is still among my favorites.

To Paris

My real education in wine and food began during two years I spent studying in France while in college. My route to France was a long and unusual one. My father was a hard-nosed German from an Amish family who believed that people learned things only through hard work. When I was fifteen I told him I would be needing a car. He told me I could have one when I could pay for it myself. The next two summers were spent baling hay for local farmers to make money for the car. By the time I was a senior in high school, I had enough money to pay for a decent old junker. My father said he would match what I had made, a pleasant surprise. After he rejected several little sports cars I wanted, we finally agreed on an old red Plymouth convertible, which I immediately fitted with loud "glasspack" mufflers popular in those days and long, low-slung wheel covers called "fender skirts."

The first day I had the car I baled hay all morning and had a long, hot baseball practice all afternoon. I didn't waste any time after practice showering or changing out of my ratty blue jeans and T-shirt. I just hosed myself off and let the wind air-dry me as I drove. I went straight to a nearby college town I had always wanted to visit by myself. There was an outdoor dance going on with a live band. The place was full of pretty girls in thin summer dresses dancing barefoot on a grass field. I asked the first girl I saw, a petite brunette, if she would dance with me. We began to dance. A couple of older guys started tapping people on the shoulder. I thought they were cutting in. The pretty girl and I danced on, enjoying both fast dances and slow dances and were having a really good time when I suddenly noticed there were only three or four couples left. "Where did everybody go?" I asked her. "This is a dance contest, silly. The rest have all been eliminated."

Amazingly, even though we did not yet know each other's names, we won the dance contest. I asked if she would go out with me that weekend. I planned to say something like "This is fate," but didn't need to. She said, "Of course, but you have to meet my mom first." As I followed her to her house I should have paid more attention and would have noticed that she was driving a new Cadillac convertible, which made my old beat-up Plymouth look pretty bad. But I was young and oblivious to such details.

When we got to her house, a big one on a hill with columns and a manicured lawn, her mother came down the long, curving front steps to greet us. I thought I made a good impression on her with my suntan and muscles, but I guess I forgot there was hay in my hair and holes in my jeans. I should have noticed how many personal questions she asked me, but I was sort of blinded by the girl and the dance experience.

I drove home. When I got there I called the pretty girl and asked her what time I should pick her up that weekend. She said, "I'm terribly sorry. I cannot go out with you. My mom says you're too *countrified*." I was crestfallen. My mother saw my face and asked what was the matter. I explained it to her. My mother, always quiet and shy, was not timid this time. She called straight out to my father without missing a beat: "Dear, we're sending Johnny to Paris to knock off his rough edges. Nobody calls *my* son *countrified*."

The transformation was not immediate. It was only after two years of college French, a summer conversation program in rural France and a summer of intensive phonetics in Quebec that I was accepted to the Sorbonne in Paris and finally went off to have my rough edges "knocked off." I liked it so well the first year that I refused to come home. True to form, my father said, "If you can pay for it you can stay." I got a job as a gofer with the Air France charter service, worked my way up to a gig as an interpreter for tourists from India going on package tours to Spain, and managed to stay in France for a second year. That last summer I even passed myself off as "Jean," a French-Canadian, and got a job bartending on Palma, Mallorca, off the coast of Spain, tasting lots of the best French and Spanish wines.

Unfortunately I never saw the girl again, nor did I get to thank her mother for having inadvertently given me such a wonderful present.

Wine Consultant?

After college, I received a fellowship to Georgetown Law School in Washington, D.C. When my wife Regan and I arrived in Georgetown, we were hurting for money. Really hurting. I headed out to get a job, *any* job. A few blocks up Wisconsin Avenue in Georgetown, just like in the movies I saw a sign that said "Help Wanted." Again, just like in the movies, I carried the sign into the store with me. Once inside I saw it was a wine shop with a cheese department in the back and a whole wall of wine books up front. I approached the man in charge and asked what he needed done. "Unload that truck," he said, gesturing toward the parking lot.

Needless to say, I began unloading the truck—for two dollars an hour. After several hours of unloading, I noticed a ruckus inside the shop. A lady was sobbing and saying things I couldn't understand. I approached and could hear that the lady was speaking French. Everyone looked puzzled. The manager said, "Go back outside." I said, "I speak French. Let me interpret." The lady turned out to be a senior secretary from the French Embassy sent there on an urgent mission: buy plenty of good wine for a big reception and *quickly*. I explained to the manager what she wanted. He said, "Since she can't speak English, you wait on her." The manager was shocked when the lady ordered several cases of the shop's most expensive wines and had the driver from the Embassy carry them out to her limousine. As I recall, it was several thousand dollars worth.

The manager called me aside after she left and asked, "How much do you know about wine?" I told him, "Not much. The wines I drank in Paris came in jugs with no labels. I love wine and food and have a lot of experience drinking wine, but no technical knowledge of it." He pulled a bottle off the shelf and said, "Read that." I read off something in French with all the accents and intonations correct. He said, "Put your shirt on. You are now a wine consultant. I'll teach you all you need to know." The pay, however, was still two dollars an hour. I worked happily as a wine consultant at the shop for three years, going there evenings and weekends regardless of whether I was at Georgetown Law School or working for Senator John Stennis as his legal counsel. They were some of the happiest years of my life.

After a month or so, I got my wife Regan a job in the cheese department so we could enjoy the shop together. The other clerks were wine-loving grad students from several countries. At closing time, which was usually eight o'clock, we would all go in the back room and eat French bread and cheese and taste great wines together, all compliments of the shop. They would never let us sell a bottle of wine we had not tasted. The manager, Fred Weck, began to tutor me every day on the finer points of wine as we tasted them together.

Wine Columnist?

We devoured the weekly wine column in the *Washington Post* until it suddenly stopped appearing. We called the food editor, Bill Rice, and asked him what happened.

"We lost our wine columnist and are looking for another, but the people who want to write the column don't know enough about it. Those who know enough don't want to write for what we can pay." After more weeks with no column, Regan said, "Look, we still need money. You are such a fanatic on wine, why don't *you* write the column?"

I called Bill back and told him I worked in a wine shop and would like to try writing the column. He said, "Okay, what's your training? What are you?" he asked. "In real life I'm a lawyer, but I prefer wine," I replied.

He said, "Oh no, no. I'm sorry, but lawyers can't write. No one wants to read what a lawyer writes." That irritated me. "Look," I said, "My writing teacher at Millsaps College was Eudora Welty." Bill was astonished, "Oh my gosh. Eudora Welty is my *favorite* writer. Listen, you write me one column on wine, anything you like, three typed pages and send it to me. I'll at least consider you since you were trained by Miss Welty."

I finally came up with a column on Zinfandel, making plays on words like zins of the fathers and cardinal zins and who on the Washington Redskins liked to drink Zinfandel. After seventeen or eighteen drafts I finally submitted my first wine column. Bill called right back. "How often can you do this?" As often as he liked. "Fine. I'll pay you $120 a column." I nearly fainted. At the wine shop, for ten hours a day I only made $20. I figured each column would only take three or four hours once I got the hang of it. I could make $120 a week. What a gig.

A Long Career

So I wrote weekly wine columns, first for the *Washington Post*, then for the *Clarion-Ledger* of Jackson, Mississippi after we moved back home. The latter columns were syndicated by Gannett News Service to over one hundred papers from New York to California. To some this endeavor seemed arduous since it had to be done entirely in evenings and on weekends because, after 1974, I had a full-time day-job as a federal prosecutor in Oxford, Mississippi. Doubters also asked: Why would anyone want to read a column on wine written in a place as remote from the vineyards of Europe and California as Oxford, Mississippi? The answer was: wide reading and tasting and travel on my day job. My law cases constantly sent me to hearings and legal conferences in cities from Washington and New York to San Francisco and New Orleans and several times to Europe where, in a few extra days at my own expense, I could eat in the finest restaurants and taste the finest wines in the world. Gannett, which started *USA Today* during this period, even began to pay my wine, food, and hotel expenses.

Readers have asked if writing a weekly column did not detract from family life with my wife and daughters. On the contrary, writing the column actually enhanced our family life. My wife and daughters often joined me on the best trips. At home, my little daughters would sit on my lap in the evening as I typed the columns and my wife would critique them. Making suggestions about what was interesting and what was not was an unusual education for our daughters. Both are now great cooks and serious and sober wine lovers.

Other benefits flowed from syndication. I was asked almost immediately to serve as a judge at several international wine competitions where winemakers, wine merchants, and enology professors award medals to the best wines each year. I still do several competitions every year. Wineries need publicity and syndicated writers give it to them for free. We are, of course, not paid for judging, or only minimally. *All* they do is reimburse our expenses, and wine and dine us like kings. How good can it get? Well, there were a couple of other things. Wine companies send wine writers samples of their best new wines to taste and write about. Every week a case or two of wine would show up on my doorstep to taste. Sometimes they would send two bottles of red so you could taste one and write about it right away and keep the second in your cellar to write about later after you saw how it aged.

Another unexpected benefit was that once you are on the list of syndicated writers, book publishers send you free copies of every new wine book that comes out. Since their lists lump wine and food writers together, you also receive every new cookbook published each year, a flood of them, and a real boon to my wife during the twelve years she ran a gourmet catering business from our home. The Veuve Clicquot Champagne company made me a judge of their annual "best wine book" competition for several years. Publishers also toss in their best travel books if they have anything conceivable to do with food or wine. It was a perfect way to build up a nice library on the subjects I was writing about, which included wine, food, travel, and even restaurant reviewing. After all, what's wine without food? And no one wants to read only about what you drink at home. You *have* to travel to fine restaurants and write about the experience.

Last and far from least, we decided to put every penny from the columns into a savings account for our children's college. That little column helped put two fine young women through college. They did develop expensive tastes for fine wine, food, and travel, burdens they now share with their willing husbands.

A Brief Update

Since these columns/essays were written, much has changed in the world of wines, but much more has remained the same. One prediction I made proved spectacularly true. Who would have thought that a restaurant in Birmingham, Alabama called Highlands would become over the years one of the finest and most respected in the U.S., or that its chef/owner, Frank Stitt, would become an international star. His second restaurant, Bottega, is now equally renowned and celebrated in a wonderful cookbook of the same name. In style, Stitt reminds me of New Orleans's new star chef John Besh, the Marine Corps combat veteran from south Louisiana who helped bring the Crescent City back from the ravages of hurricane Katrina as chronicled in his fine book *My New Orleans*. Almost as amazing is the survival of San Francisco's garlic-with-everything restaurant, The Stinking Rose, which I figured was just a gimmick theme restaurant which wouldn't last another year when I wrote about it in the 1980s. *Au contraire*, one of my law students, a former chef herself, still eats there regularly. Who would have thought it?

One sad casualty of time was Charles F. Shaw, the wealthy investor in a fancy tuxedo who vowed to make in the U.S. a Gamay as good as Beaujolais. Over-extended, he went belly-up and had to sell his winery to Fred Franzia, the clever owner of hundreds of acres of prime vines around California who snaps up bankrupt wineries like potato chips. Franzia, once convicted of wine fraud as explained in a hysterical piece in the *New Yorker* (see the bibliography), now produces some of California's greatest wine values under a variety of labels including Crane Lake. My favorite of his wines, at just five dollars for a .750 milliliter bottle, is Coastal Vines Pinot Noir, a light, delicate wine perfect for everyday. But it was under poor Charles F. Shaw's name that Franzia made his first big splash. Shortening and coarsening it to "Two Buck Chuck," Franzia scandalized the wine world—and made a small fortune—with the best two dollar Cabernets ever seen in California.

The latest big debate in the world of wines is also a new-old one: Which will prevail in winemaking, tradition or chemistry? Writer David Darlington, in his excellent book *An Ideal Wine*, casts the debate as one between intuition and romance on one hand, represented by romantic Randall Grahm of Bonny Doon Vineyard, and on the other hand modern science in the form of reverse osmosis, oak chips, and micro-oxygenation as represented by a bevy of modern wine consultants. The same phenomenon is going on in Bordeaux as described by English wine writer Stephen Brook in his fine, in-depth study *Bordeaux: People, Power and Politics*. The latest entry in the debate, *The Wine Savant*, by Michael Steinberger, takes a middle ground. His 2013 book is well worth a read as the latest word on the subject.

Flying wine gurus like Michel Rolland are now being accused of making the wines of the Medoc and Pomerol into industrial chemical products, following the taste of the ubiquitous wine writer Robert Parker. On the other side of the debate are the most experienced and traditional *negociants* and chateau owners of Bordeaux who insist that, for Bordeaux at least, highly manipulated wines like the expensive *vins de garage* made by the new-wave winemakers called *garagistes* will never in the long run equal the old-style wines produced based on *terroirs*, the unique soils and sun exposures learned by the French only after centuries of experience (location, location, location).

One winemaker who seems to win on both sides of this debate is my old friend Alfred Tesseron, owner of the venerable Chateau Pontet-Canet of the village of Pauillac, whose estate is the largest of all the sixty-two classified growths of the famed Medoc. His land adjoins both Chateau Lafite and Chateau Mouton. His wine is very highly rated both by Parker and the *Wine Spectator*, yet his winemaking methods are both the most traditional and "green" of all his neighbors. He handpicks all his grapes, uses no chemical fertilizers, and plows his land without the weight of tractors, using big Belgian draft horses instead. Thus it may still be possible to have it both ways: to please modern palates like Parker while still using traditional, *terroir*-based techniques.

One huge change in the wine market has been the emergence of the newly capitalist Chinese as *buyers* of wines. Although their wine*making* is still in its infancy, as it is in India, the Chinese, both mainland and on Hong King and Taiwan, are having an enormous impact on prices, especially prices of the biggest names of Bordeaux.

On the other end of the scale, the teetotaling mullahs of Persian Iran continue to deny that their ancient city of Shiraz was the original home of the grape of Australia's most famous red. Those new-teetotalers would probably hang their great poet Omar Khayyam if he came back to write about "a jug of wine underneath the bough" or to ask "what can wine sellers buy (with their profits) one half so precious as what they sell?"

In our own South, having at last put Prohibition and hypocrisy somewhat behind us, North Carolina is making some good wine and Virginia is making a lot of excellent wine following the advice of Thomas Jefferson to plant only the best European varietals. Mississippi, which appeared to be a leader in the Southern wine revolution just twenty years ago, has been decimated by the dreaded vine blight Pierce's Disease, which wiped out not only its best wineries but also its outstanding winemaking school at Mississippi State. The Temecula Valley of California's deep south has apparently survived its bout with the same Pierce's Disease and now has a splendid new flagship winery, South Coast, run by Jon McPherson, whose brother Kim is winemaker at my favorite winery in Texas.

An outstanding traditional dessert wine still made only in southern California is Angelica, a fortified dark-gold wine from the venerable Mission grape brought to America by Father Junípero Serra of the Spanish island of Mallorca. The best Angelica, which wins gold medals as Best of Class every year at the L.A. Fair International judging, is from the equally traditional Galleano winery, which also makes fine Zinfandels from hillside grapes, fermenting them in ultra-traditional redwood vats rarely seen anywhere else.

One emerging trend is the growth of screw-tops. Once loudly decried by traditionalists, screw-tops lined with modern plastics to prevent metallic tastes from affecting the wine, are now standard for wines meant to be drunk young. Corks, which have had significant problems with spoilage, are still used for nearly all reds meant to be aged, but their failure rate, established at nearly three percent by most studies, have caused many winemakers to abandon them for wines not meant to be kept long in bottle before drinking.

Of wine-making countries, after Australia and New Zealand, the rising stars are now in South America. Chile, long a favorite for cheap wines, has now attracted lots of French winemaker-expatriates, and their wines show it. Perhaps their biggest change came when French ampelographers (experts in vine DNA) discovered that what Chileans had always sold as Merlot turned out to be Carmenère, an ancient and honorable Bordeaux variety long thought to be extinct. It now makes lush, aromatic wines of real character and finesse, far surpassing in quality their old "Merlots."

Argentina is now even more of a player. For centuries Argentine wine-makers kept their reds and whites almost entirely for domestic consumption. Now their hundreds of reds, mostly from the Malbec grape, sell for up to two hundred dollars. The traditional "gaucho" white grape, Torrontes, a light-red Muscat variety meant to be sweet but vinified dry in Argentina, is fast losing ground to fresh, unoaked Chardonnays from the foothills of the Andes. To my taste the red Tempranillo grape of Spain's Rioja region, just recently planted in the Mendoza region of Argentina, is even more promising than Malbec.

If there is a sleeper on the Argentine scene it is Bonarda, an old red long believed to be from the Piedmont region of northwest Italy. When you visit Argentina, you quickly recognize the truth in the saying that despite its mostly Spanish origins and language, Argentina is "like Italy, only more so." Veterans speak not just of wild and crazy politics, but of a lively, enthusiastic side to Argentines that makes their current wine and food scene one of the most exciting in the world. Recent research has revealed that the supposedly "Italian" wine-grape Bonarda is not Italian at all, but the fine old French grape Charbonneau. To my taste the Bonarda has a really bright future, even if a slightly murky past.

Last and far from least are the newly emerging wine countries of central and eastern Europe. Freed from the dead hand of communism, those ancient countries are slowly recovering their ancient wine cultures. One such country I wrote of back in the 1970s, Bulgaria, is not yet much imported in the U.S. The first Balkan wine country I visited, Moldova (called Moldavia under the Russians) makes a lot of good wine but very little makes it to the U.S. Better distributed are the fine wines of the ancient Republic of Georgia. According to Hugh Johnson, the supreme expert on the origins of wines, the world's first vinifera wines were made in beautiful Georgia, at the foot of the mighty Caucasus Mountains, over five thousand years ago. Today their fine red wines from the Saperavi grape, which resembles Syrah to me, can be found in the U.S. in limited quantities by searching the Internet. Their dry white quaffing wine Rkatsiteli is now made in upstate New York by the winery of Konstantin Frank, and in Virginia by the Horton Winery, which calls it "R-Katz."

In 2006, after thirty-three really enjoyable years of research and writing, I published my biography entitled *Thomas Jefferson on Wine*. Its title was meant to convey that it was based on Jefferson's extensive writings about wine, including over three hundred letters and countless lengthy memos and journal entries written over the eighty-three years of his active life, most them as a serious wine-drinker. It definitely was not meant to imply that he was ever *high* on wine when he wrote the Declaration of Independence, as a few wags have suggested. That book, happily, is still selling well in 2014.

In 2007, I finally retired from my full-time day job as a federal prosecutor, but continue to teach trial practice and law and literature as an adjunct professor at the University of Mississippi Khayat School of Law.

In 2008, out of the blue, my old friend Layn Phillips, a former federal judge, asked if I would be interested in helping him, as lead counsel for billionaire wine-collector William Koch, investigate (in France and in French) large frauds perpetrated on Mr. Koch by the notorious German wine fraudster "Hardy Rodenstock," the alias for a man really named Meinhard Goerke. I accepted readily. To appreciate Herr "Rodenstock's" cavalier attitude toward the law, one only need consider his remark to a journalist when confronted about his crooked dealings: "What is the big deal about a little wine fraud? After all, Jesus did it!" Quite a guy.

Our team of investigators and I spent several fine, wine-soaked weeks probing the fabulous Bordeaux wine scene, interviewing stars like the Marquis de Lur-Saluces of Chateau d'Yquem about bogus Bordeaux Rodenstock sold to Mr. Koch and others for hundreds of thousands of dollars. We garnered considerable insight, and evidence, into the widespread networks of fraud in the high-end wine world. I describe that and other cases in some detail in the epilogue of the latest printing of *Jefferson on Wine* (pp. 397–404 and 429).

Unfortunately, Rodenstock had skipped the jurisdiction for Monaco just before we got there, and the unbelievably short French statute of limitations on fraud against Mr. Koch had already run out. But Bill Koch is a fighter and never quits. Brother of the well-known political activists Charles and David Koch, he was once captain of the winning U.S. America's Cup yacht-racing team and loves competition. In December 2009, just after I left his fraud-fighting team when it moved from France to the U.S., Bill Koch was featured on the cover of the respected *Wine*

Spectator magazine as the leading worldwide crusader against wine fraud. He has since obtained good settlements in other cases, donating his proceeds to entities combating fraud in the wine business.

In 2013, his testimony and expertise helped New York prosecutors convict Indonesian wine speculator Rudy Kurniawan of criminal fraud for selling bogus high-end wines (see *Los Angeles Times* and *Wall Street Journal* stories of December 18, 2013). It appears wine and law can mix well after all.

That should be enough updating for now, although readers will find, scattered throughout the essays, brief italicized comments noting important changes which have taken place since my original columns were written.

Here, then, without further ado, are the fruits of our family's years of enjoyable labor with wine, food and travel. It is hoped that rubbing elbows with interesting people and interesting places will be half as useful and enjoyable for readers as it was for us.

CHAPTER ONE

People Who Love Good Wine

Ben Franklin, Wine Lover

Much has now been written of that great wine lover, Thomas Jefferson, and of how he taught George Washington about French wine. But less is written of the man who taught Jefferson about French wine: Ben Franklin.

In 1784, when Jefferson went to Paris as American Commissioner, Franklin had already been there for eight years as American Minister and knew French wines well. As early as 1778, his Paris cellar list showed more than 1,000 bottles, including: "258 Bottles of Red and White Bordeaux; 15 Bottles of old Bordeaux; 21 bottles of Champagne; 326 Bottles of Mousseux (bubbly); 113 Bottles of Red Burgundy; and 148 Bottles of Xeres (sherry)."

Jefferson noted in his letters that it was primarily Franklin who instructed him on "wines of distinction" like Chateaux Margaux and Haut-Brion to serve his French guests. Jefferson and his fellow commissioner John Adams, another great wine lover who often corresponded with him about wines, visited the house of the invalid Franklin several times a week to talk and drink good wine.

Franklin's main ailment was gout, which is often induced by an excess of food and drink. In his "Dialogue Between Franklin and Madame Gout," he denied being "a glutton and a tippler" as she accused him, but admitted he had not always followed his rule from Poor Richard's Almanack: "Eat not to Dullness; Drink not to Elevation." But it should not be presumed that Franklin drank to excess. His health was too strong throughout his eighty-three years, and he held too many posts of dignity and seriousness before, during, and after the Revolution. Franklin did however, found a regular wine-drinking society called the Junto.

In a letter to Abbe Morellet, a frequent dinner companion who taught him French drinking songs, Franklin proposed to "edify you with a few

Christian, moral, and philosophical reflections on the same subject." Franklin wrote, "In vino veritas, says the Sage. The truth is in wine. Before Noah, men having only water to drink became abominably wicked, and were justly exterminated by the water it pleased them to drink."

Turning to the Marriage at Cana, where water was turned into wine, Franklin noted this happens every day when rain falls on vineyards so grapes can make wine, saying "wine is a continual proof that God loves us and likes to see us happy. The particular miracle at Cana was done merely to perform this operation in a sudden case of need."

The Irish writer and humorist Oscar Wilde, who didn't much like the English, had a different take on the subject, describing what he called an "English miracle": Turning wine into water.

In a postscript to his friend, Franklin concluded, "To confirm you in your piety, reflect on the position Providence has given the elbow. Man, who was destined to drink wine, has to be able to carry the glass to his mouth. If the elbow had been placed closer to the hand, the forearm would have been too short to bring the glass to the mouth; if closer to the shoulder, the forearm would have been so long that it would have carried the glass beyond the mouth. Let us then adore, glass in hand, this beneficent Wisdom. Let us adore and drink."

Wine tips of the week: For Bordeaux like Ben Franklin drank, try fifth growth Chateaux like Croizet-Bages, Haut-Bages-Liberal or Pontet-Canet, whose prices remain reasonable. For modern Mousseux, try Spanish Cavas Codorniu and Freixenet. They would appeal both to Franklin's taste and Poor Richard's sense of thrift.

A Toast to Hilarious
George Washington

Like most of the Founding Fathers, George Washington was a great wine lover, which bears remembering on his birthday. This fact is too little known today because political myth has long required that he be dehumanized into a goody two-shoes, which he never was. In spite of stereotypes, Washington's favorite supper was a bowl of hazelnuts washed down with plenty of claret.

Long before the Revolutionary War made him famous, Washington was ordering German Rhine wine and Madeira by the case, noting in letters as early as 1759 that his wines should be "secured from pilferers" on the riverboats. He also ordered dozens of cut-glass wine glasses, demanding in practical Washingtonian terms that they be "rather low and strong as well as neat, with broad bottoms that they may stand firm on the table."

Alarmed at the high cost of importing wine before the Revolution, Washington joined Jefferson and the Royal Governor in planting large vineyards of Madeira wine grapes to make good U.S. wines. Frosts, vine diseases, and wars halted this project, causing Washington to depend on imported wines throughout his life.

Washington's early preference was for strong wines from the Atlantic island of Madeira, which were taxed less by the English because technically they were from Africa, not Europe. He loved red Bordeaux and, during the war, drank it almost exclusively because his French allies insisted on it. His usual custom was to pass around a bowl of nuts at about half past nine in the evening while his chief aide, Alexander Hamilton, led French and American officers in toasting each other in silver "camp cups" full of claret.

Records reflect that during the war Washington had better wine than even Thomas Jefferson, America's greatest early wine lover. But letters reflect that Washington gave away much of his Madeira to his wounded soldiers as "the only pain-killer for poor fellows exposed to the weather." When the war was over, while posted in Europe on diplomatic missions, Jefferson and John Jay sent their boss the finest wines of France, from great Champagnes and Bordeaux to the best Burgundies.

Late in life, Washington was warned by his physician that his false teeth had been harmed by "too much acid Port," but he never gave it up, noting to a friend that at Mount Vernon "a glass of wine and a bit of mutton are always ready" for visitors. Ever thrifty, however, Washington wrote to a servant at about the same time and ordered him not to serve his best wines to the tourists who had already begun to visit, but to "re-serve my old Madeira for my own use when I get home."

Is it possible for us to recreate a scene today that Washington would recognize? Definitely. He would never know the capital city named for him. All the buildings are new, and he never lived in the White House. But if we laid a table with cut-glass decanters and silver wine coasters and coolers, and filled them with fine Champagne and good red Bordeaux like Chateau Lafite or Chateau Rausan, both of which he liked, George Washington would probably feel right at home. He deserves a toast, a tradition he loved but which has fallen on evil days in our own time.

Except for certain formal occasions, where toasts compete for the title of most pompous and boring, the institution of toasting seems almost dead in America. Now the best toasts happen mostly at celebrity roasts. It was not always thus.

Washington, a notable eater despite his teeth, and a drinker of fine vintage wines, always had a long succession of toasts at his dinners. The toasting was led by his chief aide, Colonel Alexander Hamilton. Our main allies in the Revolution being the French, they naturally were invited to these sessions. One of them, General Chastellux, an experienced soldier and a member of the French academy, left a two-volume journal of his experiences in the American War where he commented on the items of interest he saw and experienced. A Burgundian by birth, and of a war-loving family going back to the Middle Ages, Chastellux was used to drinking wine with his soldiers.

According to Chastellux, General Washington's suppers were fairly moist. Being mostly stag affairs for military officers, that is not surprising. More surprising is the way such evenings were conducted. Even during the depths of the Revolutionary War, Washington had nice suppers where he ate inordinately large amounts of dried nuts accompanied by toasts in claret or Madeira. The practice was mitigated, according to Chastellux, by the glasses, which were small, and the fact that you did not have to empty the glass at each toast.

Nevertheless, one unimpressed observer said that his drinking of "healthes" was so extensive they had little time left to eat. He said some officers even "ruined their healthes by drinking that of others."

Chastellux was one of the few French officers to speak fluent English and acted as translator for the French commander, Rochambeau, when he spoke with Washington. He said that then, as now, wine was considered something of a luxury item in America. This did not deter Washington, however, from plying visitors with fine claret in silver camp cups.

Noting that the General's supply was almost out from entertaining, Chastellux sent Washington a fresh cask of claret with a note that if the General would not accept it as a gift, his French ally would consider that "you have a little of the Tory in your composition." Breaking his rule of never accepting gifts, Washington replied that he would accept the claret only because "by your ingenious manner of stating the case I shall, by a refusal, bring my patriotism into question." Washington agreed to accept it only on condition that Chastellux would "relieve me by promising to partake very often of that *hilarity* which a glass of good claret seldom fails to produce." Hilarious George?

At first, I doubted this description of George Washington by a Frenchman—until I read later an American description of his induction into the Philadelphia Irish Society, where the initiation ceremony was a series of humorous toasts, followed by "the exterior application of a whole bottle of claret upon the head of the initiate and a generous libation to liberty and good living." Quite a different, and happier, portrait of the father of our country. Here's to you, George.

The Favorite Wines of Sherlock Holmes

Everyone needs heroes. Mine have varied from Lawrence of Arabia to baseball player Rod Carew, depending on my age and condition at the time, but one has stood the test of time: Sherlock Holmes. Of all fictional characters, this English detective exemplified enjoyment of life at its best.

Sherlock Holmes was the first man I ever heard called a "connoisseur," and it applied to everything from his taste in firearms and cigars to music and wine, of which he mentioned several favorites. No one ever called him a "common-sewer" of wine as someone did me recently, in jest I'm sure.

The creator of Sherlock Holmes, Sir Arthur Conan Doyle, was of course a medical doctor. For that reason, doctors have always had a special liking for Holmes. I am grateful to Dr. Paul Scholten of San Francisco for reminding me recently of the many wine references in the Holmes mysteries. Paul was for many years the U.S. president of the Sherlock Holmes fan club called the Baker Street Irregulars.

The most winey story of all was "Sign of the Four," in which Holmes drank not only red Burgundy from Beaune for lunch, but old Hungarian Tokay and three glasses of Port after dinner. For those wishing to emulate the great detective one hundred years later, there are some truly great Beaunes on the shelves right now. If those are too high, and most are, you can try one from Oregon, Sonoma Coast, Russian River, Santa Barbara, or the remarkably inexpensive California Pinot from Coastal Vines at just six dollars.

With Hungary now a free-market country, its Tokays are improving greatly. The main thing for beginners to know about Tokay is that it is best as a dessert wine. Each label tells how many "puttonyos," or eight-gallon vats of overripe grapes, have been added to each barrel. They vary from three (the lightest) to five (the sweetest).

For Port, which Holmes also enjoys in "The Creeping Man," I recommend a Tawny from Suarez, named for the amber color it gets from barrel-aging. For vintage Port, supposedly Sherlock's favorite, try Quinta do Noval, a 1963 if possible. They are drinking beautifully now, as Sherlock would have said. For ruby Port I've always loved Graham's. If you prefer U.S. wines, try a Port of Cabernet Sauvignon from Beringer, one of California's best.

Holmes and Watson, as Englishmen, necessarily drank a lot of claret or red Bordeaux, notably in "The Dying Detective" and "The Cardboard Box," although I found no reference to particular Bordeaux. In that case you can try any Bordeaux, but based on his other tastes I'd guess Holmes would like something classic, simple, and moderately priced from a village like Pauillac, where Lafite and Latour are still located, say a Pontet-Canet. A light, ripe vintage would be right down his line. A St. Julien might do as well, especially for lighter dishes. For U.S. equivalents, try one of the new Meritage blends like Cain Five from Napa or Langtry Red from the Lake County estate which once belonged to actress Lillie Langtry.

Dr. Doyle mentioned the name of Sherlock Holmes's favorite London wine merchant, Mr. Vamberry, and a wine salesman named Windebank, a scoundrel. Holmes's favorite white wines were Burgundies, apparently obtained for special occasions from Mr. Vamberry, especially Montrachet and Meursault. To celebrate his success in "The Veiled Lodger," Holmes chose a partridge and "something a little choice in white wines," i.e., a Montrachet.

Although still by acclamation the top white Burgundy, most Montrachet now costs as much as a used car. On special occasions it is worth it, but a Meursault from a good house like Roulot is fine at half the price.

Once again, if you are a patriot like Holmes and especially want to support the wines of our country, I suggest a rich and flavorful Stony Hill Chardonnay, which can be excellent with game birds that are not too gamey, like Holmes's favorite: goose and pheasant. For French game birds aged in brandy, a red wine would do better.

When life gets rough, you might have to turn for medicinal purposes to Cognac or a "brown" sherry, as Holmes did in "The Hound of the Baskervilles" and "The Reigate Squires." Emilio Lustau produces fine sherries available here, perhaps a Manzanilla, my own favorite and

Thomas Jefferson's. Whatever wine we try, if it is good, the connoisseur Sherlock Holmes probably got there before us in one story or another. Not bad footsteps to follow come to think of it.

The Favorite Drink
of Robin Hood

What was the favorite wine of Robin Hood and his Merry Men? The same wine that made the ancient Romans merry but turned the Vikings vicious. This ancient wine, pale and golden, is unfortunately seldom made in the United States nowadays, but mead can be surprisingly good.

Before good wine grapes were developed in Europe, especially northern Europe, the main ingredient in fermented beverages was honey. Don't turn your head too quickly. Made by good winemakers, mead is neither too sweet nor overly alcoholic, although it can be both. Modern mead is around eight to nine percent alcohol, less than most wines, and its natural sugar can be fermented out. The aroma is like Sauternes.

Reading Prince Valiant cartoons growing up, I often wondered what that golden liquid was that the knights and serfs alike drank from big goblets in their mead halls. Now I learn that the places they sat were called mead-benches and the great drinking vessels they passed around were called mead-horns.

When I worked at a wine store in the early 1970s, we sold a half-dozen meads, mainly from England and the Scandinavian countries, although the best I ever had came from France, from the old seaside province of Normandy, named for the Norsemen who drank it there with such pleasure. Until then I'd thought any wine made from honey must be pretty wimpy stuff, but if the Vikings drank it, who knows?

It goes without saying that the Vikings were not exactly gourmets. The word "vike" after all is a verb that means "to pillage." The appearance of Hagar the Horrible cartoons with his "shopping trips" to England for wife Helga have begun to soften their image a little. But Robin Hood is another story. The Sherwood Forest crowd included at least one lettered churchman, Friar Tuck, and it is well known that monks loved mead right up to the time of Queen Elizabeth, and monks were among the most discerning of European wine drinkers.

Of course taste was not the only reason medieval people drank mead. Its other name was Hippocras, named for the father of medicine. The Welsh name for mead, still seen today on many English meads, was *metheglin*, their word for "medicine."

Pure, old-time mead was made from water, honey, and yeast alone. The juice of lemons was often added to make it less bland. The use of fruit juice, either lemons or oranges, to replace water makes mead into what is called *melomel*. An intriguing drink favored by the Romans was Oxymel, wine made from fermented mead and vinegar. Oxymel still existed in the Middle Ages when the English mockingly called it "Italian" wine. Sailors under Queen Elizabeth liked to add rum to their mead. When made entirely with wine instead of water, mead was called Pymet, and usually had spices added.

About the only country still having mead as its national drink is Ethiopia. A few years ago, while dining at the Red Sea restaurant in Washington, an Ethiopian friend, now a lawyer in Tucson, introduced me for the first time to mead as a food wine. It was not a big hit with every diner, but I thought it made a decent after-dinner drink. It was called Tej and was made in Canada of all places.

For those brave enough, my friend passed on this recipe for homemade mead:

2 gallons of water
10 pounds of uncooked honey (no comb)
1 ounce of yeast
Flavor for acidity with 3 lemons and 3 oranges.

The wine should ferment for twenty-one days, and then be fined with fresh egg whites after the scum (really) is skimmed off the top. Mead is somewhat unstable, so it should be allowed to rest for six months in strong bottles with wired-on corks before drinking. The other great modern mead-makers, the Masai of southern Africa, require their winemakers to remain celibate during the entire fermentation. This practice is optional, but the strong bottles are a necessity.

Julius Caesar's Favorite Roman Wine: Still Around?

Ancient Romans liked their wine. In Pompeii, their resort near Naples, there were more than one hundred wine bars and twenty wine shops in a city of twenty thousand. We know this because a volcanic eruption of nearby Mount Vesuvius suddenly buried the city under nine feet of ash in A.D. 79. Many Pompeians were buried alive at their tables, and thousands of large wine jugs, or amphorae, were preserved in place.

Murals of wine drinkers at banquets were also preserved, showing the colors of Roman wines to be about like today, from light whites to deep reds. The first real Roman wine-and-food writer was Pliny the Elder around two hundred years before Caesar. Cato also tackled the subject. Horace made a careful study of which wines did not give hangovers.

Julius Caesar's favorite wines were Greek, but his Roman favorite, called Mamertine, is still made today. It is now a strong, dry white, usually of no special quality. The modern wine which most resembles Roman wines is probably Lacryma Christi (tears of Christ), which is still made in quantity on volcanic soil on the slopes of Mount Vesuvius, giving it the same unusual taste Romans often wrote about. It comes in both red and white.

Romans drank their wines according to the seasons; whites were cooled by adding stored snow in summer and heated with hot pokers in winter. Romans liked to drink wines while strolling around the city snacking rather than seated but insisted you not drink wine on an empty stomach, just like dietitians today. The best wines had leather identification tags around their necks, indicating the vineyard and year of harvest.

Roman wine bars stored their wine in large jars buried up to their necks in the ground, cooling and preserving them much like a cellar.

Beer was scorned by the Romans, who said it was only good enough for people living north of the Alps (like the French). A wine server, or *cellarius* filtered their wines before serving.

Everywhere Romans went, from Israel and Syria to Germany and France, they planted grapevines and made wine. Herod, the Roman King of Judea, had at least ten different kinds of wine at his palace. To keep wine from tasting spoiled, Romans made many concoctions using raisins to sweeten wines, a classic preservative. They even added sea water, like the Greeks, to "preserve" wine by salting it. They added honey to cover vinegary tastes.

Eventually they developed a taste for vinegary wine, and a common refresher for soldiers was a wine-vinegar sponge carried on the march to moisten their lips periodically. Some scholars contend it was such "vinegar" that was given to Jesus on Calvary, as a kindness rather than cruelty.

For a deep-colored red somewhat like the Romans made, try Taurasi from Mastroberardino. It is rich-tasting and easy to find most anywhere. For lighter whites, try Robert Mondavi's Moscato d'Oro, also a Roman favorite. For a Roman "smoked" wine, substitute a Madeira like Malmsey or Verdelho. For something Roman but still modern-tasting, try a fine Chateau Ausone from Bordeaux named for the native Bordeaux professor Ausonius, tutor of the Emperor Gratian. It is certainly as good as anything the Romans drank, probably better.

Agoston Haraszthy, Father of California Wine, Enjoyed a Vintage Lifestyle

A few weeks ago I promised to tell the story of the "Father of California wine," the incredible Agoston Haraszthy, who brought the Zinfandel grape to California and founded Buena Vista, the winery that makes some of the best wines now available. Several readers have repeatedly reminded me of that promise, and I herewith make good on it.

Haraszthy was born in 1812 in the region of Backsa, Hungary. His family was country gentry and also winemakers of some renown. At that time, Hungarian wines were better known and more respected than they are now, especially the Tokay dessert wine, favorite of the Russian czars. Their Slavic spelling "czar" of the Latin title "Caesar," which they bestowed on themselves, tells you a lot about their self-image.

Haraszthy studied law in Vienna but quit for the more adventurous life of an officer in the Guards of the Emperor of Austria, a political realist and survivor who was both the nephew of the guillotined Marie Antoinette and the father-in-law of Napoleon. Haraszthy himself had a foot in each camp, being both an aristocrat and a revolutionary, some-what like the better-known Lafayette. While an officer in the Imperial Guard, he secretly joined the Hungarian nationalists under Kossuth (for whom the town in Mississippi is named) and eventually had to flee to America to escape the heat generated by his revolutionary activities.

Upon his return to Hungary in 1842, Haraszthy sold his family's estate and brought his wife and parents to America, where he bought ten thousand acres of land along the Wisconsin River. There he began calling himself "Count," which some historians say was a title he simply expropriated, but coats of arms have always been cheap, and titles were easily purchased in those days. Haraszthy also founded a town with the unpronounceable name of Szepta, which is Hungarian for "beautiful view." Later, more practical and less esthetic settlers renamed it "Sauk City."

Haraszthy planted vineyards of European vinifera grapes on his new land, but they all died from the harsh winters and vine diseases. Undaunted, he started a ferryboat line across the Mississippi and also ran a steamboat from St. Paul down to Galena, Illinois, supplying meat and grain from his farms to the troops of the Northwest Territory. Quickly wealthy, he entered politics and helped Wisconsin gain statehood. The climate, however, gave him asthma, so in 1848 Haraszthy emigrated again to the healthier climate of Southern California.

He chose to go by the "easy" southern route via the Santa Fe Trail. He was accompanied by his mother, another real survivor, who had married the U.S. attorney for Wisconsin, and his wife and six children. By then a big man with coal-black hair and a bushy beard, Haraszthy was wagon master a la Ward Bond of a twenty-wagon train of Conestoga prairie schooners pulled by teams of oxen. He led his wagon train safely through the American Indian tribes of Kansas, Texas, New Mexico, and Arizona, and arrived in San Diego in 1849. It was then a town of 650 people.

His friends in Wisconsin got word that Haraszthy had been massacred by American Indians en route and sold all his businesses and lands in Wisconsin and sent the money on to his "widow." Haraszthy took the proceeds and bought the estate of the son of the former Mexican governor near San Diego.

There he planted yet another vineyard, this time with vinifera "mission" grapes that had been brought to California from Spain centuries earlier by Franciscan friars. This time his vines lived, but the wine was so mediocre that he vowed to import the best European vinifera grapes as soon as he could afford it.

In the meantime Haraszthy and his family planted orchards, opened a livery stable and butcher shop, and began speculating in land. He quickly became wealthy again and entered politics. By late 1850 he was elected the first sheriff of San Diego County and later a delegate to the state assembly. He began calling himself "Colonel" instead of "Count." His mantle as heroic pioneer began to slip a little, however, when his first real scandal arrived. His stepfather, as chairman of the City Council, approved Haraszthy's bid, which was double that of any other, to build a county jail. Its walls promptly fell down, but the taxpayers paid Haraszthy to rebuild it anyway, a monument to his gifts of persuasion.

On his first trip north to meet the state assembly at Vallejo, he saw the Gold Rush in full bloom. To an entrepreneur like Haraszthy, it seemed the Promised Land. The climate also looked better for vineyards, being sunny but less hot, similar to the best winelands of Europe. As he put it, the problem at San Diego was that the winters were so warm that "my vines don't get their rest." He also sensed certain social differences between the two regions and introduced a bill to divide California into two territories, north and south. The bill failed, but it was probably as sociologically sound then as some say it would be now.

Still pursuing his dream of making great wines in America (and a little money on the side), in 1852 Haraszthy sold everything in San Diego and moved his family to the San Francisco Bay area for yet another new start among the new wealthy of Gold Rush-era northern California. The new wealth of the miners was mingled with the already opulent lifestyle of the powerful Spanish grandees who owned most of the best land. Far from the Mexican government and its control, the high-living, free-wheeling land barons of old California held lavish fiestas for hundreds of guests that lasted for weeks at a time.

Life on their semi-feudal estates was apparently much like that portrayed in old Zorro movies. To Haraszthy, those scenes of elegant rowdiness no doubt had great appeal. He saw a tremendous market for wines among both the old grandees and the newly rich miners, and he planted a large vineyard of some two hundred acres south of San Francisco. Again it failed, this time due to the great fogs in the area, which kept the grapes from getting enough sun. As he had everywhere else when his vineyards failed, Haraszthy went into business, this time building a gold refinery. If alive today, he'd no doubt be making oil rigs or computer chips to finance his winemaking. His gold-refining skills, coupled with his even more developed political skills, procured him the post of Assayer of the San Francisco Mint. There he supervised the processing of more than one hundred million dollars in gold from 1855 to 1857. He built an elaborate Italianate mansion and adopted a lifestyle that was lavish—and suspect—even for that era.

In 1857 he was indicted by a federal grand jury for embezzlement of more than one hundred thousand in gold from the mint. Four years later, after a lengthy Treasury Department investigation, during which the smokestacks of his refineries were thoroughly scraped, the indictment was dismissed because the missing one hundred thousand in gold was all found in soot stuck to the insides of the refineries' chimneys.

Rich again and relatively free of scandal, Haraszthy found the perfect land and climate for the only project he was ever really interested in: winemaking. He bought six thousand acres in the foothills of the Mayacamas Mountains, which separate Napa from Sonoma. The area was called the Valley of the Moon because of the way the moon appears and disappears repeatedly behind six different tiers of mountains. Mayacamas itself is said to mean "howl of the mountain lion," which indicates this was not exactly suburbia at the time.

Grapes had been grown in the area commercially by the provincial Comandante General Vallejo since at least 1834, but from poor quality Mission grapes. Haraszthy revolutionized the California wine industry forever by introducing finer grape varieties and new farming methods. Instead of planting in the rich alluvial valleys, as the others had done, he planted his vines on the mineral-rich hillsides and made the *vines* struggle for their water, producing less but finer juice. One historian said his changes affected northern California much as the cotton gin did the South.

Haraszthy purchased his estate from the brother of General Vallejo, whose twin daughters married Haraszthy's sons, Arpad and Attila, whose name is a reminder of who put the "Hun" in Hungary. The Haraszthys soon had four hundred acres planted in fine varietals, including Riesling. In a single year they planted more than eighty thousand vines on more than one hundred acres—by hand. Anyone who has ever tried to plant or tend grapevines will realize the enormity of this accomplishment. Of course eight-dollar-per-month Chinese labor helped. The tenacious Chinese, with their legendary industry, working by moon-light on the hottest days, also dug eight enormous wine cellars, each one hundred feet deep, into the limestone of the mountain faces, and built two large stone wineries that are still in use. Haraszthy named his new winery Buena Vista. It still thrives today.

The vine which did best at Buena Vista was something of a mystery. It had been sent to Haraszthy by a Hungarian friend in New York. Because of its origin, Haraszthy assumed it was also Hungarian, but was puzzled because his family had been winemakers in Hungary for generations and he had never heard of the grape before he saw it written on the box: Zinfandel. Today its origins are known to be Croatian by way of Italy's southern Primitivo grape. It is undoubtedly California's most distinctive grape and still makes some of the state's best wine.

In the late 1860s the restless Haraszthy developed an interest in Central America and decided he could make yet another fortune there by harvesting sugar cane and mahogany. He obtained a lease on one hundred thousand acres and moved there, leaving his sons Arpad and Attila in charge of Buena Vista. But in 1868, tragedy struck. His wife, not surprisingly, came down with yellow fever, as did so many other new settlers to the mosquito-infested new country. Then old Colonel Haraszthy himself, trying to cross an unbridged coastal river by climbing across a tree limb, fell in and drowned in July 1869. It was a sad but typical end to a life filled with amazing adventures.

Hemingway at the Oyster Bar
with Wine

In that string of months with "r" in their names, oysters are said to be in season. All foods are better with wine, but none profits so much from it as the oyster on its own shell.

Much debate can be had as to which wine goes best with oysters. Many favor Champagne, sparkling or still, with fine oysters. Others say only true Chablis will do. I agree with both, gladly taking turns as each dozen is ordered. Still others, most notably the voracious wine lover Ernest Hemingway, preferred Sancerre, a lean but ripe Sauvignon Blanc from the upper-most reaches of the beautiful Loire River of western France. French kings for generations chose it as their preferred summer playground, and the nearby wines were their favorites.

In 1961, while spending the summer nearby, I discovered the medieval town of Sancerre with its narrow streets, ancient buildings, and sweeping vistas. At the same time I discovered its unique wines, before discovering that Hemingway had long since called them favorites.

One good thing about modern Sancerre is that it is not a scarce or expensive wine. Over a half million cases are made each year of the white alone, with another 300,000 of red from Pinot Noir. Of course for oysters, only white Sancerre will do. The quality of the red is a matter of taste. I've always loved both but preferred the red, except with oysters.

Sancerre the village gives its name to the whole region, but the best wines actually come from neighboring villages and vineyards, whose names often appear in larger letters on labels than that of Sancerre itself. Chavignol, Les Monts Damnés, and Verdigny. Good producer names to look for at the bottom of the labels are Cotat, Reverdy, Roger, Delaporte, and Thomas. The most available nationwide is the excellent Michel Redde.

When I was a teenager, the idea of eating an oyster in any form, especially raw, was scary at best. I therefore actually began my experience with Sancerres tasting them with cheeses, especially goat cheeses, which often go better with white wines than reds. Given my reluctance to attempt raw oysters at the time, my first Sancerres washed down some little Crottin cheeses, which were terrific. Little did I then suspect that I was eating goat cheese, probably as gross a thought to the teenage American mind as an oyster. Even worse is the translation of Crottin (little white turds)—very French. In fact, way too French. As my father used to say: "If you have to use a French word to say it, it's probably nasty."

Fortunately, my oyster-phobia passed at age twenty, and most Sancerres I've known since then have accompanied dozens of that most self-sacrificing of shellfish. Aromatic, distinctive Sancerre is very hard to beat with oysters. Julius Caesar is said to have chosen Sancerre as one of his main regional capitals on the beautiful upper Loire River. With nearby oak forests for making casks and some of the most beautiful scenery in all France, one could never go wrong in choosing Sancerre, whether for a real visit or just an imaginary one.

As has been said by extreme gourmets, man's best friend, the most unselfish of animals, may be not the dog at all but the oyster, preferably on the half-shell. Prepackaged, ready to eat, bite-size, delicious with just a taste of lemon juice as seasoning, what could possibly match the oyster for sheer generosity toward humans?

About the only thing oysters lack is their own wine-in-the-shell to go with them. But there are plenty available. One traditional oyster wine has been true Chablis from the French region of that name. Old U.S. imitations labeled "Chablis" are not good, being blends of lesser grapes and often sweetened. Of American wines, the driest, leanest Chardonnays and Sauvignon Blancs are probably best. But as much as I love American wines, for some reason (like Hemingway and Julius Caesar) I've always preferred certain French wines for oysters; their acid balance is so good.

Next to Chablis, which is often too expensive for my budget, some classic oyster wines are the steely dry, clean whites of Muscadet, from the region where the Loire River meets the Atlantic Ocean. One is even called "l'Huitriere," or "the oyster one."

A French wine that is an especially good value in the United States, because it is not as well known, is Aligoté, made all over Burgundy. Although not as subtle as the classic Chardonnay-based wines of Burgundy, the modest Aligoté sort of "comes out" when matched with good oysters. Because they are not made from the noble Chardonnay grape, legally the Aligoté wines from around the village of Chablis cannot call themselves "Chablis," but only Aligoté, after the grape from which they are made.

White Bordeaux are to my taste often a little too soft and mellow for oyster companions, except for certain Graves. The otherwise undemanding oyster seems to require something with a bite of acid to set it off just right. Bordeaux's most inexpensive white, from the sandy region known as Entre-Deux-Mers (actually, "between two rivers"), is another answer. Most Bordeaux shippers bottle at least one good Entre-Deux-Mers. Another choice is a dry Sauvignon Blanc from the upper end of the Loire such as Quincy, Reuilly, or Pouilly-Fumé, not to be confused with the softer and more expensive Pouilly-Fuissé of lower Burgundy.

The most difficult choice is what to drink with oysters accompanied by a hot, spicy red sauce, the kind you eat with boiled shrimp. To me, oysters on the half-shell are much more subtle and tasteable, if that is a word, with just lemon juice or with nothing on them at all, especially when fresh and salty from the sea. But if you like the hot sauce, for some reason a softer, fruitier white seems to go better. It is at that point that I really like one of the leaner, unoaked American Chardonnays, something like a Beringer, a BV, or a Fetzer.

For those who feel compelled to commit *huitrecide* by cooking them, and like my wife enjoy extremes like oysters Rockefeller, a whole new ballgame presents itself. Despite old saws to the contrary, I have often observed in New Orleans, the heartland of oysters Rockefeller, slightly chilled light, inexpensive reds being enjoyed with them. After all, I say grumpily, if you're going to ruin oysters by cooking them, you might as well compound the felony by chilling a red to go with them.

Thomas Jefferson: Wine Expert

The foremost American wine expert of his time was our third President, Thomas Jefferson, who tasted and left written comments about most of the wines of the eighteenth and early nineteenth centuries. Surprisingly, most of those wines still exist today, and the detailed descriptions of them left by Jefferson are generally applicable today (with some notable exceptions), since the same wines are still made in the same places and even now bear the same or similar names.

My interest in Jefferson as a historical figure dates back to the period when I worked in Washington as an aide to Senator John Stennis, a graduate of the University of Virginia Law School and a great admirer of Jefferson. My particular interest in the wines of Jefferson dates back to 1973, when I was writing a wine column for the *Washington Post*. As a result of one article on old Madeiras, I received a call from James Bear, then curator of Jefferson's mountain home, Monticello, near Charlottesville.

Bear had been systematically collecting, as he came across them, all of Jefferson's references to wine, which had turned out to be considerable. Jim asked me to join him in what sounded like a modest project of producing a little pamphlet on Jefferson's wines for distribution at Monticello. Needless to say, I readily accepted, jumped in my VW convertible and headed to Monticello for a visit.

The variety of Jefferson's interests and expertise, from architecture to patent law, was vaguely known to me, as it is to most Americans. But I had never imagined the breadth and depth of his knowledge of wines. His tastes ran from Sauternes and Champagnes (which he insisted *not* have bubbles) to well-traveled Madeiras and classic Bordeaux, which he would buy only if bottled by the chateaux and only direct from the owners of the chateaux—to avoid adulteration.

Jefferson constantly searched for bargains among the lesser-known "country" wines of France and Italy, and imported his own "jug" wines, mostly from Portugal, to keep costs down.

After collecting and studying literally hundreds of letters and memos by Jefferson ordering and discussing wines, Jim Bear and I somehow never finished the project of the pamphlet. In 1983 we let the Vinifera Wine Society of Virginia have our research, and they published some of it in a volume of their journal, which is now out of print. Because of my continued interest in the project, however, or perhaps just out of sheer cussedness at leaving something unfinished, I began in 1985 a full-length book on the subject.

It was finally published in 2006 by the University Press of Mississippi as Thomas Jefferson on Wine *(the title refers to Jefferson's writings on wine and does not mean to imply he was "high on wine" as some suggest).*

Jefferson: "Disguised in Drink?"

Shortly before writing the Declaration of Independence, Thomas Jefferson noted in his account book: "Broached a pipe of Madeira, 1770 vintage." By 1826, the year of his death, he had left written comments on hundreds of the world's best wines, nearly all of which still exist today under the same names. In an era when price lists of Virginia taverns offered "small beer, bad rum, and Madeira lemonade," Jefferson had a cellar as varied as any in Europe. He knew and drank nearly all the great wines: Lafite, Margaux, Yquem, Chambertin, Montrachet, Hermitage, Tokay. And he paid for them: During his first term as president, when his salary was $25,000, he spent $13,000 just on wines.

He also knew the depths. During his last year as president he spent only $200 on wines, and when he died, nearly bankrupt, the once-great Monticello wine cellar contained mainly Scuppernong and a handful of the cheaper wines of southern France. In the interim, Jefferson tasted the gamut of the world's wines. In his youth, "wine" in colonial Virginia usually meant a sweet dessert wine drunk after dinner, not with it. Only during his years as American minister in Paris did he learn really to appreciate dry dinner wines.

Returning to America, he found that a sweet wine like Sauternes still "hit the palate," as he put it, of Americans most favorably, but Jefferson himself went on drinking the dry ones, establishing at his table the rule that "you drink as you please, and converse at your ease." Jefferson never liked liquor or brandy, and kept old Antigua rum only for his servants. He was a veritable evangelist of wine, which he felt promoted moderation, saying in an often-quoted letter: "No nation is drunken where wine is cheap." He was himself moderate in his consumption, noting, "my measure is a sober one of three or four glasses at dinner, and not a drop at any other time." Wine glasses passed down through his family indicate his glasses were fairly small, from three to five ounces generally.

One record says Jefferson drank three glasses of Champagne at a single toast during Lafayette's retirement party, but his favorite servant Isaac insisted that he had never known Jefferson to be "disguised in drink." His enormous political and intellectual accomplishments themselves certainly belie any excessive indulgence in alcohol.

Whatever the intemperance around him, there is no evidence, despite his love of good wines, that Jefferson was ever troubled by physical addiction to alcohol nor suffered any related disease, such as gout. In fact, his interest in wine definitely had its moral side. He wrote many times to Hamilton, Monroe, Washington and the Swiss-born Secretary of the Treasury Albert Gallatin, urging that the government lower wine taxes to encourage drinking of wine in place of intoxicating liquors such as rum and whiskey, which were then gaining great popularity, much to the detriment of eighteenth-century American society and morals.

Several of Jefferson's own employees, servants, and family, some of them personal favorites, were problem drinkers. For these reasons Jefferson was a lifelong advocate of wine drinking as a substitute for spirits, since wine contains, now as in Jefferson's time, only about ten to fifteen percent alcohol, compared with forty percent or fifty percent in the case of whiskey and rum.

Jefferson specifically attributed his longevity (he died at eighty-three) to moderate wine drinking and light eating of a mostly vegetarian diet, especially in his later years. As he once said, he liked meat mainly to flavor his vegetables. One of his canons for a happy life was that one rarely regretted eating too little.

Thomas Jefferson's Wine Cellar

During an early visit to Thomas Jefferson's spectacular home at Monticello, the curator lent me the key to the wine cellar for some "research." The key was a large, sturdy, incongruously modern one, and not rusty at all, as I thought it should have been. It fitted into an equally modern deadbolt lock set into a large iron-barred door, there to restrain thirsty visitors.

The wine cellar itself has recently been restored but back then was left in more or less its original state: dust, cobwebs, and all. This cellar was not idealized, but left more or less like the rather messy Jefferson and his family actually knew it. With Jefferson away so much of the time holding public office, the wine cellar at Monticello was often supervised by his older daughter Martha. She wrote to him many times about how they had more wine than they had either bottles or corks.

It was Martha who accepted the large casks of Portuguese wines from the muleteers and riverboatmen who delivered them to Monticello in Jefferson's absence. It was she who drew the wine from the casks into bottles and knocked in the corks (or *had* them knocked in). Later her son Jefferson Randolph became the Monticello cellar master.

The day of my first visit to the cellar was a Saturday, always a busy day for Monticello. This one was also a University of Virginia football weekend and visitors were swarming like ants over the grounds and in and out of the buildings. Although I had locked the door to the cellar behind me, it was still open to view between the bars. Seeing my notebook, the groups of visitors assumed I was there as a sort of docent to explain the cellar to them, or that I at least knew something about it. They bombarded me with questions about Jefferson and his wines all afternoon, to the point that I got very little work done. The questions, however, were probably at least as useful as the "research" would have been. They taught me that visitors knew much more about Jefferson and his love of fine wines than I'd expected. Many knew, for example, of his correspondence with winemakers in Bordeaux and of his coach and barge tours of the vineyards of southern France in 1787. They also knew the names of some of the wines he liked and wanted to know more about what those wines are like now.

In general, people of our era have a tremendously respectful attitude towards Thomas Jefferson, almost to the point of obsequiousness. A similar attitude once existed toward George Washington, typified by the cherry tree story. Eventually Washington got such a goody-goody image that people lost interest in him as a real person—except perhaps for his teeth. The same thing could conceivably happen one day to the reputation of Jefferson, who has been nearly deified by some. On the other hand, the very opposite might happen. The intense speculation and ribald humor, produced by the book about Jefferson's active sex life with beautiful concubine Sally Hemmings, and the equally vociferous denials of it by his defenders, may have the effect of trivializing him into a sort of eighteenth-century soap opera.

Jefferson's cool, somewhat musty wine cellar can bring one back to earth. It tends to balance the image of him as an inquisitive, bookish man seeking new experiences in esoteric wines with the rough-and-ready world of colonial Virginia, where most destinations could be reached only by horseback, and both wolves and American Indians roamed free. If you read Jefferson's lengthy cellar lists and his many letters ordering wines, it sounds like a huge area would be needed under Monticello to store it all. But his biggest quantities of wine by far were actually stored and consumed in the White House during his eight years there.

The cellar at Monticello is only a single, rather average-sized room. Although cool and mostly underground, it has a small, high window to the outside like an English basement, and is nothing like a wine cellar in Europe or California. The floor is simply the ground. All along one wall, square wooden bins have been reconstructed according to Jefferson's notes, and filled with laid-down bottles. On the top shelf there is plenty of room for the large, round eighteenth-century bottles that won't lie down for aging, the kind that were already old-fashioned in Jefferson's day. There is also room on top for wines that must be stored standing up, like Ports and sherries, because their high alcohol content eats up their corks if they are stored on their sides. The floors under the bottom bins are made of damp sand, an excellent cooling device Jefferson said he learned from a wine merchant's cellar he visited in Marseilles.

On the wall opposite the bins, behind a table with corking gear, is an old bricked-up fireplace. On both sides of it remain the old pulleys of the dumbwaiter, which Jefferson used to bring wine upstairs without going down to the cellar. Some of the finest wines in the world rested in that cellar and rode ancient dumbwaiters to Jefferson's dining room. From that cellar came the Champagnes he drank with Lafayette, the Bordeaux he shared with Madison and Monroe, and even the Greek wine of Samos he drank as an old man with visitor Daniel Webster.

Of all the multitude of subjects which Jefferson took an interest in, I know of none which allows one more completely to recreate the atmosphere and spirit of what has been called the "lost world" of Thomas Jefferson than a visit to his wine cellar at Monticello.

Indeed, if Thomas Jefferson returned to America today, he might well feel more at home in a wine cellar than in any other place in our fast-paced modern word he might choose to visit.

Wine Won't Do? Try Cider

Even the most dedicated wine lover gets tired of wine on occasion. It happened to me recently. Other times you end up in a spot so remote and dry that there is no wine to go with a meal that badly needs it. What can the wineless do? Certainly not turn to Pepsi.

As in most matters concerning wine, Thomas Jefferson left in his letters some excellent advice on substitutes. As the greatest wine lover of the Founding Fathers, and the most-informed president on wine and food generally, Jefferson still speaks with authority.

Late in life, as he neared bankruptcy, Jefferson could no longer afford the fine wines he had once enjoyed, so he turned to cider for what he called his "table drink" with meals.

But Jefferson's cider was no ordinary commercial stuff. As his overseer Edmund Bacon once complained, "Every March we had to bottle all his cider. Dear me, this was a job. It took us two weeks. Mr. Jefferson was very particular about his cider. He gave me instructions to have every apple perfectly clean when it was made."

Jefferson left many letters on cider-making, often noting how he enjoyed a "smart cask of cyder." One letter, written just before he became president in 1800, said the best cider came from a blend of red Hughes and golden Wilding apples, "pressed immediately upon picking," and "not overripe." Seventy bushels made one hundred and twenty gallons.

Jefferson's most detailed comments on cider came after his retirement, when he had hoped to enjoy a cellar full of fine wines, but was prevented from doing so by the War of 1812, which stopped imports of his favorite French, Italian, and Spanish wines for some three years. In 1814, being left "without a drop of wine," he wrote to a friend in Philadelphia to describe his favorite cider, saying it had "more body, less acid, and comes nearer to silky Champagne than any other wine." Jefferson, who loved wine jargon, could not discuss even cider without sounding like a wine connoisseur.

He complained in 1816 that his cider supplies from Norfolk had been watered down by "rascally boatmen," who drank part of the barrels and refilled them with river water. In the year of his death, 1826, when his finances had cut his consumption of fine wine almost to zero, he was still praising cider in a letter to his granddaughter Ellen, calling one cask "more like wine than any liquor I have ever tasted that was not wine."

Virginia, like the Pacific Northwest, has long been known for fine apples, including colorful-sounding varieties like "Northern Spy." In my experience some of the best cider in the world can still be bought, homemade, along rural Virginia roadsides. But if you don't have access to such fine stuff, as I no longer do since my mother's family left Virginia, what is next best? There is much good fresh hard cider from Normandy, the center of France's cider country, that is available nationwide in the U.S. Some English ciders seem to travel pretty well too.

In Vermont and other New England states, small lots of apple wine are still made. If you like mild brandy then Calvados, the apple brandy from Normandy is the best. To my taste, however, cider brandy is to wine brandy as cider vinegar is to wine vinegar—a distant second.

For a table drink, when wine is unavailable or unwanted, my favorite is non-alcoholic, sparkling cider. The easiest to find is Martinelli from California. It has brightened many a meal for us. If you want to see something in your glass that *looks* like red wine, a fairly decent substitute is cranberry juice, odd as it sounds.

One nineteenth-century recipe suggested adding beet juice to make "red-wine" cider, but that is a bit much. The thought alone has caused me to stick to wine.

French Chef Matches Wine
with Grits

Those who have read John Grisham's best-selling novel *The Firm* already know about the beautiful old Peabody Hotel in Memphis. A great chase scene takes place just a few feet from the Peabody's elegant Chez Philippe restaurant, whose wine list has given pleasure to my palate and pain to my wallet for years.

Last week, near where the embattled hero of John Grisham's thriller *The Firm* leaped from the balcony, a group of us had a more sedentary, but equally unusual, adventure. Famed chef Jean-Louis Palladin came to the Peabody to cook a meal with his Gascon friend, Peabody chef Jose Gutierrez, recently honored as one of the United States' best new chefs in *Food and Wine* magazine.

At his own restaurant, Jean-Louis, formerly located at the Watergate Hotel in Washington, Palladin was known for his ingenious experiments with unusual U.S. foods. Now a good eel (a long, skinny fish and *not* a snake) is fine with me, but what wine goes with mountain oysters? Palladin had promised us not only sea urchins and Georgia caviar but stone-ground South Carolina grits with the meat course. But what wine goes with grits? It promised to be a challenging meal.

We started off traditionally enough with Charles Heidsieck Brut Champagne, which went just fine with minuscule mouthfuls of quail eggs wrapped in brioche. We wondered if we could survive six courses, but when some consist of only two bites it's not so tough. A gulp of caviar, a bite of Maryland crab cake, two sips of Champagne, and we were at the soup course.

The soup sounded like something a Frenchman would think of: sea urchin consommé. It was, however, wonderful, as subtle as the scary-sounding but delicious shark fin soup of Chinese cuisine. Some purists won't drink wine with soup, but this one was different. In the soup were morsels of floating stuffed pastry called *flans*, which went beautifully with the Champagne. So far, so good.

Next came a tougher challenge: seaweed salad in sesame with a *croustillant* of sea scallops. The wine was an inexpensive favorite of mine, Pinot Blanc from Alsace by Gustave Lorentz. The seaweed was gelatinous and crunchy in a sort of Japanese style. One disrespectful wag compared its appearance to Gummy Bears, but all praised its taste.

The scallops, however, were my favorite dish of the evening. Encrusted with a light emulsion of shaved and browned ginger, this was a dish to die for. The Pinot Blanc, poor man's Chardonnay, equaled its subtlety for half the price.

The fish course was Chesapeake Bay rockfish over basil, lemon confit, dried shad roe and tomato. Its saltiness and spiciness pretty well killed the delicate Pinot Blanc at first taste, but a tablemate had sneaked in and hidden under our table another bottle of Champagne, a Krug reserve, which made it all better.

Next came filets of lamb and with them the grits. Now I love my cheese grits for breakfast, but with wine? Palladin's grits, instead of being smooth like I'm used to, were very coarse-ground, with a consistency like bulgur wheat, the way they apparently like them in South Carolina. They were served with a consommé and tasted more like barley or oats than corn or polenta. Surprisingly, grits are good with red wine, in this case a Cotes du Rhone from the famed Domaine Goubert.

We polished off the evening easily with a glass of Muscat Canelli from Kendall Jackson, light and almost clear, and a crisp pastry filled with nectarines in honey. It was worth my rapidly increasing weight in gold.

In Cajun Country with Wine

There was a time, not so long ago, when Cajun food could be found only in Louisiana, and most Americans who had never been to New Orleans had never tasted it. Then, thanks to chefs like Paul Prudhomme and modern media hoopla, blackened redfish threatened to become our national dish. Everywhere you went in America, from California to New York, Louisiana restaurants had sprung up. All of this was great, since the food is outstanding, but it presented problems. What wine, for example, do you drink with crawfish?

My rule in choosing wines to match foods has always been to go with informed tradition. Find out what the local people who first cooked the dish like to drink with it. By that system you end up drinking Italian wines with Italian foods, French with French, and so on right down to the regions and towns where both the foods and wines originated and became wedded in taste over many generations.

Having lived in New Orleans for two years while in school at Tulane, and having traveled widely in the bayou country of south Louisiana, I knew that there was no such thing as Louisiana wine. Even New Orleans, the city with the finest food in America (take that, New York), has never been known as a wine-drinkers' mecca.

To review our prejudices, my wife and I recently traveled to the Cajun capital, Lafayette, for a refresher. We decided on Mulate's in nearby Breaux Bridge after consultation with a bellman with a strong Cajun accent. He explained you pronounce Mulate's as if it were an order to a cow: "Moo lots." That, plus the alliterative quality of "Bro" Bridge, with its ethnic ring, won us over. Mulate's was also said to have lively Cajun bands, and our daughters were along and wanted to dance. At real Cajun restaurants everyone dances together, from grandpas to three-year-olds.

The exterior of Mulate's looked promising. The door handle was carved to look like a giant shrimp, not to attract tourists but from real homey devotion to the idea. The large parking lot dispelled my fears of tourism, being filled exclusively with Louisiana license tags. Large, hand-painted signs out front accurately described the atmosphere inside. The first said *"Bon Manger, Bon Temps,"* meaning "Good Eating, Good Times."

The atmosphere of Mulate's was what we had expected and hoped for—happy and lively without being raucous. The music helped, but sounded more Irish than French, the fiddles and old-time accordion giving it a sort of hypnotic, ancient effect as the evening wore on.

The Irish-bar feeling is not surprising. The Cajuns of Louisiana are descendants of the French-speaking Acadians of Canada, exiled to the southern swamps by the British. But the Acadians' original home was Brittany, the Celtic part of France, so it is natural that their music still sounds oddly Gaelic despite its French words.

The biggest surprise at Mulate's was the "Cajun" wine list. It was the only thing on the menu in English and featured Chardonnays and Cabernets from Jordan and Fetzer Wineries of California and Ste. Michelle of Washington state, and carafes of Robert Mondavi rosé. In one sense they were typically Cajun: simple, suited to the food, and excellent at four different price levels. There was not a French wine on the list—very American *these* French.

The menu was similar. There were few dishes, but all were good and all were fresh, local specialties. Crawfish are only in season from January to June, so we laid aside the *cuisses de quaouarons* (frogthighs) and *bouchees de barbue* (catfish bites) and got into huge plates of crawfish *etoufee.* Mulate's did not over-spice the already spicy crawfish, and the accompanying sauce of onions and peppers was among the best I've tasted in years. The word *etoufee* literally means "stuffed," but in this case the term "smothered" would be more accurate.

All the Chardonnays won with this version of crawfish, the buttery Jordan being the best. This was something of an exception. For Cajun food, my theory has been to order what you like to eat and drink inexpensive wines since most of the foods are spicy. If you insist on making wine the centerpiece, then order the mildest thing on the menu.

In a last-minute folly, my wife ordered us some red-hot Cajun andouille sausage, which was served with hot mustard on the side—as if it needed more spice. The waitress rightly suggested that only beer would go with it and brought along a slice of lime to rub around the rim of the glass. The lime sort of married the hot sausage with the cold beer. It was not a gimmick—it really served a purpose. No wonder Cajun food seems to be taking over the country.

Bayou Rouge:
Wine in the Deep South?

One Saturday long ago on a hot and dusty Delta day, a new winery opened in Mississippi—our fifth since the Native Wine law took effect. The newest effort was promising, being planted in a mixture of vinifera and French hybrid grapes. It was called Claiborne Vineyards after its owner, Claiborne Barnwell, a civil engineer who also farms cotton and soybeans, or did until the vineyards devoured all his time.

The winery was located in the deep Delta just north of Indianola on Highway 49 West North (one direction per highway would have been enough). The sales room was an old plantation office, mercifully air-conditioned, but still bearing from earlier times a round metal sign proclaiming membership in the "Seed Improvement Association." The vineyards were located behind it, on sun-baked land as flat as a table, in appearance every bit like the San Joaquin Valley of central California.

What was a man like Barnwell doing in the wine business? Perhaps it is the wave of the future. It was not so long ago that growing rice or sunflowers in the Delta was thought slightly eccentric. And Barnwell did go to Mississippi State, whose beautiful School of Enology was once the parent of a whole new generation of grape-growers and winemakers in the long Mississippi growing season.

Claiborne Barnwell and his wife Marion, a writer and professor at Delta State, also fit the demographic profile of so many new winemakers all over America: professionals in other fields seeking new challenges in the hard but satisfying labor of a family winery, one of the few real family-farming operations still possible.

The instinct for fine wines may also just be in the blood. Claiborne Barnwell is the nephew of the late Craig Claiborne, America's finest food writer, the former food editor and restaurant critic of the *New York*

Times, and Sunflower County's best known native son after quarterback Archie Manning. His autobiography, *A Feast Made for Laughter*, was a best-seller for months. The Claiborne in Barnwell apparently runs deep because his first wines definitely showed it.

The winery was a family one in more than its name. In addition to Uncle Craig Claiborne, who came all the way from New York for the opening, brother Bobby Barnwell, whom I had not seen since Millsaps College days, returned from thirteen years in Saudi Arabia for the occasion. The Barnwells' son Will faithfully handled the guest register for hours and ably answered questions of all kinds. Their daughter Craig (these names can get a little confusing) took visitors on rolling tours of the vineyards in the family golf cart, an excellent idea until she had a flat tire.

Next to the wines themselves, which were a big success, the appearance of the vines was the most encouraging part of the entire day. They looked in terrific health, as neat and well tended as a maiden aunt's bedroom during a Deep South Pilgrimage. Claiborne allegedly talked to his vines when needed, and sat up with them like sick children when it was believed they had contracted the dreaded Pierce's Disease. The vines, alas, never recovered.

While the vines were thriving, especially Cabernet Sauvignons planted in 1983, they held huge clusters of healthy young grapes. Some Chardonnays, planted only the year before, were growing almost like kudzu.

The winery's capacity was a small five hundred cases per year, but a large expansion was likely if the first wines were well received, which they were. From a preliminary tasting of eight, including Cabernet Sauvignon, Pinot Noir, Marechal Foch, Seyval Blanc, Villard Blanc, and others, the future of Claiborne Vineyards looked bright.

Bayou Rouge, their blended, everyday generic red, was named with an appropriate Delta sense for mixed metaphor and had a nice balance of acidity, especially for a wine just made last fall from a blend of ten different French hybrids. At just five dollars it could have become the everyday dry dinner wine Mississippians are always looking for.

Sad to say, Pierce's Disease, which once threatened to destroy the vineyards of Southern California's Temecula Valley, was just too endemic for

Mississippi, and its once promising wine industry is now just a poignant memory. But wine in the South is not dead at all. The fine wines of Virginia, North Carolina, and Texas are now thriving, bless them.

Chef Frank Stitt at Highlands in Birmingham with Wine

Some of Arthur Conan Doyle's most famous mysteries are the ones he never got around to writing. In several Sherlock Holmes novels, his associate Dr. Watson asks Holmes about some intriguing titles that Doyle never followed up on by actually writing the story. *The Giant Rat of Sumatra* is one such title I recall. What a loss.

Less of a loss is a book that probably will never be written—*The Great Wines of Birmingham.* Some have even said that if such a book were published, the pages would be blank anyway.

As friends have noted, the protector of Birmingham is Vulcan, not Bacchus. Yet friends of mine seem to keep moving there. First, it was my neighbor and law dean Parham Williams; then Sam Knowlton, neighbor and former D.A. from Perthshire. What would Parham and Sam do for wine in Birmingham?

For one thing, they'll find that Alabama, like Louisiana, allows wine to be sold in grocery stores, unlike Mississippi where they used to live. For another thing, they'll find that lots of what some call Yurpies (Young Rural Professionals) have moved there. They demand not only such amenities as quiet air conditioning and free trash compactors, but mellow Chardonnays and smooth Cabernets.

During a visit to Birmingham on legal business, I went to the lovely restored area known as Five Points, a tony name for a place where several streets intersect. To my surprise, there was a restaurant called Highlands that had a surpassingly good wine list. With your smoked Scottish salmon or Apalachicola oysters on the half shell, you could get several outstanding wines by the glass: Acacia Chardonnay from California, Puligny-Montrachet from Burgundy, or Muscadet from the Loire. Unbelievably, Highlands also had its own *private* bottling of several wines from Joseph Phelps winery of Napa Valley.

To clear your palate, Highlands had its own fresh watercress supplied by a little old lady in a nearby county. In all, the wine list had seventy-three items, all well chosen. Of German wines, they had Thomas Jefferson's favorite, Brauneberger, from the Mosel Valley across from Berncastel. In red wines, the Cheval Blanc from Bordeaux was naturally a little steep, but there were Duboeuf Beaujolais and a fine Rhone from the village of Gigondas.

Add a dozen of the finest California Cabernets and several excellent wines of every type from Meursault to true Champagne in *half*-bottles, and one can begin to understand a little better the appeal of the Highlands. With all due respect to Birmingham, the atmosphere and wine list at Highlands reminded me a lot more of the Commander's Palace in New Orleans than it did Birmingham. If this keeps up, the city will soon merit a detour to it instead of around it. Maybe Parham and Sam will invite me for another visit.

The Hochar Family and the Wines of the Middle East

Even before the Gulf Wars, it was hard to get a good bottle of wine in the Middle East. The heavy, teetotaling hand of Islam has long stifled wine production in most nations in that region, which was once the heartland of fine wines. Only in moderately Islamic Turkey and in the Christian parts of Lebanon and in Israel is wine still a staple of everyday life.

One of the most courageous wine-making families in the world is the Hochar family of Lebanon. Their winery, called Chateau Musar, is located in the beautiful, war-torn Bekaa Valley, near the bloodiest battles of the seemingly endless Lebanese and Syrian civil wars. Somehow the Hochars have managed to continue producing and exporting to the United States their great wines, which for character and quality rival the best reds of California and France's Rhone Valley.

Just to the north of Iraq, Turkey produces a fair amount of wine. Some of it comes from the northern part of the country near Armenia, where Noah supposedly had his vineyard, close to Mt. Ararat. Turkey in fact is now the largest wine producer of the eastern Mediterranean. The most common Turkish brand now available in the United States is Kavaklidere, which is generally not bad, and its colorful labels are outstanding for collectors. A Turkish white called Trakya, made from the Semillon grape, was also pretty palatable when I tasted it recently in Baltimore.

From Ancient Times

The Egyptians once made some of the greatest wines in the world. Even the wine-loving Romans enjoyed them. Egypt still produces some wine, most of it pretty ordinary stuff. The labels nostalgically recall former glories with names like "Cleopatra white" and "Ptolemy red."

A great little paperback called *King Tut's Wine Cellar* by Egyptologist Leonard Lesko tells the story of ancient Egyptian wines interpreted from murals in unearthed tombs of several pharaohs. They depict vintages and even describe preferred growths much as in modern Bordeaux.

The Israelis now make better wine than anything from Babylonia or Egypt. Largely with wineries and vines donated by the Rothschilds of Bordeaux, the Israelis make some very pleasant wines from classic vinifera varieties like Cabernet and Sauvignon Blanc. It seems frivolous to talk of wine with wars going on, but most great generals, from Alexander the Great to George Washington, were ardent wine lovers. The Crusaders brought back to Europe a taste for Persian wines like Shiraz. German troops "liberated" many French wines, and vice versa, and returning GIs helped start the wine revolution in the United States after World War II, discovering wine in Europe and bringing it here a full decade before tourists discovered it.

Choice of Generals

One of the most surprising of wine lovers among generals was a former Kansas farm boy who was also a secret ladies' man: General Dwight David Eisenhower. Long before he was president, Eisenhower loved wine from his European campaigns.

Once, when visiting the White House, I asked a longtime employee who was the greatest wine lover of the presidents from Roosevelt to Reagan. "Eisenhower, by far," was the answer. "He loved Sauternes from Bordeaux, and even knew the chateaux and vintages, not to mention lots of Mosels from Germany." Those must have tasted especially sweet, even when not late-picked, after taking them away from the Nazis.

The Basques and Their Wines

One of my favorite regions of France is the Basque Country. Unfortunately, nowadays about the only time we hear about the Basque Country, or Basques in general, is when a terrorist bomb goes off. That is not the Basques as I know them. Basque cuisine, with its crawfish, spicy sauces, and Spanish influence on a French base, reminds me more than any other of our uniquely American Creole-Cajun food of south Louisiana. And the ancient Basques, on both the French and Spanish sides of the border that divides them, are generally peaceful people.

There are actually a substantial number of Basque ranchers in our own West, and most people would be surprised to know that powerful former Nevada Senator Paul Laxalt was of Basque origin, as was former Reds' catcher Andy Etchebarren. At their ancestral home, on the Atlantic coast by their main resort of St. Jean de Luz, in their commercial city of Bayonne, or in their Pyrenees Mountains strongholds, the Basques do a lot more than play outdoor Jai-Alai, their national game, and wear their national hat, the beret, and their native rope-soled shoes, espadrilles.

On the French side of the mountains they make some of France's best, least known and least expensive fine wines. To go with them, they have dishes like grilled fresh salmon, fresh game, and poulet basquaise, a spicy chicken dish I swear would be just as at home in New Orleans.

They also make some very fine dishes from eels (long, skinny fish that are *not snakes* at all, believe me). The best Basque white wine is Jurancon from the region near Pau (I know it's now technically in the Béarn department, but it's still Basque). Jurancon was the wine that was rubbed on the lips of French King Henry IV when he was born, and it still takes credit for his having been the famous stud that he was.

Whatever the merits of that claim, Jurancon is a uniquely fine white wine. In its modern form, it is a dry wine of considerable finesse, with an aroma every bit as subtle as Riesling, and equally memorable in its subtle way. It is odd that so few U.S. wineries have tried to grow it here from its Manseng grapes.

The old-fashioned style of Jurancon, also still available, was a dessert wine of fairly high alcohol and a pleasing light sweetness perfect with the Basque national dessert, *gateau basque*, a moist pound-cake-like concoction. Both types of Jurancon may be found by almost any wine store willing to go to a little trouble to find them.

There have been several Basque restaurants in many U.S. cities, notably the old Cote Basque in New York. Most are opulent, general-French, and resemble more a Basque seaside resort than the rustic mountainside inns I associate with the spectacular views of the emerald-green Pyrenees. You can also drink the rich, heady red wine for which the Basques are most famous: Madiran.

Like the white Jurancons, the red Madirans are made from Tannat grapes grown nowhere else in France and recently mildly popular in small quantities in the U.S. Like Jurancon, they are relatively inexpensive and not hard to obtain, but they must not be drunk too young. At least eight years from the vintage date should have elapsed before you try them. But once they are ready, they are a rich and hearty treat, excellent with a steak or rich stew. Like the Basque people themselves, they are well worth getting to know.

An excellent book on these fascinating people is highly recommended: *The Basque History of the World*, by Mark Kurlansky.

My favorite Basque restaurants currently are Chez l'Ami Jean in the 7th arrondissement of Paris and Centro Basco in Chino, California, in the L.A. area. The Centro has real down-home Basque dishes like home-grown rabbit and also has its own boarding house where lots of Basque gardeners live. Worth a detour. Ask for tips on specials from the owner, Bernadette.

The *Wine Spectator* Staff Stocks a Dream Cellar

What would you do if someone gave you ten thousand dollars to stock the wine cellar of your dreams? This scenario was presented a few years ago to editors of the *Wine Spectator*, the wine magazine. Their choices differed tremendously, but their tips are worth considering.

Publisher Marvin Shanken chose entirely red wines, and from just three regions: classified growth Bordeaux, California Cabernet, and vintage Port. Shanken also admitted for the first time, even to himself, that he cellars only wines that he thinks will appreciate in value. His selections show that he is, consciously or not, a "label" buyer, from Chateau Mouton to Opus One. For ten thousand make-believe dollars (this is journalism, not television), Shanken got eighteen cases of wine, at an average price of about forty-six dollars per bottle.

At the other end of the scale was senior editor Per-Henrik Mansson, who got thirty-nine cases, more than double Shanken's. Mansson, perhaps because he travels incessantly and often has a one-year-old son's diaper to change in mid-tasting, has little time to wait for his wine to appreciate in value. He seeks wines with "distinctive personalities," classic examples being Pinot Blanc from Alsace, Jurancon from the Basque country, a Rosemount Shiraz from Australia, a Nalle Zinfandel, and a Meridian Pinot Noir from Santa Barbara. Mansson concluded with a reasonable Chablis, a good red Burgundy value from Nuits St. Georges, and four cases of red Bordeaux "futures" (bought before bottled) for a cellar that really appealed to me.

For Sentimental Reasons

The most radically different was New York bureau chief Thomas Matthews, who got only nine cases for ten thousand dollars or nearly one hundred dollars a bottle. Matthews chose his wines entirely for reasons of sentimental association: 1953 Chateau Margaux for his birth year, 1959 Vouvray for that of his wife, the best Merlot from his native Long Island, etc. That's a lot of sentiment.

More my style was Harvey Steiman, the editor-at-large, who often concentrates on wine-food matches, loves to cook, and entertains nearly every weekend. Steiman got forty different wines, often buying just a few bottles of one wine to have more variety. Good Steiman picks are Benziger Cabernet, two great Fattoria di Ama Chiantis (Thomas Jefferson liked Ama), Chiantis from Farneta and Talosa, and an Italian dessert wine of Verduzzo grapes from Friuli, near the Austrian border. A stroll through Steiman's highly individual choices was alone worth the newsstand price of the *Spectator*.

James Laube, who wrote the excellent *Spectator* books on both Chardonnay and Cabernet, devoted most of his budget to Pinot Noirs from California but "bought" only four cases of Cabernet and two and a half cases of Chardonnay. His Pinot choices: Acacia, Chalone, Hanzell, Mondavi, Saintsbury and Williams Selyem.

Revealing Choices

Former editor Jim Gordon had perhaps the most classic wine cellar, featuring Cheval Blanc of Bordeaux (my favorite), two cases of German Saar wines (another favorite now legally called Mosel but still easy to find), a great white Chenin Blanc Savennières from the Loire, a Vieux Telegraphe Chateauneuf, and a really old Louis Martini Cabernet. Gordon says he rides the bus home across the Golden Gate Bridge every day reading retail wine catalogs. Sounds like it was worth it. Some bus ride, too.

James Suckling, the now-retired *Spectator* European editor, doesn't believe in vintage charts, and several of his picks contradicted the *Spectator* scoring system. His only goal? "Optimum drinking pleasure." Suckling never buys less than a case, liking to watch his choices mature over several years, even if there are fewer of them.

All in all, this issue was one of the *Spectator*'s best, revealing a lot about its own writers in an interesting and personal way.

James Suckling has now gone modern after retiring to Tuscany and writes an excellent wine blog at JamesSuckling.com

Barefoot Boy

Davis "Barefoot" Bynum went upscale several years ago and sold his famous "Barefoot" label. He makes only premium wines now, not the Sonoma County blend he once called Chateau "Lafeet." Bynum's former winemaker, Gary Farrell, was named Winemaker of the Year by Dan Berger, then the wine writer for the *Los Angeles Times*.

Davis Bynum was always of special interest to me because he is one of few winemakers who was a writer on wines first (for the *San Francisco Chronicle*) who later became a full-time winemaker. In 1951, he bought fifty pounds of Petite Sirah grapes from Robert Mondavi, made three and a half gallons of pretty good wine, and was hooked. By 1965, Bynum was crushing in his garage a ton of grapes into wine. In 1971 he bought land in Napa, but in '73 changed his mind and moved to Sonoma County's cooler Russian River Valley, where he renovated an old hop-drying kiln into a winery and residence. When I first visited the place in the late 1970s, it was rustic at best, but a good family place with good honest wines.

Since the sale of the Barefoot line, Bynum has concentrated on the growing parts of the market: top grape varietals at reasonable prices and exports. It will come as a surprise to some, but fine wine is now a rapidly growing American export. Bynum now exports to more than fifty restaurants in Belgium and to the Oriental Hotel in Bangkok, one of the finest in the East.

From one ton in 1965, Davis Bynum now crushes about 450 tons annually and sells 22,000 cases, about the same as many Bordeaux Chateaux. Bynum's grapes also come from gravelly soils like some near Bordeaux, giving them good drainage. Proximity to the Pacific Ocean also helps, with sea breezes coming up the river just twelve miles to cool the vines on hot summer nights, keeping the wines' acidity levels high enough for good balance.

At a long-ago dinner at the classic old Harris restaurant on Van Ness

Street in San Francisco, I once tasted the gamut of Davis Bynum's releases with him and his son. With oysters on the half-shell, his Fumé Blanc was perfectly matched. With crab meat, his Chardonnay was smooth and medium-bodied. My favorite, as it often is, was his Pinot Noir, which had classic Pinot aroma and a good finish. A barrel sample was excellent, somewhat fuller and richer, and promised to be hard to find soon after release. A perfect accompaniment to prime rib was his Merlot.

Davis Bynum has marketed his wines from the winery to most states by son Hampton Bynum and has an unlimited future. There is a lot more to Bynum than Barefoot.

Pharmacy Prof Tries
to Simplify Wine Labels

Do you like wine labels? Hate wine labels? Sometimes I feel both ways at the same time, loving the pictures but hating the words. Often, beside a stunning picture of a clipper ship sailing the seas, you find chemical jargon like "contains sodium metabisulfite." Who really wants to know that? Other labels tell you wines are dry when they are really sweet. We need a cure for such labeling practices.

John Juergens, a friend and wine lover who is also a pharmacy professor, has applied for a patent on a labeling scheme called VinTest (it wouldn't be wine if it didn't have a little French) that might make things easier. VinTest labels have a small, simple bar graph with four ten-point scales that look like a row of thermometers. They show each wine's sweetness, acidity, astringency, and body, thus giving an objective, chemically verifiable picture of what's really in the bottle. It took ten years of study and consumer research to convince Juergens that these four basic elements are what cause most people to like or dislike wines.

Process of Elimination

Unfortunately, his system had to omit aroma, bouquet, "nose," or whatever else you choose to call the smell of wines, the most subtle part of their evaluation. This makes VinTest more of an "E-li-mi-nate the negative" exercise than an end-all wine-chooser. With VinTest you find out what you dislike. Then you seek out the wines you like most by traditional trial-and-error, but within the much smaller group of wines you like in a general way.

My favorite scale, because it gives the most new information, is the one for astringency. Called tannin by wine lovers and complex polyphenols by chemists, astringency is experienced as the "pucker factor" by anyone tasting a wine that is too tannic for them. Like the other three scales, astringency goes from zero to ten and looks like a thermometer. A "perfect" ten may be well-nigh undrinkable. In this case a zero, shown on the scale California-like as "mellow," may well be too soft.

Most people, it is said, actually like sweet wines labeled "dry." Juergens's scale eliminates that illusion by telling them how much sugar the wine really has, measured from zero to ten.

Acids, which produce tartness but are often confused with tannin (bitterness), are also measured simply, without any excruciating explanation of pH, from zero (3.8 pH) to ten (3.0 pH) on the simple bar graph.

In Pursuit of a Good Body

One of the most disputed of wine characteristics is the elusive term "body," which refers to the weight or substance of a wine as felt rather than tasted. It is produced by the interaction of sugars, tannins, and alcohol. With wines like Chablis (light) or Cabernet (heavy) you can often judge body just by holding the wine in your mouth. But body is deceptive, often causing the politically incorrect French to refer to it in terms of female anatomy. They say wines with heavy bodies have not just "legs" but "thighs," referring to the breadth of the streams of wine that run down inside a glass when you slosh wine around. Really.

Old-time critics use words like "elegant" for light bodies and "beefy" for heavy ones. With John Juergens's system, you know scientifically the body weight of your potential evening's partner from the label alone. Detractors say chemical tests will remove the poetry from wine and are a Puritan plot to make wine hygienic and dull. Is that really true? Naah.

There is just too much romance and whimsy in wine for anyone to remove it all. This was illustrated in one of those *New Yorker* wine cartoons which, like Greek philosophers, eventually explain all of life if you study them enough. In this cartoon, a yuppie offers his friends "a really *gifted* young Zinfandel." If you want to know more about your Zinfandels than whether they're "gifted," you can write VinTest's inventor direct at 309 Wishing Tree Lane, Oxford, MS 38655 or call 662-234-2957.

Winetasters

Several years ago, when wine prices were much lower, a dozen of us experienced wine fanatics once sat down in groups of three to taste blind some three hundred and fifty wines from eight countries and six U.S. states. The event was the annual wine judging of The Tasters Guild, a group that seceded from the old Les Amis du Vin Club.

Fittingly for rebels, the Guild event was held in Memphis, Tennessee at the cozy restaurant of the late wine guru John Grisanti, who thought nothing of paying thousands of dollars for a wine he truly coveted (if it was for charity and tax-deductible).

Wine "judgings," which I prefer to think of as impartial evaluations by neutral veterans, always have a competitive air with clear winners and losers. Some expensive wines do pretty poorly; some very cheap wines show up their betters.

Rankings for the Guild judging were simple. All wines were scored on a French scale of from 1-20 points. A score of 18-20 won a gold medal; 16-17.9 won a silver; a score of 14-15.9 merited a bronze. Wines scoring below 14 weren't mentioned further. No point rubbing it in.

All wines were tasted in groups by type and price, from "whites under five dollars" to "wines over thirty dollars." Price/quality ratio was critical. A five dollar wine that tasted very good got more points than a fifteen dollar wine that tasted the same. Panels were used to reduce the influence of personal prejudice.

One reason I keep participating in what my friends consider a frivolous activity that should be summarily dropped in favor of turkey hunting or golf is that it shows you where the values are in the wine market.

Sleeper of this tasting, for example, was a Merlot from Whitehall Lane of Napa Valley. It was well worth twenty dollars and won a gold. I had once visited Whitehall, which is near Mondavi, and wasn't that impressed. Now I am. Whitehall Lane also won a pair of silvers for its Cabernets. All were super wines and super values.

Of the expensive stuff, I was on the panel that gave a silver to the only over-thirty-dollar medal winner, a worthy 1977 Rebello Valente vintage Port. Bollinger Champagnes nonvintage blends, won well-deserved medals in the tough twenty- to thirty-dollar category.

Of the lowest priced whites, there were no golds awarded, but Gallo won five silvers for their Sauvignon Blanc, Chenin Blanc, and Gewurz. Glen Ellen's white blend and an unusual Monterey Zinfandel also took silver. My favorite inexpensive white was steely-dry Galestro, a proprietary white from Tuscany by the great, innovative house of Antinori.

Readers often ask how wine judges themselves are judged. Two experiences stand out. In Texas once we were presented with a dozen wines to judge on a scale of one (lowest) to twenty (highest). We were not told that the same wine was among the twelve under separate numbers. Luckily for me, I called it a fourteen once and fifteen the other time. Another would-be judge was not so lucky. He rated the same wine an eighteen in one glass and a measly four from the other glass. He was dismissed faster than a spoiled wine.

Our second surprise test was at the elite L.A. County Fair where uber-strict Chief Judge Nathan Chroman insisted we never swallow any of the wines. After tasting nearly two hundred wines one day, we were lined up by Nate before a California Highway Patrol officer and given a breathalyzer test. All of us passed except one really famous California winemaker. When Nate threatened to toss him out like a bad wine, the rest of us from his panel of five all swore (truthfully) that the famous winemaker had saved his favorite wines on the back of the table and drunk them only after the tasting was officially over. Based on our testimony Nate pardoned our friend but made him walk the mile and a half from the tasting pavilion back to our hotel. A tough profession.

Giants of the Bible

Wine bottle sizes have always been a puzzle for me. With wine's slow slide into the slough of metrics, it has gotten worse. But even before metrics, there were those giant wine-ageing bottles with Biblical names like Methuselah and Nebuchadnezzar. Who were those guys, anyway? Could remembering their stories help us to associate which bottle size each one represents? Probably not, at least not for me.

Some purely bookish research into the question has convinced me that neither history nor metrics is much help in remembering the relative sizes of those venerable giants. No one knows for sure how the names first came to be used. Nor does anyone seem to know why the biblical Belshazzar came to be the bottle called Balthazar, but all wine authorities agree that he is the source. As it now stands, these bottle names are like Latin—they must simply be memorized. Or you can carry a little chart around with you, like a vintage chart, if you really think the question may come up that often.

Despite their idiosyncrasies, or perhaps because of them, giant oddball bottles have always held for me a certain perverse charm. Maybe it was the cheap thrill of thinking what it would cost to drop one that contained, say, a dozen bottles of 1949 Bordeaux.

Because of their great size, sometimes as large as twenty regular bottles, such bottles were reserved for great and festive occasions, and by definition had to be shared with good friends to be enjoyed. One theory behind their existence was that being so large, the wine in them was exposed to less air around their corks and thus aged more slowly and with greater finesse. That is the theory, although no one really knows for sure if it is true even now, but it has always made a good story.

Under the old pre-metric system, the quantities of the old giant bottles varied according to regions. In Bordeaux a Jeroboam was a six-bottle bottle, while in Champagne it held only four bottles. Recently the European Union and our own Treasury Department have undertaken to abolish such discrepancies, or at least to standardize the confusion, by converting all bottles to uniform metric sizes.

As a result, abolished from modern American shelves along with the giants is the traditional little Beaujolais bottle known as a "pot." Pronounced "poe" as in Edgar Allan, it held two-thirds of a standard bottle. They say it will be revived here under the title five hundred milliliter. It still exists in France, however, where they have refused to give up the poetry of its old size, shape, and name. The annual award in Paris for the cafe with the best wines is still called the "Best Pot" (meilleur pot) award.

In America, the name still exists even if the size does not. The resourceful winemakers of Beaujolais have met the American challenge by keeping the old rounded shape of that bottle while enlarging its size to a standard bottle and its price to match. Remember "Piat en Pot"?

Perhaps for old times' sake, several other incongruities have been preserved from the pre-metric world of king-sized bottles. The new nine-liter bottle is for some reason still named Salmanazar for an obscure Assyrian king with no known liking for wine. Nebuchadnezzar, the king of Babylon who violated the temple at Jerusalem, has been unjustly rewarded by having the largest of all bottles, the fifteen-liter, named for him.

The more deserving Methuselah, who lived longer than the oldest of wines, was relegated to a mere six-liter bottle. Even Balthazar, son of Nebuchadnezzar and his successor as King of Babylon, doubled Methuselah and had the ample twelve-liter named in his honor. But maybe that is fair. From what we read about Balthazar in the Book of Daniel, he liked his wine plenty.

Greatest casualty of all was the noble Rehoboam. As readers of the Book of Kings will recall, Solomon's son Rehoboam, King of Judah, was at war with Jeroboam, King of Israel, "during all their days." Well, Jeroboam has finally won, on the fields of wine anyway. The Treasury Department has abolished the Rehoboam altogether for wines bottled after 1978, since its traditional sizes came out in an uneven number of liters, a no-no in the wonderful world of metrics.

Like rewriting the King James Bible, the changeover from the old language may have made a few things more accurate, but too many of the best and most poetic parts have gone missing. The noble Rehoboam, filled with the equivalent of six bottles of fine Bordeaux, had brightened many a fine winter evening in bygone days, and some not so bygone, in several of which I was a joyous participant. Down with metrics. Up with King James and the ancient bottles made for kings.

Who Owns the Wineries?

One pleasure of old-time wine drinking was thinking how a little old winemaker made the wine in his own ancient family cellar. There are still more family wineries than there are family farms, but giant corporations are now swallowing up wineries like new Beaujolais. They also dump them when the wineries don't produce dramatic profits. A couple of bad vintages and you're gone.

Yet it is not corporate takeovers that trouble experts most—it is *foreign* corporate takeovers. Did the Japanese toast their purchase of Rockefeller Center with sake? Not likely. They already own Chateau St. Jean, not to mention Ridge Vineyards, perhaps America's best Cabernet Sauvignon producer. Sanraku, Japan's largest winemaker, bought Markham, one of the most American of all wineries. Sapporo brewery owns St. Clement of Napa, and Kirin brewery owns Raymond Vineyards.

Yet we must put all this in perspective. One seems to recall it was the same Raymond family that a few years ago sold Beringer to the Nestle Company of Switzerland. Nestle, it must be admitted, improved the wines. Buena Vista, Franciscan, and Mt. Veeder are now owned by Germans, and none seems to have suffered thereby, nor have Clos du Val and Lost Hills, both owned by French companies, nor DeMoor, which is owned by Belgians.

Foreign Ownership Widespread

Cuvaison of Napa is owned by a Swiss family and Cambiaso of Sonoma is owned by an outfit from Thailand called Four Seas Investment. All this raises the usual question: Is our concern about foreign owners just a cover for "yellow fever," that feeling some Americans get every time the Japanese buy something we would not mind the Canadians owning? This time I don't think so.

By 1987, twenty-five percent of all "California" wine sold here came from foreign-owned U.S. wineries, but most of these belonged to Canadian outfits such as Seagram (Sterling, Monterey Vineyards) and Hiram Walker (Clos du Bois, Callaway). The biggest shock was when the British conglomerate Grand Met PLC (talk about a faceless corporate name) made a blockbuster acquisition of all these U.S. wineries: Christian Brothers, BV, Inglenook, and Almaden.

It's Not Foreigners We Fear

So it's not Japanese and other foreign ownership that is shaking everyone up. Foreign investment has generally been welcome. When Moët built Domaine Chandon in Napa decades ago, it showed that the French finally thought fine Champagne could be made in the United States, and they staked their money and reputation on it. Then the Spanish house of Freixenet ("Fresh-net") built Gloria Ferrer Winery in Sonoma County and began making even better sparking California wine than the French.

The great Burgundy house of Drouhin pleased the state of Oregon by buying several hundred acres of prime Pinot Noir land there, put their name on it, and began to make the difficult and sought-after Pinot Noir, a real breakthrough. Now the owners of Bordeaux's famous Chateau Mission Haut-Brion have sold their stunning chateau and moved to Napa Valley, believing it to be the wine country of the future.

These winery purchases are all in the finest U.S. tradition. These people have built their own wineries with their own money in their own way and many of them now live here. What most wine people seem to resent and fear is not foreign presence at all, but the coming of flinty-eyed MBAs, foreign and domestic, whose fast-buck, quick-kill, short-sighted mentality could do irreparable damage to the U.S. wine industry, whose future is currently one of the brightest in the world.

It is not foreign influence we need to fear, but universal corporate greed.

CHAPTER TWO

Going Places with Wine

Wine Attics of New Orleans
Old Madeira
Wining and Dining at the Peabody Hotel
Wine at the Napoleon House in New Orleans
Mellow Memories of an Oxford Poolroom Rival a Fine Wine
Without the Bubbles What've You Got? It's Still Champagne
Armchair Wine Travels
Fine Wines of China?
The Story of "A": Traditional Chinese Food and Wine in Paris
Kublai Khan: A Chinese Feast with Wine
Merlot Among the Magnolias: K.C. Joe's Restaurant
The Rose of San Francisco: Red Wine and Garlic Breath
Napa Valley: An American Eden?
Napa Valley: A Local Auction for Everyone
Monticello West
Is Wine-Tasting a "Profession"?
Best Wine Bars and Bistros of Paris
The Wines of New Zealand
Spain's Whites Catch Up with Its Great Reds
Sea Air Cools Temecula Valley
The Wines of Texas Are upon Us
Wine in Yosemite: The Ahwanee Hotel
The Dark Side of France
Never Heard of Chenin Blanc? You've Got Company
The Wines of Chateau Biltmore
Irish Wines in Bordeaux

Wines from Bulgaria
All Is Ducky at the Peabody
Cool Reds for Summer
In New Orleans the Cajun Tide Ebbs, as French and Italian Wines Flow
A Deep South Winemaking School Thrives—For a While
A Mouse-Jump for White Burgundy
Red Wines Flow When Chill Winds Blow
The Great Old Reds of Italy
The Great New Reds of Italy
America Conquers Pinot Noir, the Holy Grail of Wine
A Friend Comes through with Spanish Treasure

Wine Attics of New Orleans

You can often tell more about a restaurant's food by visiting its kitchen than by studying its menu. The same is true of its wines. A visit to the cellar may tell you a lot more about the restaurant's wines than its wine list will.

In the case of New Orleans restaurants, wine "attic" would be more accurate than wine cellar. Because of its unusually high water table, New Orleans generally lacks underground cellars, and most restaurants store their wines above ground, sometimes in rooms as elaborate as the city's famed marble mausoleums, but much more cheerful.

The most extreme example of a New Orleans wine attic was at the classic old Pontchartrain Hotel on St. Charles Avenue, whose renowned Caribbean Room restaurant had its cellar on the eighth floor. More typical was Galatoire's on Royal Street, whose second-floor walk-up cellar was in an attic right out of Tennessee Williams, complete with peeling plaster, musty furniture and window air conditioners. When I visited it several years ago, the attic had all the charm of a condemned nursing home, but the many fine wines lodged therein did not seem to mind at all. Galatoire's is still a favorite of mine for food, although its wines are still more limited than Antoine's or Commander's Palace.

I used to pay little attention to wine competitions or "judgings," but my attitude changed dramatically when I became a wine judge myself at the wonderful L.A. Fair. The experience has also strengthened my faith in the restaurant wine list competition sponsored by the *Wine Spectator*. Many times in strange cities I have relied on the *Spectator*'s recommendations from its yearly "Top 100" restaurant wine lists in the United States and have rarely gone wrong with them.

Its selections for New Orleans one year so totally confirmed my long-standing preferences that I now have even more faith in them. The three New Orleans restaurants whose wine lists made the *Spectator* cut were Antoine's, Brennan's, and the Commander's Palace. Brennan's, once my favorite for wines and unfairly underrated among the greats in certain food guides, once merited a separate article in the *Spectator* about its wine selections. Sadly, it recently closed. My preferred replacements are now Mr. B's Bistro ("B" for Brennan) and the several fine restaurants of master chef/entrepreneur John Besh.

Antoine's, another New Orleans great that certain food writers shoot at unfairly as "inconsistent," has a wonderful traditional wine list. Its cellar is at ground level, but the optimum conditions there, not to mention the obvious age of the place, which cannot be faked, give you the feeling from inside the cellar that you are not on top of a swamp but under the cool soil of Burgundy.

Authenticity is one of the charms that bring so many people to New Orleans. It is not a city of instant "theme" restaurants like so much of America, and the same is true of its wine cellars. New Orleans's best wine cellars, like its buildings, have that distinctive patina of age which only time can give. Wine cellars, like architecture and wine itself, need time to mature. There is no such thing as "instant" aging, although my children seem to produce it in me pretty fast sometimes.

New Orleans possesses in some abundance the old wine cellars that newer cities are trying to create overnight, artificially, and you notice it, especially when you're in New Orleans. It's like the lady from Texas who said, "What do you mean we don't have culture? We *bought* two symphony orchestras last year." Or it's like the pilot who had just bombed the ancient Italian monastery at Monte Cassino. With utter faith in modern technology and no sense that the past can be lost, the young American pilot tried to comfort a devastated old monk by telling him, "Don't worry about it, Padre, we'll build it back for you *older* than it was before."

Of the old, traditional cellars, Antoine's is for now probably the finest in the city. You can even dine at certain tables looking down its endless corridor of old bottles. Another old New Orleans cellar, and a marked exception to the attic rule, is the cellar under the Rib Room of the Royal Orleans Hotel. Kept watertight by nineteenth-century feats of engineering now seldom attempted, the Rib Room cellars are also unique in another way. They maintain the old and now mainly extinct tradition of dual wine cellars, one for the reds and another ten degrees cooler for the whites.

The Rib Room also has special cellars designed for private dining with large, handsome tables, low ceilings and an atmosphere that could only be duplicated in a chateau. Normally, it is no more difficult to get reservations for one of these dining rooms than for any other sought-after spot in the city.

The winey atmosphere is something that C.P. Snow's academic lawyer Lewis Eliot would have enjoyed, although he might disapprove of the color TV and the telephone inside a wine cask protruding from the wall. Last time I was there, however, the TV was broken and not about to be fixed. Perhaps by now, reason has really prevailed and the telephone wires have been cut too.

Traditional as it is, New Orleans has kept pace with modern wine trends, its cellars leaning ever more heavily toward California wines. Always a white wine city because of its natural preference for seafood, its tastes are currently going even more toward whites at the expense of traditional reds. I asked a waiter at the Rib Room, whose specialty is, after all, red meat, if the trend was the same there. In the Latin American accent increasingly heard in New Orleans restaurants he replied, "Mister, people drink white wine with beef now. They don't go to the old school no more."

Old Madeira

Madeira was once the most popular American wine, the personal favorite of Franklin, Washington, and the other Founding Fathers. Shakespeare said Falstaff liked it so much that he "sold his soul to the devil on Good Friday last for a cup of Madeira and a cold capon's leg."

Madeira is still one of the world's great wines but is not sufficiently appreciated in America, where it first gained its fame. Madeira is also versatile, since the drier types may be served before dinner as an appetizer like dry sherry, and the heavier types after dinner as dessert wines. Good bottles of Madeira may now be had very reasonably in every major city.

Zarco the Blue-Eyed, a sea captain for Prince Henry the Navigator, discovered the island of Madeira in 1419 some four hundred miles due west of Casablanca, Morocco, in the South Atlantic. Calling it "steep as an iceberg, green as a glade," Zarco named the uninhabited volcanic island "Madeira," the Portuguese word for "wooded" because of its incredibly dense foliage, which was so heavy that sailors were unable to hack out a clearing for settlers.

In one of the great anti-ecology acts of all time, Zarco burned the entire island to clear it. After burning for seven years, the fertile soil of Madeira was allegedly so impregnated with smoke and ash that natives claim, somewhat implausibly, that the great fire imparted the unusual and characteristic smoky taste that all Madeira wines retain to this day. It more likely comes from how they use heat to age the wine.

Madeira became the most popular wine in colonial America by geography and politics. First, the trade winds that pass Madeira carried sailing ships naturally toward our ports. Then, in 1663, Charles II of England put heavy taxes on all European wines going to British colonies in America. Since Madeira was technically in Africa, its duty-free wines swept the colonies. By the late eighteenth century it was considered patriotic to drink Madeira and thereby avoid taxes to England, and Madeira became a symbol of the American revolutionary spirit. John Adams declared that a few glasses of it made anyone feel capable of being president.

Madeira was especially popular in the South, and Natchez and Savannah were for years the leading ports of entry for Madeira wines. Thomas Jefferson had dozens of barrels of it at Monticello and the White House. Madeira caught on in England only when returning redcoat soldiers carried back a taste for it acquired in America.

Today little Madeira is drunk in America. Most is exported to Scandinavia, Germany, and France. Americans now seem to want light, dry, quick-drinking wines, and Madeira is heavy and must be sipped and savored at leisure. Really fine Madeiras are today the Ford Edsels of the wine world: a handful of fanatics cherish them and talk about them, but most people have never tasted one, let alone bought one.

Madeira is made much like Port or sherry. It is a "fortified" wine, i.e., brandy is added to stop fermentation before complete dryness. In Madeira the brandy is made from sugar cane, and raises the alcohol content to roughly twenty percent, compared to ten to fourteen percent for normal table wines. After fermentation, Madeira is heated for months in *estufas*, stove-like rooms that darken this basically white wine and give it a smoky, caramel quality and color unlike any other wine. Because of its high alcohol content and stoving treatment, Madeira is very stable, travels better, and lives longer than any other wine. Hundred-year-old Madeiras are commonplace, and a few still exist from the eighteenth century. Last year I presided over a fundraiser tasting of nineteenth-century Madeiras for the Historic Preservation Society of Charleston. It was quite an event.

In the days of sailing ships, casks of Madeira were deliberately sent on long, rough sea voyages around the Capes to the East Indies and South America because the heat of the ship's hold and the jostling of the sea voyage seemed to improve them. Old bottles often had parchment labels listing the bottles' various ships and voyages, like pedigrees. Nowadays, like most wine labels, those on Madeira seem better designed to confuse than inform. Like laundry detergents, they describe themselves with a certain poetic license as "rare," "fine," "famous," and even "splendid" and "superb." These words have no legal meaning. The worst case of damning with faint praise was a bottle I saw labeled simply "imported."

As for the island itself, much has changed in Madeira. Politically, it is now an integral part of Portugal, an island province much as Hawaii is an island state. "Informed opinion," in the wine world also has it that Madeira now faces difficult problems: labor costs rising sharply, new European Union regulations, and islanders leaving winemaking for better-paying jobs. At the same time, Madeira winemakers are trying for a comeback. Methods are being modernized and better grape varieties like the fine old Terrantez replanted. So, on balance, future Madeiras will probably be good although they may cost more, but then what doesn't? Best advice for now is to buy the old and good ones while supplies last.

Wining and Dining
at the Peabody Hotel

For several months, it was my duty to review and sample all the wine lists of the finest restaurants of New Orleans and write a series of articles thereon, to be called "The Wine Attics of New Orleans," because the city's water table is too high for cellars. The task proved demanding but infinitely pleasant.

Then came an interruption from my editor, asking if I'd "mind" attending a special dinner for wine and food writers at the Peabody Hotel's fancy Chez Philippe restaurant. Being a good soldier, I laid aside my New Orleans wine lists and trekked dutifully to Memphis.

Chez Philippe is, to put it mildly, no ordinary hotel dining room. It has a very unusual setting, being located on three tiers of marble overlooking the South's most opulent lobby. On the far wall of the ninety-seat restaurant is a striking, full-length mural depicting a masked ball of an Italian mood which my daughters immediately claimed was right out of their favorite Harlequin book. Old Peabody hands will recognize it as the former Venetian Room.

Reliable sources within the Peabody, who shall remain nameless, told me that certain of the masked faces were those of the Belz family, owners of the hotel who, like Alfred Hitchcock, could not resist a cameo appearance in their own production.

Although there was no Philippe at Chez Philippe, there is a Daniel. Daniel Palumbo, the maitre d', although young, was experienced, relaxed, and unlike so many maitre d's in the stuffy French restaurants that infest most large American cities, he sincerely tried to make diners feel more comfortable rather than less. A maitre d' is, after all, basically an enforcer in a tuxedo whose job is to look elegant while exerting discipline and meting out punishment for incompetence by the staff. Good maitre d's are one of the main reasons why some French restaurants in

France give such excellent service compared to the sloppy, snobby treatment they often inflict on us in this country.

Palumbo was a pleasant and marked exception. He was able to maintain a good-natured, bantering mood with the waiters, perhaps because his Corsican name alone put fear in the French-speaking members of the staff. Not that he would actually put out a hit on a chef whose mousse collapsed or break the leg of a waiter who poured Champagne down some dowager's cleavage, but there was a toughness and decisiveness beneath Palumbo's relaxed demeanor that kept the service smooth, efficient, and unobtrusive.

When the dining room began to clear out around one o'clock in the morning, we got bold and asked if he'd join us for a drink at our table. A certain tightness around his eyes led me to suggest instead a large glass of Perrier. That offer he accepted, accompanied by two large aspirins.

The wine list at Chez Philippe, as befits an expensive and French-oriented menu, offered several bottles at stratospheric prices and has sufficient vintages of Lafites, Latours, Pommards, Corton-Charlemagnes, and Bernkasteler Doktors to satisfy the richest and most discriminating wine-drinkers. Of the roughly seventy wines on the list, however, there are always numerous moderate and even inexpensive ones such as Soaves, LaCour Pavilions, San Martin Zinfandels, and sparkling Freixenet.

Thus one can still dine well at Chez Philippe without fear of breaking the bank on wine. The majority of the list consists of medium-priced and excellent selections from French Vouvrays and Pouilly-Fumés to German Schloss Vollrads and Steinbergers, as well as many of the best California wines.

In charge of the kitchen at Chez Philippe was chef Jose Gutierrez, who apprenticed under Paul Bocuse, and who is not Spanish, as his name implies, but a second-generation Frenchman from Aix-en-Provence. I realized he was French when he invited my wife for a private tour of the kitchen without me.

Gutierrez is still thin, which the great chef Fernand Point always said was suspicious in a chef, but Gutierrez is still young and certainly the food he prepares does not reveal any tendency toward meagerness in his character. His evolving menus are elegant and lean toward traditional French cuisine. His cuisine is serious and authentic enough to be called *haute*, but definitely not of the esoteric hummingbird-wing school still prevalent in some restaurants that my father and Humphrey Bogart both used to call "clip joints," a useful term that should be revived and used loudly where appropriate.

At one November dinner for Thanksgiving, Gutierrez began with a consommé of pheasant. I wondered what they did with the pheasant itself. A consommé's basic purpose in life is to be subtle, and this one was subtle to perfection. It was accompanied by what looked like bread sticks, but turned out to be sticks of puff pastry, or *pâte feuilleté* as Gutierrez correctly called them.

Next came some beautiful scallops of salmon, that least fishy of fish, accompanied by a mousse of some of the most delicate spinach I ever recall eating. My wife said only her mama in Issaquena County ever grew any spinach that fine. Following the salmon was a plate of endives in walnut oil, upon which I looked with suspicion. The endive is a naturally bitter vegetable and perhaps the world's easiest to serve badly. Inexperienced cooks often serve absolutely inedible endive dishes just because they are "different." These endives, however, were mild and pleasant, a brightish yellow, and well matched with their sauce. Though "only a salad," the endives may well have been the most deceptively challenging dish of the evening, and Gutierrez made them look easy. Like most vegetables, they are hard to match with wine. I usually just go for a simple white.

Next came the main course, sometimes called, in a rich variety of mispronunciations, the "piece de resistance." It was Scottish venison, which is often so tough and overcooked that it should be called "a piece *of* resistance." The venison, in small round slices the French call "medallions," simmered in a Pommard wine sauce, was excellent. It was accompanied by, of all things in the Peabody, little swans made of toast, pureed turnips, and caramelized pears. My wife liked them somewhat more than I did. She likes broccoli too.

Of course no one will ever eat a duck at the Peabody; it would be sacrilege and cannibalism to eat your symbol, the Peabody duck. For its game bird, Chez Philippe serves a nice squab, which fits well with Mississippi traditions, being not a common park pigeon as sometimes loosely rumored, but a special breed of fowl described classically by Larousse as "a sociable granivore of the dove family."

During the swans, after having polished off a whole bottle of Muscadet Sur Lie with the salmon, and while concentrating intensely on an entire bottle of Jordan Cabernet, I persisted with steady professionalism in tasting a large glass of Nouveau Beaujolais with every dish so as to be able to report how it went with each course (it went fine). It occurred to me I should memorize the way back to our room before it was too late.

Just then the dessert arrived, an apple tart at least nine inches in diameter, which momentarily shook my confidence. I asked our waiter, Captain John Harris, one of the most sincerely helpful food and wine professionals I have encountered, if they had any provisions for diners unable to leave the table under their own power, claiming weakly that I had a bad back. He said, without batting an eye, "Yes sir, we have specially padded wheelbarrows for just those occasions."

With that assurance, knowing we were in good hands, we ate the whole tarts, which were surprisingly light, then followed them with a glass of Port and retired to our room with that careful-stepping dignity of the over-indulged, thoroughly convinced that when the time comes and our money is right, Jose and John and Daniel had better have their wheelbarrows ready, because we are coming back to the Peabody for more of Chez Philippe.

Years later, in 2012, Jose opened his own restaurant in east Memphis, a cozy bistro named River Oaks, located on Poplar just off the intersection of I-240 and I-55 South on the road (conveniently for us) to our home in Oxford, Mississippi. It quickly became the hottest restaurant in town, the favorite of doctors, lawyers, and corporate executives looking for a taste of France. Reservations, not surprisingly, are usually required.

Wine at the Napoleon House in New Orleans

I return to New Orleans, once my home, now a place I can visit mainly when business, such as reviewing restaurants, takes me there. It is a city that takes food more seriously than wine, as it should be. As a matter of fact, this city takes food more seriously than almost anything. Perhaps for that reason, it is a place where I enjoy wine most. Let me explain.

Wine was developed to complement food and not the other way around. In a New Orleans restaurant you first discuss at length what you are going to eat, then order the best wine you can reasonably afford to go with it. Rarely do you see a tableful of people haggle over which is the greatest wine on the list, then compromise on what foods might make it taste better.

This tradition continues at my favorite New Orleans cafe, the Napoleon House, a classic French Quarter spot. Built in 1791 as a residence for the mayor, the pirate Jean Lafitte joined other patriotic Francophiles in 1821, bought the house, and offered it to the exiled Emperor Napoleon as a New World refuge, planning to rescue him from St. Helena. Napoleon died before they could pull it off.

Winds of Change

Ever since I have known the place, more than forty years, it has been a unique neighborhood bar. The atmosphere is Mediterranean with tile floors, ceiling fans, small tables, and quiet, unobtrusive waiters. The last time I was there it was closed for renovations, which was ominous. Worse yet, a salad bar with "fresh-squeezed juice" was opening next door.

My return allayed my fears: the Napoleon House is still as dark as a Corsican cave. You can still select your own classical music, the only music available, although now on CDs rather than old-time vinyl records. Their cigars are still the finest and their desserts are Italian, from torrancino to cannoli. For food you need not get too serious. Better to relax with long, multi-meated muffaletta sandwiches and delicious antipasto salads.

It doesn't get any simpler than this and the wine list is to match. You could put the Napoleon House wine list in your wallet without folding it. I did, as a matter of fact. It specializes in practical half-bottles and carafes, with white Gavis and red Corvos by the glass to complement its Mondavi Pinot Noir, Fetzer Chardonnay, and a few modest Bordeaux and Burgundies.

The Napoleon House is across the street from the old Royal Orleans Hotel, a gaudy wedding cake of Bourbon ostentation, and just a block from Paul Prudhomme's fashionably seedy Cajun restaurant K-Paul's, but the Napoleon House remains the same. One guidebook once called the Napoleon a "crumbling ruin," another said its crowd was "somewhat intellectual." Neither image really captures its peaceful, soul-restoring atmosphere.

After half a muffaletta, a whole carafe of red wine and some long cigars, my friends and I left the old cafe totally relaxed and reassured that some things will not change. Former owner Pete Impastato, now deceased, still looked down on us from a dark old oil painting above the bar, still wearing the same white apron, black bow tie and benevolent expression I recall from so many good evenings in his place. Never once in all those years did Pete show any interest whatever in which wine we chose, but never served us a bad one. Never once did he fail to show an interest in our well-being and the state of our families. Pete was a man who enjoyed his wines, but had his priorities straight. May he rest in peace, and his soul always hover over the bar at 500 Chartres Street, corner of St. Louis.

Mellow Memories of an Oxford Poolroom Rival a Fine Wine

Writing a weekly wine column for years on end is a challenge. Occasionally, you just can't think of anything to write. I once asked another veteran columnist what he did on those occasions. His reply was amusing: "I just lower my standards." The dreaded columnist block struck me once back in late 1983. But rather than lowering my standards, I just changed the subject totally, leaving the title of the piece its only link with wine.

Recently I read a column about old-time poolrooms that really took me back. It described the apparent disappearance of these unique institutions from Jackson, Mississippi.

My assignment as a columnist is supposed to limit me to writing about wine and food for the Leisure section, but the piece provoked me, and after all, what could be more leisurely than a slow winter afternoon shooting snooker with friends? I therefore offer to the piece on poolrooms what our oft confused U.S. Supreme Court might call "a concurring and dissenting" opinion.

First the concurrence. Yes, it is true that many poolrooms were the dirty dens of iniquity our mothers said they were—while our fathers remained strangely silent. Yes, these once uniquely male institutions formed an ominous rite of passage into manhood unsurpassed even by one's first hunt. On the other hand, their effects could also be positive, far from sinister, and in north Mississippi good old-time poolrooms are not yet entirely gone.

There is a good one right here in Oxford, an over-studied little town that has been unduly romanticized by many, unfairly condescended to by some, and rightly criticized by others. One place generally overlooked on tours, however, is Pete's Pool Room. Just off the famous town square, it is known to the many who have never been inside as Tom's

Recreation Center. Pete never bothered to change the old name on the sign out front.

Pete's is a poolroom that belongs in the hometown of William Faulkner. Although decidedly no candidate for the National Register of Historic Places, it has a spare, samurai-like simplicity. The floor is clean, the cue sticks are straight and there are no dead rails or low corners on the tables, all of which are a true, pool table green.

While the games you see there are not exactly ESPN material, the level of the nine-ball is sometimes quite high. The snooker table is equal to most you'd find in Cajun country, where snooker seems to dominate over straight pool, Cajuns being experts at the better pleasures of life, from the dinner table to the poolroom. They are the only ones I know in America who write popular songs about food and drink, as in "crawfish pie and file gumbo."

Pete's is actually operated by *James* Purvis, an intelligent and worldly man with impeccable poolroom manners. A lot of people call him "Pete" either by mistake or from an unwitting sense of alliteration. "Pete" Purvis respects your privacy, tells good but short stories at the right moment between racks, will hide your favorite cue stick where no one else can find it, and still possesses many other fine points of poolroom etiquette too numerous to detail here.

In contrast, the 1950s poolroom I grew up in, figuratively speaking, was much different. Behind dirty curtains was the back room. Off limits, but in view of us teenagers, there was a table covered with green felt where dice were shot and cards were played for cash. Several of the regular players were liberally tattooed and had seen the penitentiary from the inside. They had nicknames like "Ropey."

Pete's Pool Room in Oxford is exactly the opposite kind of place, and probably more typical of the institution as a whole. During the 1960s, when law students were much more laid back and less earnest than they are now, certain friends (now Jackson attorneys) and I rarely missed our afternoon snooker session at Pete's.

In those days there was a small jukebox stocked entirely with old Ray Charles records. His songs are especially well suited to the mood of snooker-shooting, snooker being a subtle game played on an expansive table with small, unusually colored balls that strongly resist all efforts to drive them into narrow, almost chaste pockets.

The soul and sort of maitre d' of Pete's in those years was a gaunt, white-haired man whose true name I have long since forgotten, but who was referred to by one and all as "Greasy." The old gentleman, who was not the least bit greasy and was really quite neat, stood at least six feet four inches despite a pronounced stoop from too many years of hardscrabble farming.

Always unfailingly courteous and cheerful, he seemed grateful for his modest job racking balls. More pampered people would have considered it a low-status job, but to him it was a pleasant indoor sinecure, cool in summer and warm in winter, where he could joke with energetic young men the age of his grandchildren. He was wise enough never to moralize or raise his voice, and he easily kept order all by himself over a typical crowd of twenty or so working men and rowdy students averaging two hundred pounds each. We never really liked his established name "Greasy," since it was so opposite his character and demeanor. We never learned its origin. Others no doubt felt the same way without saying so, but poolrooms are bastions of tradition, and the name stuck.

Although the old man himself never developed any great skill at pool, and declined to shoot snooker at all, he was a fine student of the game and periodically instructed my friends and me on certain tactical errors we made. He even began to issue us occasional oral "report cards" on our progress, causing us to call him "Professor." We apologized for "cutting" his classes on the rare afternoons we missed snooker to take law exams.

The old gentleman's best advice, given with his usual mixture of deference and gentle mockery, was that we young fellows counted too much on offense, always trying to sink the difficult shot rather than on deftly boxing in or "snookering" the opponent with defense. Only years later, in the elegant alley fights aptly called "trials" by lawyers, did we begin to appreciate how he was teaching us real tactics more useful in real courts than the more abstract concepts of the law professors.

A solution to the problem of his name that we'd never thought of was finally invented by one of those raw-boned and boisterous but goodhearted kids footfall coach John Vaught always seemed to find somewhere. The boy came into Pete's with some of his buddies for the first time and shot simple "slop" pool for awhile, watching as the professor racked the balls, undoubtedly hearing everyone for some reason call this kind old man "Greasy."

When his turn came to pay and ask for another rack, I watched as the new boy tried unsuccessfully to catch the old gentleman's attention with hand signals alone. Failing that, he finally had to address him directly. After hesitating a couple of times, the big, awkward boy came up with an instinctively courteous phrase that would have made his mama proud. "*Mister* Greasy," he said, "would you mind giving us a rack over here?" The old gentleman gave a sort of gaunt chuckle at this striking example of respectfulness from youth and wordlessly complied.

I recently went back to Pete's, where I had not been for several years. Middle age has its good points, but long, lazy afternoons of snooker-shooting do not seem to be among them. To my pleasant surprise, the atmosphere of Pete's had hardly changed at all. The jukebox and its Ray Charles records were gone, but at least there were no pastel table covers and all else seemed remarkably the same. James Purvis was still there and people still called him "Pete." He remembered me and came over to greet me. He told me that the "Professor" had died peacefully in his sleep a couple of years ago, but had often asked Pete what ever became of his "students."

While telling me this, Pete reached into one of those dark recesses real poolrooms have, pulled out my old cue stick and handed it to me as if I'd never been away. The stick, a short, thin, perfectly balanced and very hard one, made from an old broken pool bridge or "crutch," had always been exactly right for snooker. I rolled it across the nearest table. It was as straight and true as ever.

Decadence may have removed the last true poolroom from Jackson, but in William Faulkner's hometown at least one real poolroom still exists. And in one corner of Oxford, the spirit of Mister Greasy still presides.

In a sad compromise with modern life, Pete's poolroom was bought out when he retired and is now a raucous Sports Bar with heavy cover charges on big-game weekends. Ray Charles and snooker have given way to giant-screen TVs and instant replays. Mister Greasy must be spinning in his grave.

Without the Bubbles What've You Got? It's Still Champagne

To most of us, Champagne is a bubbly white wine you drink on festive occasions. That in itself is a great blessing to us all, but that is not all there is to Champagne.

For hundreds of years, Champagne was a still or non-bubbly wine. That changed only when Dom Pérignon, the eighteenth-century monk-cellarmaster of the Abbey of Hautviller, discovered how to trap bubbles in the bottle during a second fermentation. Now it is hard to think of Champagne that doesn't bubble. Yet Thomas Jefferson said that bubbly was just a fad that would never catch on. "Persons of taste" he said, pompously for him, would never drink such stuff and it "would never catch on."

For years I thought that "still" Champagne was one of Thomas Jefferson's few crazy notions. I should have known better. Once I tasted non-bubbly Champagne, I saw what he meant. Non-sparkling Champagne is every bit as good, if not better, than bubbles. It is now legally called Coteaux (hillsides) Champenois and is one of France's better wines. It comes in two types: white and red. Each is a highly unusual and desirable wine, but I personally prefer the white.

Tiny Bubbles, Big Profit

Still Champagne is made only by a very few of the seven thousand Champagne producers because it is so much more profitable to make bubbly. Still Champagne sells for less than the cheapest Champagne which bubbles, even though the white is required to be from one hundred percent Chardonnay grapes and the red from one hundred percent Pinot Noir.

Consistently the best still white Champagne is that made by the ancient house of Ruinart, named for Dom Pérignon's cousin and fellow monk Dom Ruinart. It comes in squat little eighteenth-century bottles easily recognizable by their tiny necks and a yellow label saying Coteaux Champenois "still" white wine rather than "Champagne." It is one of the best wines I've ever tasted with oysters on the half-shell, better even than Chablis, which it resembles. Another good one is called Chateau de Saran, produced by the giant Moët et Chandon house in taller, darker, but similarly shaped eighteenth-century bottles.

For years I had read of the supposedly great non-bubbly red Champagne called Bouzy Rouge. The old restaurant reviewer of Paris's best newspaper, *Le Monde*, in his annual "Guide Courtine," always favored any restaurant that carried it. For years I searched for Bouzy (some say it is the origin of the name "booze"), finding only a few examples in the United States, but never a really good one. Last month, during a visit to the Champagne harvest, I found at last what Courtine was talking about. Bouzy red can be one of the world's most subtle wines. Made from one hundred percent Pinot Noir, the temperamental wine-grape responsible for red Burgundies, Bouzy red can be a wine of high quality. It is delicate, of a light color like a Romanée-Conti, and has an aroma like violets immediately noticeable upon uncorking.

The flavor of a great Bouzy is as subtle as a Frenchwoman's logic and as lingering as her perfume. It goes well with mild cheeses, but is too light for peppery or salty steaks. To me it is perfect with veal or pork, but that's a matter of taste. My favorite Bouzy, tasted by chance during a series of winery tours, is that of Alain Vesselle. The 1986 Vintage cost only twenty dollars when I first tasted it years ago, but well worth three times that. Vesselle has at least nine cousins who also make the wine, one of which I have found at Paris's Dodin-Bouffant and other top restaurants. In the United States you have to ask for it, or even have it ordered specially, but it is well worth it if you want a truly fine wine experience.

At last I see that Jefferson was right again: Champagne does not live by bubbles alone.

Years later, during another visit to Bouzy, I was chatting with a ninety-year-old winemaker when a carload of American ladies arrived. They spoke little French and he spoke no English, so I was asked to translate. Finally, one lady asked him, meaning to speak of wine, what had been the most delicious of his life. He asked in return, "The most delicious? She an-

swered, "Yes." He thought, smiled broadly, then replied firmly: "The young women of Thailand." When I stopped laughing, I tried to translate. The ladies didn't know how much to laugh, but when I explained the confusion to the old gentleman, he laughed harder than anyone. But he didn't change his answer.

Armchair Wine Travels

How can you learn about wine without leaving your living room or asking embarrassing questions using words you can't pronounce? Through Internet websites or, for dinosaurs like me, by watching wine videos. One of my daughters recently saw on cable a segment of "Vintage," the classic PBS television series on wine, and asked if there wasn't something like it for beginners. My other daughter noted that the popular TV program "Funniest Home Videos" has said wine had better "get on the stick."

I informed her that wine was already, as she termed it, "on the stick." There are dozens of wine videos in catalogs and on Netflix. I just hadn't gotten around to watching them. This challenge led me to spend much of my free time the last three weekends watching the things, and I am happy to report that I can recommend some of them. I can also recommend laying in a good supply of snacks and inviting friends to bring over wines and watch them with you.

Of the crop, we found four sets that are truly outstanding. These are films you can watch at home without worries for weather, lost passports, gastric distress, or any other of the ills that often accompany visits to foreign wine countries. And, like modern TV sports, they have instant replay as often as you want it.

The best: *The Wines of Bordeaux.* Some real wine heroes like the late Alexis Lichine guide five gurus from Robert Parker to Michael Broadbent through the chateaux and cellars of Bordeaux. My favorite parts are about ancient St. Emilion, a medieval town that hides many excellent bargains suggested by these relaxed experts. Home of a wine society founded by King Richard the Lion-Hearted, the best of these wines is called by Parker "a privilege to drink." This video is a privilege to watch. "Bordeaux" also encompasses the towns of Graves and Pomerol as well as the famous Medoc region (pronounced "may-duck"). This video is the best, least painful tool for learning Bordeaux wine I've seen. Watching these guys taste and analyze wine is unique.

Hugh Johnson's *How to Enjoy Wine* (one hour). The pick of the litter for short wine videos is a comical romp through the cellars of English wine-writer Hugh Johnson, who tells you more about wine in less time with more pleasure than anyone else anywhere, anytime. He begins by knocking the neck off a bottle with a stuck cork using a sword, then decants it through a coffee-filter over a flashlight, saying the traditional candle is "too watery." To preserve his labels in a damp cellar, Johnson sprays them with hair spray, and later decants a jug of supermarket wine into a crystal decanter to fool his friends.

Johnson's video also contains a ten-minute skit reminiscent of early Alec Guinness where he portrays an invisible wine-advisor who can be seen only by "Wally," a lecherous boss out for what Johnson calls a "spot of dalliance" with his comely secretary. He is saved by Johnson's wise tips on handling wine lists and waiters. A classic.

The Wines of Burgundy: Anthony Hanson, perhaps the greatest living expert on Burgundy, and Robert Joseph, perhaps the funniest, explain Burgundy with a number of their earthy French winemaker friends. This video has tons of information on the soils in Burgundy and how they affect so dramatically the quality of its wines. They go to washed-out places and examine exposed roots in different layers of soil, something not even an in-person tour would usually do.

Equally good are tastings of great Burgundies by people like Louis Latour, Robert Drouhin, and other local experts, who make comments like, "Tradition is an innovation which succeeded." Why did Charlemagne plant so many white grapes? Because his wife complained that red wine stained his white beard. I may even believe that. *Burgundy* explores in two two-hour tapes all the best wines of the two major areas, the Beaune hills and the Nuits hills, with the experts prattling cheerfully as they taste. The cameraman captures the unique beauty of perhaps the world's greatest single wine area. Highly recommended.

Best of All

Vintage: A History of Wine. This video, a compilation of Hugh Johnson's masterful thirteen-part TV series, is the *Masterpiece Theatre* of wine. It cannot get better than this. Beginning in the newsworthy Republic of Georgia, Johnson explores the beginnings of wine in the Caucasus Mountains, which "dwarf the Alps." Near the place where Noah's Ark is said to have landed, Mt. Ararat, Johnson tastes wine as it was made 4,500 years ago. This is an unreal trip with an unreal guide. I made two lengthy wine-tasting trips to beautiful Georgia myself and can vouch for the authenticity of Johnson's observations.

Johnson passes on to examine wine in Rioja, Spain, picks frozen grapes on New Year's Eve for icewine in the Moselle Valley, and ponders John Kennedy's favorite poet, Alan Seeger, who was killed in World War I fighting to save Champagne from the Germans. If I had to pick two favorite parts from this magnificent video, they would be Johnson visiting the wine bars of ancient Herculaneum, the resort city of Rome buried and preserved under the ashes of Mt. Vesuvius, and a wine-tasting in Japan conducted by Johnson, who gamely tries to tell them why we take wine so seriously. "It is a sort of ritual," he concludes. That, they can accept.

Fine Wines of China?

For years my daughters have asked my why there were no Chinese wines in Chinese restaurants. The French have French wines and the Italians have Italian wines, even the Japanese have plum wine, so why are there no Chinese wines? Is green tea all there is? When I try to tell them that China was the one great civilization that never had wine as its main beverage, they correct me: "But Pop, didn't Judge Dee always drink wine at dinner and to celebrate solving cases?"

Judge Dee, the famous Chinese magistrate of whom they spoke, really lived in the Tang period, and was later fictionalized into a sort of judicial Robin Hood by Robert van Gulik, a Dutch diplomat writing in English. His detective novels are said by sinologists to portray traditional Chinese culture better than any other western source. If Judge Dee drank rice wine, why do modern Chinese no longer do so? Is it some kind of Communist plot?

To answer my daughters' question, I visited expert Michelle Chao Louie, born in Hong Kong and educated there in British schools, who came to the United States for college and stayed on to run her own successful interior design firm. Later she took over as general manager of China Swan, the first U.S. importer of Chinese wines in decades. Catalyst was her father, a native of China's best wine-growing region, Tianjin.

Our interview, which evolved unexpectedly and pleasantly into a wine-tasting, took place in an unusual setting: a boardroom table in a glass-walled office on the top floor of a bank building overlooking San Francisco's Chinatown. Louie laid out a tall, fluted green bottle with a striking label that said "SPRING MOON, Imperial Cuvee, produced and bottled by Heavenly Palace Winery, Tianjin, People's Republic of China." The poetic title was complemented by an unusual picture of a quarter moon, set in a red sky and bordered in gold.

The wine itself, when poured, was a pale green-gold with a slight effervescence on the palate. It was pleasant, rather neutral, and reminiscent of a restrained Gewurztraminer if anything, although *sui generis* like Chinese food. The label fairly described it as "medium dry." It might go well with Chinese food, I thought. When Louie said it had won a gold medal at Vin Expo in Bordeaux last June, I could not resist asking what the grape was. "A Muscat," she replied a little diffidently, since that family of grapes once had a dubious reputation in the United States after Prohibition because its cousins were making cheap "Muscatels." But no more.

After a few glasses of the pleasant Spring Moon, shared with Louie and Charles Cross, an English venture capitalist and partner in China Swan, he said, "What could be more venturesome than importing wine from China?" We began to talk of many things, in particular my daughters' question. "It is true the Chinese have always drunk wines, but not always in the Western style," Louie explained. "Chinese wines were often made from fruits other than grapes, and usually drunk warm or even hot." I recalled that was how Judge Dee drank his.

"Our wines, while FROM China, are not traditional Chinese wines necessarily," she made clear. "We are now experimenting with small quantities of other grapes, notably the Chardonnay and Riesling," she added. After some urging, she produced a bottle of each.

The labels were strikingly different from the first. Each pictured vast, healthy green vineyards under a bright blue sky, which might have been in France, but in the center stood a large, many-storied pagoda. The labels read "East China Winery, TSINGTAO." Being accustomed to many a glass of excellent Tsingtao beer with my Chinese dinners, its appearance on a wine label was a pleasant revelation. The memory of how quickly Tsingtao beer swept the United States, via the vast network of Chinese restaurants here, made it dawn on me like nothing else that this modest project of importing a few hundred cases of Chinese wine into California could well become a major industry over the next decades.

Tasting the Chardonnay confirmed the impression. It had excellent fruit, a full character, and a natural, lemony acidity that would match well with the strong, complex sauces typical of Chinese cuisine. I suddenly wished I had a plateful to try it.

Since this column was written, both China and India have become serious wine producers. It is as wine investors and collectors, however, that the Chinese have gone wild. They now buy most of the sky-high classified growths of Bordeaux. Their new capitalist millionaires are the biggest players in the high-end wine market. Who would ever have thought it?

The Story of "A": Traditional Chinese Food and Wine in Paris

Watching former Soviet states enjoy their new freedom always reminds me of how Chinese democrats lost their most recent attempt in 1989. Along with their freedom, the Chinese in their disastrous Cultural Revolution lost irreplaceable portions of traditional Chinese culture, including much of their classical cuisine and wines. These now exist mainly outside the mainland, in Taiwan and Hong Kong, in Europe, and even in the United States, where many say Chinese food is now often better than in China.

My most vivid experience of this irony was in the fall of 1989, in Paris, in an unusual little Chinese restaurant near Notre Dame. It was called the Restaurant "A," a French abbreviation of its full name: Chinese Cuisine in the 18th Century (Au 18eme). Its name referred to the Golden Age of Chinese food and wine, a period of peace from 1736 to 1796 under the gourmet emperor Qian Long, who constantly traveled the country in disguise seeking out the best foods and wines.

The chef of Restaurant "A" was Huynh Kien, who was born in Vietnam to Chinese parents. His family fled the Japanese only to have to run from the communists again as boat people a generation later. After tiring of his Western-style Chinese stir-fry restaurant in Paris, Kien decided to seek an education in the disappearing art of classical Chinese cuisine. From master chefs in Hong Kong and Canton, Kien learned both traditional eighteenth-century simmered meat sauces and classic food sculpture, which reached its height under Kublai Khan when Marco Polo was at his court. It is truly dramatic when performed tableside as Kien does it. From bright red, gold, green, and black sticks of rice flour, cut in lengths like stiff spaghetti, Kien makes dragons, lotuses, mandarins, and swans. Customers often request Mickey Mouse or Donald Duck, but Kien calls them "too easy." He says that fewer than two hundred chefs in the world can perform this art.

Allegedly less difficult but equally impressive were his vegetable sculptures. Using only a razor-sharp cleaver to cross-cut a very large carrot, Kien makes—in three minutes as you watch—a flexible, woven lantern which expands and contracts like an accordion. To learn these arts he practiced seven hours a day for three years under Chinese master chefs.

What wines could suit such foods? Most classical Chinese chefs now match teas with their foods, not wines. But Kien gave me a traditional Peking Aperitif, or appetizer wine, perhaps the best I ever tasted. Called "laurel wine," it is made by soaking laurel leaves in sorghum alcohol for three years, buried in a bottle underground. The result is an exotic, gold, utterly subtle drink, which should be much better known in Chinese restaurants.

Also on the table were hot crock pots in which a rabbit and a duck had been marinated in Tsingtao rice wine and simmered forty-eight full hours in an eighteenth-century meat sauce of almost indescribable complexity. An old red from Chateaneuf-du-Pape drank perfectly with it. Surely this was Chinese heaven.

Wine tip: In a Chinese grocery you might find Kuei Hua Chen Chieu laurel wine. If not, you'll have to make do with Japanese plum wine. The Gault-Millau Guide called "A" the "most refined" of the more than two thousand Chinese restaurants in Paris, but it is now too late to learn the story of "A" by going there in person.

Sadly, Mr. Kien recently retired and supposedly returned to China. A new restaurant is in his old place, but bears no resemblance to his uniquely wonderful establishment and I've been unable to find anything remotely resembling it in Paris or anywhere else.

Kublai Khan:
A Chinese Feast with Wine

One day years ago I was invited to a luncheon-tasting of the wines of a California winery then new to the Deep South: Estrella River. Generally I avoid such events because drinking wine at lunch makes me fall asleep, but this one intrigued me for several reasons.

First, one owner of Estrella was Rocky Bleier, former Pittsburgh Steelers halfback and Vietnam veteran who overcame severe wounds to help make Franco Harris famous. Second, Estrella was located near where I used to live on the central coast of California. Its grapes have been the backbone of some renowned wines at Zaca Mesa Winery. The last but most compelling reason for my interest was that the wines were to be tasted with *Chinese* food—at the fine Kublai Khan restaurant on Beale Street in Memphis, which had one of the best wine lists in the area.

Choosing Chinese foods to showcase new wines is risky because matching wines with Chinese food is a lot like gathering honey bare-handed; mistakes are rarely fatal, but you get stung a lot. The wines themselves were promising: a true Syrah red, one of the first in California outside Joseph Phelps; a medal-winning Chardonnay; a much-praised Zinfandel; a new Fumé Blanc; and most promising of all an estate Cabernet Sauvignon. Cabernets of the fine '78 vintage have mostly disappeared from local shelves, and I was curious why this one was still around. There were some possible negatives to make things interesting. The latest Connoisseurs' Guide implied that Estrella had an overproduction of red wines it needed to sell. How could you ever have a "glut" of fine '78 Cabernet?

Add another ambiguity: both the Cabernet and the Fumé Blanc were being served on certain airline flights. Since in-flight wines are often even worse than in-flight movies and have screw-tops, that too gave me pause. One final bad omen was that instead of concentrating on the one or two wines it makes best, as wine countries have done for centuries, this winery took the MBA approach: first check the market for what will sell, then try to make products to fit it by fielding a whole line of wines. This habit is responsible for many of the mediocre American wines on the market.

But not to worry. On this occasion the exception proved the rule. The wines were fine and the food near superb. With the Fumé Blanc a sort of double first course was served, consisting of two kinds of shrimp. The first was fried in batter and called Golden Corn Shrimp, which was spicy and delicious but overpowered the wine. Its partner was another story. Some extremely fine shrimp were wrapped in subtle-tasting deep-green seaweed and shaped like the curved and tapered tail of a dragon. The dish was named, with a kind of reassuring obviousness, Green Dragon Shrimp. I could not find it on the menu, but I'm sure you can order it in advance. It was a rare example of a typically Chinese dish perfectly matched to a subtle but equally typical California wine.

I told my young daughters, known region-wide for their slavish devotion to shrimp, about the Green Dragons. The word "seaweed" made them wince, and the name "dragon" made them suspicious that I was trying to trick them into tasting eels again, but they agreed that if I would let them stop at an amusement park on the way home, they would cover their eyes and taste the dragons—*next* time we're in Memphis. Still, that's progress. I can't even get most adults to eat eels with me, even though I keep telling them they are fish and have nothing snaky about them.

The second course, perhaps my favorite of all, was Szechuan scallops. In theory the dish had all of wine's worst enemies: hot peppers, ginger root, wine vinegar, and a spicy sweetness. The dish was beautiful and succulent but just about killed the Chardonnay, which was on the lighter, "food wine" style. An old-time, buttery blockbuster of a Chardonnay would probably have gone better. But I had hoarded on a bread plate some of the Green Dragons, and they matched up well with the Chardonnay.

The third course was a beautiful Peking duck. Owner-chef Bernard Chang explained how air was blown by a sort of Chinese bicycle pump between the meat and the skin, making it crisp on the outside and moist but not oily (like too many ducks) on the inside.

Served with the Peking duck by the "book" of Chinese food-wine matches was the Syrah, which was okay, as good as most Cotes du Rhone, but no Hermitage (which it did not claim to be). A Zinfandel was also served, but since the shipper goofed and sent its bottom-line, nonvintage bottles and not the top estate bottling, it was spared close scrutiny. Kublai's fourth course was tangerine beef, one of those glistening, lacquered dishes the Chinese do so well. Although the dish had both sweetness and acidity, a robust Cabernet Sauvignon stood up to it well.

I had kept all my wines and small samples of all the courses, and at about this time started tasting back and forth, trying each wine with each dish and clearing my palate with water in between. Conclusions: The Fumé Blanc and Chardonnay went well only with the lightest and most unspiced dishes. The Cabernet went very well with both the duck and the beef and their respective sauces.

I had also been eyeing Kublai's wine list. It had a modest fifty-something items, but they were uniformly excellent: from Burgundy a Puligny-Montrachet and a Meursault; from Bordeaux, Lafite and a Chateau Filhot Sauternes; Taittinger from Champagne. A sampling from California included Raymond and Stag's Leap Chardonnays, Acacia and Iron Horse Pinot Noirs, and Jordan and BV private reserve Cabernets.

With a wine list like that, unusual for restaurants in my area, let alone a *Chinese* restaurant, I was curious to know which of the Estrella wines owner Bernard Chang preferred. To my pleasant but not total surprise, he replied, "the Cab." I agreed. With all due respect to the venerable Chinese detective Judge Dee, Mr. Chang's occidental wine list clearly wins out over jugs of hot rice wine.

Restaurants are among the most transitory, even ephemeral of human institutions, blooming brilliantly then dying like exotic flowers. Such was the fate of Kublai Khan. Bernard Chang could not find enough repeat customers to support it and changed its name to Ghengis Khan *and installed huge Mongolian firepots which were a big hit until Bernard's premature death. Estrella River Winery had a happier outcome. Rocky Bleier sold it to fellow pro football veteran Gary Eberle, whose eponymous winery is still a huge success, especially for its Central Coast Rhone varietals, led by wonderful estate-grown Syrahs. If you haven't tried them yet, it is time.*

Merlot Among the Magnolias: K.C. Joe's Restaurant

One year I saw the East meet the West in the South, and it was not a football game.

Chris Benziger, young heir to California's wildly successful Glen Ellen Winery, grew up in the affluent atmosphere of White Plains, New York until his family moved to California. One week long ago he introduced their fine Chardonnays, Cabernets, and Merlots to one of the most unique of all restaurants in the United States: K.C.'s, a Chinese-American restaurant in the Mississippi Delta. It was a classic U.S. evening.

As explained in the fascinating book *Lotus Among the Magnolias*, an enclave of Chinese has thrived in Mississippi for more than a century. Planters with a yen for dim sum have found happiness for years at the restaurant of K.C. Joe, a former Hong Kong dentist relocated to the cotton fields of the Deep South. K.C.'s sons, Don and Wally, having gotten business degrees from Ole Miss, steered the traditional Cantonese menu not only toward a newer, more California cuisine, but toward the finest wines.

Upon arrival at K.C.'s in Cleveland, you would notice first a display of bottles: Heitz Cabernet from Martha's Vineyard, Phelps Insignia, Chardonnays from Grgich, Far Niente, Chalone, Mondavi's Opus One.

I had driven nearly three hours on a cold, dark night to get there and once inside, awaiting dinner with a glass of Champagne, I began to ponder just where I was as young Benziger explained his wines to the Joe brothers. Then, in walked a tall man in Confederate uniform complete with sword and muddy boots. This was after only one glass of Champagne.

It turned out he was a local radiologist with the quintessentially Southern name of Culver Craddock, who was returning from a Civil

War re-enactment. He put his Confederate glove around a glass of Benziger Cabernet and we went in to an extraordinary black-tie dinner. It began with delicate lobster ravioli in lemon dill sauce that would have made any San Francisco restaurant—U.S. or Chinese—proud. A ripe Benziger Chardonnay went exceedingly well with it.

As the courses progressed from wild boar ham and veal chops in green peppercorn sauce to poached pears in Muscat Canelli, Chris Benziger gave a counterpoint with the history of his family's entry into the wine business. He unabashedly admitted that his grandfather started as a bootlegger during Prohibition, smuggling hooch from Canada to New York. Less than a decade earlier Chris had moved with his family, including six brothers and sisters, to Sonoma County, where his father directed the making of their first vintage by the headlights of milk trucks when all else failed.

Ever since then their winery, Glen Ellen, has been one of California's most successful. When father Bruno Benziger died, his children and twenty-five other relatives continued the business. The family used the huge profits from the sale of its inexpensive Glen Ellen line to launch upscale, estate-bottled Cabernets and Chardonnays under the family name. Their latest effort at the time of the dinner, a 1986 Merlot, was the favorite of Don Joe, who ordered it and got it to the Delta by sheer persistence despite its rarity, even in California.

As I savored the Merlot, the whole scene recalled to mind the first time I saw the Chinese Baptist Church in Cleveland, Mississippi, emblazoned with Chinese characters, as well as the first time I heard a Mississippi-Chinese Ole Miss cheerleader with a native Southern drawl. Now, thanks to the Joes and the Benzigers, we could have Merlot among the magnolias. The United States truly is an amazing place.

Since the above column was written after that glorious evening, much has changed in Cleveland, Mississippi, where K.C.'s once reigned. First, the restaurant burned, but the Joe brothers built it back better than before. Finally, seeking a bigger market, Wally moved the restaurant to Memphis where it now thrives under the name Acre. Like K.C.'s, it is well worth a detour.

The Rose of San Francisco: Red Wine and Garlic Breath

Red wine has been recognized as a healthy drink in the United States ever since Thomas Jefferson called it "the most healthful beverage" and "an antidote to the bane of whiskey." But it was not until *60 Minutes* anointed it as the miracle cure for clogged arteries that red wine sales began to catch up with white. Now it has an unexpected health-food partner: garlic.

Every time you turn on the television, someone is advertising the health benefits of garlic pills, which supposedly make you healthy without giving you bad breath. Until recently, such ads passed by me as unnoticed as that little rabbit beating the drum for flashlight batteries. Then I read *National Geographic*, where a serious study found that babies nurse better when their milk is flavored with garlic. Really?

While walking up Columbus Avenue in San Francisco's North Beach years ago, I passed a restaurant whose sign said, "The Stinking Rose, a Garlic Restaurant." The menu was startling. For appetizers there were garlic soup, garlic chili, escargots with garlic butter, baked brie with roasted garlic bulbs, and a pot of steamed garlic with clams and mussels. The salads featured garlic croutons. You did not have to order garlic bread—it came with everything. A sign on the wall said, "We season our garlic with food."

The Rose featured a pizza with roasted garlic cloves on mozzarella and a garlic sausage pizza. Their pastas, chicken, rabbit, and even sea bass were all covered liberally with—or marinated in—garlic. With every dish you could get a side order of garlic mashed potatoes, marinated garlic olives, or whole roasted garlic bulbs. Their brunch featured "eggs over garlic" washed down with a garlic-flavored Vampire Mary. That was too much, even for me.

My first question was whether red wine or white wine would go better with garlic. I first just stuck with the tried-and-true formula of white wines with fish and red wines with beef and lamb, since there was garlic in everything. The Rose had a long list of wines by the glass, and my friends and I tried a little of everything, both wines and foods. A surprising result emerged: the red wines definitely went better with everything.

For some reason, if you put enough garlic on something, most white wines seem to have a slight bitter or metallic aftertaste, or at least they did that night. With red wines, however, the sweetness of the garlic seemed to come out and its harsher qualities retreated.

With really garlicky dishes like whole roasted garlic cloves, red Zinfandels from Caymus and Sausal went well. With most dishes, to my surprise, the unanimous winner was the supposedly delicate Pinot Noir. Both La Crema and Acacia were perfect. Although the Rose did not have them, I suspect inexpensive Pinots like Mirassou would have been fine as well. Of the Chardonnays they had, Morgan and Meridian went best. Maybe it's a Central Coast thing.

With a good red wine that has spent a long time fermenting on its skins, and thus has the most heart-preserving chemical resveratrol in it, you can get good health and bad breath at a single sitting.

A few months ago one of my law students went to San Francisco for spring break. When I asked her to check on the Stinking Rose, mainly to confirm it was probably closed by now, she surprised me by saying, "It's not closed. My boyfriend lives there now and we eat there all the time." Another surprise from the unpredictable world of wine and food.

Napa Valley: An American Eden?

Ever since Robert Louis Stevenson lived there in the nineteenth century, the Napa Valley north of San Francisco has held a special aura for wine lovers—and for all who visit there, for that matter.

My first time there was in 1953 with my parents, when I was a child and it was all orchards and ranches. I next saw the valley during a law school vacation in 1967 when it had a couple of dozen wineries but was still incredibly peaceful and unspoiled. Now it has hundreds of wineries and is one of the most famous and expensive wine-growing regions of the world, and its history has been written.

Writing the story of Napa was no doubt a daunting task. If too full of gossipy family stories or "sagas," as they seem to be called nowadays, it could have been just another script for an evening soap opera. The job required a writer with not just a knowledge of wine and a feel for human drama, but also familiarity with contemporary history. Such a writer was found: James Conaway, a Southerner who is both novelist and journalist, and who earlier chronicled the amazing career of Leander Perez, political boss of south Louisiana's Cajun country.

What Conaway produced in *Napa: An American Eden*, is not just an exposé, although it has murders, suicides, adulteries, gangsters, lunatics, lechers, and lawsuits. Its best chapters contain factually detailed vignettes worthy of the literary journalist John McPhee. Unfortunately for Conaway, a former *Washington Post* wine columnist, he probably ruffled so many feathers on so many powerful birds that he will return to Napa, if at all, at his peril. He savages some of the corporate "barbarians" (his word), whom he describes as "not knowing wine from Alpo," and removes from several closets some dark stories that certain prominent families would rather forget.

Yet this book was not written to be sensational. It is no *War and Peace*, but it has the feel of an early Balzac novel. Conaway has a definite gift for imagery, calling the social atmosphere "more like Iowa than

California," and Napa newcomers "Anglo Saxons with Mediterranean delusions." He has captured Napa's curiously mixed atmosphere, which combines a visual calm with intense capitalist striving. He notes how the first hippie-looking enologists who came there in the 1960s seemed "as exotic as Mongolian herdsmen" to the valley populace of farmers and ranchers.

Conaway's book also resembles somewhat *The Winemasters* by Englishman Nicholas Faith, which told the story of the Bordeaux wine trade and its juicy scandals several years ago. Napa has enough interesting personalities to appeal to those who know little about wine, yet has enough special insight into the wineries to satisfy the most jaded aficionado. The gossip isn't to be overlooked either.

The villains were easiest to spot. The heroes evolved more slowly and were more detailed and satisfying. The male leading man is probably Richard Peterson, an honest, competent idealist who comes off as the bloody but unbowed victim of a lifetime of corporate abuse. The heroine is clearly Robin Daniel Lail, inheritor of the Inglenook tradition, once also a partner in Dominus, which pairs Chateau Petrus of Bordeaux with the classic Napa vineyards of Inglenook.

But the true hero of the book is the Napa Valley itself, still an endangered Eden, and as Conaway concludes, "If the Napa Valley can't be saved, then nothing can."

American Eden, written in 1990, is still excellent reading, all these years later in 2014 as this book is written. In 2002 Conaway wrote a sequel, The Far Side of Eden, which details the bitter war between its preservationists and its bulldozers, which continues to this day. Napa is less pristine now, but to me still well worth visiting. If you find it too crowded, try Sonoma, or better yet Mendocino—while they're "still there," as they say.

Napa Valley:
A Local Auction for Everyone

St. Helena, California—Here in the Napa Valley, where the finest wines in America have been made since the days of Jack London and Robert Louis Stevenson, the annual wine auction has just ended. Although not yet as rich or as famous as the "Hospices de Beaune," its French counterpart in Burgundy, the charity auction this year was a rousing success. It grossed more than $400,000 for local hospitals. As its name indicates, that is exactly how the famed Burgundy Hospices tradition began.

Auctioneer again this year was Michael Broadbent of London, England's greatest gift to the pun since Dr. Johnson. Broadbent's quips and jibes at indecisive bidders alone were nearly worth the price of admission. Up for grabs were some five hundred lots of the best and rarest wines ever produced in the Valley.

Wine auctions in America are a relatively recent phenomenon, bursting on the scene about a decade ago with much fanfare and megabuck bids for single bottles of rare vintages, as in the ten thousand dollar range for a single bottle of Chateau Lafite from the 1870s. For some reason, perhaps a reaction against such flagrant conspicuous consumption, or perhaps just from a desire to move on to the next fad, other wine auctions seemed to lose popularity in the past couple of years. Not so in Napa Valley.

As other auctions moved yearly from city to city, trailing extravagant press releases, the Napa auction stayed home with local wines featured and stayed strictly for charity, just like the Hospices de Beaune. In doing so, it built a solid base of regular supporters who come every year, buy a few cases, watch high-rolling collectors and restaurateurs buy the sensational bottles, then look forward to returning the next year.

In its slow and orderly progression, the Napa auction is helping build the sort of serious wine-drinking public among "normal," non-rich citizens that England once had, the people that made claret and Port household words. Today the English and even the French accuse Americans of destroying the wine market by ridiculously bidding up the prices of the clarets that their wine-drinking publics helped develop. Whatever the merits of that charge, we now seem to be building a similar solid public base in America for the best California wines, with Napa leading the way.

I was curious to know how the California papers would report the event and was surprised to read their reactions. A famous newspaper from a nameless city on a large nearby bay headlined the auction thus: "Wealthy Wine Buffs Swelter in Napa." It wasn't like that at all. The weather, to this Mississippian at least, was very pleasant in the shade, where everybody was anyway. In the evenings it was positively cool. The crowd of twelve hundred that attended was not limited to wealthy wine "buffs" at all, whatever they are. For example, near our room at the Motel 6, two ladies in one-piece swimsuits were sitting beside the three-foot-deep pool studying the handsome, silver-covered 128-page auction catalogue. Beside them were their bidder's paddles, meaning they were part of the select four hundred people who paid $150 each for the right to bid on the choice wines at the charity auction.

At some of the pre-auction dinners and tastings earlier that week (which to me were a greater attraction than the auction itself), the same thing was evident: the Napa Valley wine auction is not a hoity-toity wine-snob event (not yet, at least). It is still relaxed and open, everyone has a good time, and everyone wants to return. My wife especially wants to return to the motel we switched to after the first night: the lovely art deco classic run by a French woman, but named "El Bonita." It is as classic as the only fast-food place in St. Helena, Taylor's Refresher, where you can get fine wines by the glass with your sushi-burger.

At one dinner, our tablemates included a fireman and the parts manager of an auto dealership from southern California. This was the fifth straight year they had attended the auction, and they had carefully studied the catalogue and selected exactly what they were going to bid on and buy for their own cellars at home. Another couple had made their hotel reservations a year in advance. They knew this event was one of those rare times when even the most select wineries have open houses and the owners, no matter how jet-setish, are present in person, ready to offer their choicest wines for tasting if you know where to look and plan ahead.

Curious as to why local headlines about the auction were so at odds with my own perceptions, I asked a local columnist. Without the least note of condescension, he explained that when some famous person pays ten thousand dollars for one bottle of wine, that is news, but no one will buy a paper to read an article titled "Regular Joes Buy Wine."

Seeing how well informed he was on life in California generally, I decided to ask him something serious. My wife and I had by then eaten seven meals in California, at seven different places, and all seven of them had featured snow peas in one form or another. Why was that? Were snow peas the new official vegetable of California or something?

The columnist gave me a look of patronizing condescension that shows how far Californians have really come. It was a look that only really practiced French waiters can normally master. "Snow peas are *in season*," he replied.

Obviously this Mississippian still has much to learn about life in California.

Monticello West

Thomas Jefferson left us an amazing heritage in areas beyond his lifetime of public service. The thousands of letters he wrote, received, and dutifully preserved, are some of the treasures of America's past, an exact description of the people and events of his day unequalled in history. Among the least known are his voluminous writings on wine, a subject in which he was intensely interested throughout his eighty-three years.

As regular readers of my syndicated column know, I have been working for more than ten years editing and in many cases translating from the French, all of Jefferson's letters, memos, and account book entries on wines, which comprise several hundred separate entries. Last year I overconfidently promised that the work would be finished for publication this year. I had overlooked my talent for procrastination and underestimated the vastness of Jefferson's ability to pursue every possible facet of a subject.

As his tastes as a wine-drinker developed, Jefferson went from Madeiras to Champagnes, Sauternes, Burgundies, Bordeaux, Chiantis, and literally hundreds of other wines, scattering tasting notes as he went. Even in his old age, as he fought bankruptcy and tried to raffle off Monticello to pay his debts, he never ceased tasting and writing about new wines.

By necessity, he turned more in later years to the less expensive wines of Italy and southern parts of France from the ancient province of Languedoc (pronounced "long duck") and the Midi (like "mee dee").

Alexis Lichine, author of the excellent *Encyclopedia of Wines & Spirits*, called Jefferson "a true wine expert" who shared his knowledge and enthusiasm with other wine lovers among the Founding Fathers, including George Washington, Benjamin Franklin, James Monroe, and John Jay.

Jefferson actively promoted an American wine industry, planting several vineyards at Monticello, albeit unsuccessfully due to his constant absences and various vine diseases for which there were then no treatments. He also wrote scores of letters encouraging wine production by Italian, French, German, and Swiss settlers in the Ohio Valley, Pennsylvania, and the District of Columbia. Ironically, despite his intense interest in the Far West—he sent his personal secretary Meriwether Lewis and neighbor George Rogers Clark on their famous expedition—Jefferson never mentioned and probably never knew about America's greatest wineland: California.

During the last years of Jefferson's life, experiments with winemaking were being carried out in California not only by Junípero Serra at the missions of the Catholic fathers, but also by Frenchmen and others who found the California climate ideal for wine grapes. So far there is no indication that Jefferson was ever aware of their efforts. But now the two worlds have come together. In the wine-rich Napa Valley north of San Francisco, near the spot where the old town of Monticello, California once stood, a beautiful new winery now stands. Founded by Virginian Jay Corley, a wealthy real estate investor with an interest in wine almost as intense as Jefferson's, Corley has built an outstanding state-of-the-art winery. In front of it, in the middle of some of Napa's finest vineyards, stands the visitor center, a Palladian building modeled on Monticello.

Complete with a beautiful dining room and kitchen that serves full Jeffersonian meals based on authentic recipes preserved from Jefferson's old Georgetown shopping lists and Paris recipes preserved by his granddaughters, Monticello West is a fitting tribute to the greatest wine lover of all the Founding Fathers.

This past June (1984) I visited Monticello West with my wife Regan (who has her own catering business, Cuisine To Go, and likes to prepare Jeffersonian dishes to go with my Jeffersonian wines) and sampled the foods and wines. Jefferson would not have been disappointed.

In the glory days of the great migrations to California, some Virginians left their own Shenandoah Valley (who in his right mind would do that?) and headed west. In the Sierra foothills, they nostalgically named one valley, neither so green nor so beautiful as the Virginia one they had left behind, the Shenandoah Valley. Today it produces some of the finest Zinfandels of all California, wines of unique depth and character.

Other Virginians ventured nearer the coast, above San Francisco, into the peaceful Napa Valley, which is to wine in America what Bordeaux, Burgundy, and Champagne would be in France if all were located in a single valley instead of being scattered from one corner of the country to another. This second group of Virginians, homesick and mindful of their heritage as Virginians, founded a little village and named it "Monticello" after the home of Mr. Jefferson.

It takes a lot of stubbornness to make an American pronounce any foreign word the way foreigners pronounce it. Jefferson had that kind of strength of will and always made people pronounce the name of his house "monti-chello" as in the stringed musical instrument. The Virginians in Napa were not so persistent, however, or perhaps they just didn't care, and there the name has always been pronounced "monti-sello," like our own town of that name in Mississippi.

After semi-thriving for around a century, the village of Monticello, California, met an adversary that has been fatal to many small U.S. towns: the Army Corps of Engineers. The little town now lies under a large, rather ordinary-looking lake that does, I suppose, help flood control. But not all reminders of California's Virginians are yet dead. The road to the old town had been called Monticello Road for so long that at least the name survived.

Then came Jay Corley, a native Virginian who had, to put it bluntly, gotten rich in California in real estate. In 1970 Corley bought two hundred acres of prime vineyard land in the cooler, southern end of the Napa Valley and started growing premium wine grapes and selling them to fine Napa wineries such as Mondavi and Domaine Chandon. Corley, who definitely knew how to make money, considered *making* wine an unwise investment, a business that gave a whole new level of meaning to the term "capital venture." Perhaps from being around winemakers, or perhaps from deciding belatedly to get an MBA from Pepperdine, Corley changed his mind and in 1977 sunk a big chunk of his money into his own winery.

Drawing on his Virginia heritage, and with forgivable poetic license, Corley borrowed the name of the old Monticello Road, which was several miles away but was at least in the same county, and named his new winery "Monticello Cellars." Corley says you can pronounce it either way, so long as you buy his wine. Founded in 1980, the winery began with one of the most technologically sophisticated plants in the Napa Valley, which is saying something.

Proceeding prudently, Corley kept a low profile at first (I'd never heard of him) and was more businessman than dreamer—as so many winery owners are—he built slowly and solidly. His vines were in an ideal microclimate and matured well. The times, like the grapes, were right for a winery named Monticello.

Corley hired Alan Phillips, one of Napa's most talented young winemakers (I base that statement on tasting personally a wide range of his wines and not on press releases). Phillips had previously been with Rutherford Hill, whose fine wines are recommended to both consumers and restaurateurs as good values. He had also been with the downscale, jug-oriented Bear Mountain Winery and thus experienced the whole spectrum of California winemaking. At Monticello, Phillips walked into the dream situation for a young winemaker: Corley wanted the best possible winery and let Phillips design it with him. The results show it.

In 1984, the low profile disappeared (I heard of them), and Monticello burst on the Napa wine scene as if newborn, even though it had been there all along, carefully building. In the middle of the vineyards, on Big Ranch Road on the east side of the valley toward the old Silverado Trail, Corley opened a new visitor center, a brick, vaguely Palladian structure modeled after Jefferson's home at Monticello.

During this year's Napa Wine Auction, my wife Regan and I spent a day there, including a memorable tasting-luncheon featuring Phillips's wines matched with foods from the visitor center kitchens. It was what an old friend of mine used to call "a fine moment."

Now, thirty years later, Monticello West still thrives. Jay Corley, after visiting Mississippi several times to see his close friend Tom Storey and me and bringing his wines with him, retired and left his winery in the capable hands of his sons. Thus the Virginia tradition of Jefferson in California continues.

Is Wine-Tasting a "Profession"?

Wine-tasting is not an exact science. Some grumpy souls deny that it is a science at all, or even an art. They accuse us wine-tasters of frivolity and of trying to make something serious out of mere pleasure-seeking. A recent book entitled *One Hundred B.S. Jobs* even ranked our profession in the top ten, ahead of even food and travel columnists.

As I contemplated this important issue the other night, over a pretty fair glass of vintage Port, it occurred to me that both sides have valid arguments. But wait a minute. Was a case of the dreaded situational ethics coming over me? Not really. Different ideas of the value of wine-tastings come from real differences in the nature of the tastings and of the tasters.

When we get together with good friends to uncork some well-aged bottles, we are, let's face it, mainly there to have a good time. When, on the other hand, we descend into a cold and musty cellar to taste some acidic new wines from big, smelly barrels to advise a client which of these young devils will be great as mature adults in ten years or so, we are definitely working and not amusing ourselves.

Somewhere between the neighborhood wine-whoop and the professional barrel-tasting are the well-publicized commercial judgings of wines. In those, winemakers, professors of enology, wine wholesalers, retailers, and serious amateur collectors try to evaluate bottled wines by awarding them gold, silver, and bronze medals, just like at the Olympics or a state fair cattle-judging. As a matter of fact, most wine competitions so far take place at state or county fairs. In France they have even had a Wine Olympics sponsored by the famous food-and-wine critics Gault and Millau (pronounced "Go" and "Mee-oh").

Each year I participate as a judge in several of these curious wine events, which combine classic Yankee commercial hoopla with our equally American love of sporting competition, whatever the subject matter. The main contest is of course between the winemakers, but there is a secondary competition, friendly but fierce, between the judges. Each one seems to compete with the others to sniff or slurp out something more uniquely esoteric in the taste or bouquet than the others could discern or describe.

The outcomes of these unusual rituals have important commercial consequences for both the winning and losing wines, since wine shops nationwide post the results for months thereafter in the form of prominent gold and silver medal stickers on the bottles and "shelf-talkers" hanging from them. They also figure heavily in the wineries' advertising of the medals their wines have won, very much like horse breeders list the placement and winnings of particular thoroughbreds.

Lately these practices have been decried as examples of rampant American commercialism in the otherwise staid old wine business. Others say too many medals are awarded too easily and that it is all just advertising and not real competition at all. But we didn't start the practice, and the complaints are not new. Some famous and respected French wines still sport on their labels the gold medals they won when they were drunk by our grandfathers long before we were born, even though the current releases under the same labels may have no more resemblance to their noble ancestors than a pearl does to a rutabaga. Wine judgings are well-aged and no doubt here to stay. We long-nosed, leather-palated veterans of the tasting-table and spitting-bucket plan to stick around with them.

Best Wine Bars and Bistros of Paris

Last month, on a long break from a business trip, I set out to find the best wine bar in Paris. To those of you familiar with the growing number of wine bars in the United States, like the former Flagons in New Orleans or the London Wine Bar in San Francisco, these are institutions where you go to taste really great wines by the glass and then can buy a case or two to carry home. Such places were for centuries unknown in France, where you usually bought your wine directly from its maker and drank it only with dinner.

In the 1970s however, an Englishman named Steven Spurrier founded in Paris an English-style wine bar and restaurant very similar to ours in the U.S. It soon caught on with not only visiting Americans but Parisians themselves. Spurrier's Blue Fox wine bar was in an odd little Dickensian corner of Paris called the Cite Berryer near the Madeleine. When last I visited it, you could get a great Saumur from the Filliatreau brothers or a superb Jurancon from Cauhape.

Spurrier's partner in the Blue Fox, Mark Williamson, now has two other wine bars in Paris. The best known is Willi's Wine Bar at 13 rue des Petits Champs near Palais Royal, where you can taste an array of great wines like Avignonesi Montepulciano and red and white Hermitage, both old Thomas Jefferson favorites.

Willi's younger brother, as it were, is the wine bar Juveniles, located nearby at 47 rue de Richelieu. Run by Willi's brother-in-law Mark Collins (he calls himself "Emile" for French clients), this little place is one of my personal favorites of all wine bars in the world's winiest great city. They have International Herald Tribunes to read for free and a terrific selection of wines for rainy Paris days.

Best glasses last month were a Rioja from Remelluri and a one hundred percent Chenin Blanc Coteaux du Layon from the Loire. Juveniles is one place in Paris where you can get American, Australian, and Italian wines, not just French, as in most French places here.

One other wine bar is Le Repaire du Bacchus at 13 rue du Cherche-Midi near the Sevres-Babylone metro station. If you make it to Paris anytime soon, their Pacherenc de Vic Bilh dessert wine from France's Deep Southwest is almost alone worth the trip. But if you don't, one of life's great pleasures is dreaming you're in places you'll never get to visit. I do that a lot about China and India. Each time I leave Paris I assume I'll never return and fantasize about it a lot while I'm at home in Oxford, Mississippi. Someone said Paris is the world capital of nostalgia, and I believe it. But last month I made it back again and have some fresh tips on the best Paris wine bistros to visit this year in person or in your dreams.

A bistro is a sort of cafe/short-order restaurant but better, serving hot simple meals at all hours at reasonable prices. There are, of course, exceptions. The name *bistro* comes from a corruption of the Russian word for "hurry up" adopted when Cossack soldiers briefly occupied the city during the Franco-Prussian war in the 1870s. Bistros specializing in wines usually identify themselves on their awnings as being a "bistro à vins" or as having a "spécialité de vins."

The best bistro wines by the glass I have found recently are at a bustling spot called Au Sauvignon. Located at 80 rue des Saints Peres, near the Sevres-Babylone metro stop and some of Paris's fanciest shops in the 7th arrondissement, the Sauvignon itself is as unpretentious as when I used to stop there in the 1960s when I was a student at the Sorbonne. I usually wade through several platefuls of patés, terrines, and foie gras with large glasses of Quincy whites, Loire reds, and new Beaujolais. On a recent return visit I enjoyed delicate Burgundies from Savigny and a smooth St. Emilion from Bordeaux. They're with it at Au Sauvignon.

At the other end of the scale, you can try La Tartine at 24 rue de Rivoli. Despite its tony address in the Marais neighborhood, the Tartine ("buttered bread") is nothing short of grubby. Trotsky once hung out here and they probably haven't painted it since. This cozy bistro serves outstanding cold platters for lunch that merit a long detour and has a broad wine list at good prices.

Another terrific workingman's bar is Jacques Melac at 42 rue Leon-Frot near the Bastille. Melac is from Auvergne, an old-style country part of France that they regard somewhat like we do the remoter parts of the Ozarks. On the wall are signs saying "Water is reserved for cooking potatoes" and "If you must have water, please order a day in advance." Their best reds are from Cahors and Syrahs from Gigondas. They have really fine Sauternes by the glass as well. Melac has won the "Meilleur Pot" for being the best place in Paris to stop for an informal glass of wine with friends.

The Meilleur Pot—meaning best jug or flagon, you can translate it several ways—is a rotating award given each year to the proprietor serving the best wines at the best prices to a jury of dedicated wine-tasters who visit each bistro ten times in a six-month period.

Another personal favorite of mine was once Le Valencay on the Boulevard du Palais directly across from the entrance of the Criminal Courts or "Palace of Justice." I spent lots of time there with the barristers and it also had good lunches. The best wines there were the outstanding Loires in pitchers. *[Alas, it has since closed]*.

Across the Seine at 15 Quai des Grands Augustins is L'Ecluse, the best bistro in Paris for tasting Bordeaux. *[And it's still open in 2014]*. French-owned, the Ecluse (which means "lock," as on a canal) has now become a chain, but so far a good one. Another branch is at 120 rue Rambuteau near the old Les Halles market area. There you can taste everything from old Margaux and other classified growth Bordeaux to good little Petits Chateaux and food that matches them. Like all good bistros, they rush you at lunch, but you can linger as long as you like afterward and read a book all afternoon on the typical cold, rainy days of Paris—or on the rare and much-coveted sunny spring days of Paris for that matter.

If you want to fantasize that you're in a bistro beside the Seine in another century, try either Au Franc Pinot at 1 Quai Bourbon, a stone's throw from Notre Dame, or the Taverne Henri IV at 13 Place du Pont Neuf near the Louvre. For the best high-quality bargain lunch with wine by the pitcher, try La Rotisserie du Beaujolais at 19 Quai de la Tournelle, which shares its kitchen and food with La Tour d'Argent across the alley. *[La Rotisserie is, mercifully, still thriving in 2014]*.

Most useful of all in finding wine bars and bistros in Paris is the new 2014 edition of The Food Lovers Guide to Paris *by Patricia Wells, columnist for the* International Herald Tribune *since 1983. It is her first update of this classic guide since 1999. It is a book to savor and whose footsteps I will be following across Paris this summer.*

The Wines of New Zealand

Just as we had finally memorized the exotic names of Chilean and Australian wines, there came into the U.S. market a new challenger: New
Zealand. When last I tasted the wines of that beautiful South Seas island some years ago, they were rather ordinary. Today they are vastly
improved and well worth a try. But how to choose among new names?
Here are some guides.

New Zealand is a Dutch name, but some of its best winemakers now
came from Dalmatia, on the Adriatic coast across from Italy, once part
of Croatia.

The grape varieties of modern New Zealand are classics like Chardonnay, Cabernet, Sauvignon Blanc, and Riesling. Their most exotic
grape is Pinotage, a good hybrid of Pinot Noir and the Cinsault of south
France, a favorite brought in from South Africa, where it was first developed.

Despite its mixed origins, New Zealand is an English-speaking
country, which makes its wine labels easy to read. At a series of tastings during one annual Memphis In May Festival, New Zealand was the
honored guest country. There I met New Zealand's hereditary Maori
Queen, who was built like a linebacker and amply tattooed, but that had
no effect on her appreciation of the wines. I also met their Ambassador
to the United States and their Deputy Prime Minister. All were relaxed,
charming people. Perhaps that is their job, but I came away with the
impression of a mellow South Pacific temperament instead of the more
rugged Australian one.

Their wines seemed to be similar. Perhaps it's because New Zealand,
with its steep emerald-green mountains and spectacular coastal fjords,
is greener and cooler than Australia and did not start life as a penal
colony as its neighbor did.

Of the two dozen or so New Zealand wines tasted recently, my favorites have been from Nobilo and Kumeu River wineries, both operated

by Dalmatian families. The Nobilo Sauvignon Blanc, made at Huapai on the North Island, from South Island grapes from Marlborough, was excellent. A Nobilo Pinotage red was smoother than most, but full-bodied enough for steak. Kumeu River, operated by another Dalmatian family, made the best New Zealand red I tasted, a Merlot/Cabernet, which seemed influenced by the winemaker's training in the St. Emilion region of Bordeaux. Their importer was Wilson-Daniels of Saint Helena, California, which also imports Romanee-Conti.

Another fine New Zealand white is the Nautilus Sauvignon Blanc from Hawkes Bay. In fact, all of the Sauvignons I tasted were better wines than all the Chardonnays I tasted. Prices are no cheaper than California, but the quality of the best is comparable.

In buying New Zealand wines, it is well to remember that their southern hemisphere vintages are a year older than ours due to their seasons being reversed. Their "fall" harvest is in March and April. With whites especially, this can make a big difference.

There is an excellent book predictably called *The Wines and Vineyards of New Zealand* by Michael Cooper. It is out of print but still available on the Internet. Introduced by English master of wine Jancis Robinson, this readable book is probably worth its forty dollar price for the serious explorer of new wine regions.

Of course New Zealand is now best known for its luscious Pinot Noirs, a wonderful new development which began not long after this old column was written. And, oh yes, the beautiful Lord of the Rings movies were filmed there.

Spain's Whites Catch Up with Its Great Reds

Spain is a land of many wines, some of them cheap, many of them ancient. Spain has more acres of vineyards than any other country in the world, including even France and Italy. For years now it has produced some of the world's most prized reds, especially those of the northern Rioja and the famed old Vega Sicilia winery.

Until recently, however, Spain's white wines were made for the taste of another century: over-aged in barrels and maderized. Now all that has changed. English wine expert Hugh Johnson, perhaps the greatest living wine writer, calls the best new-style Spanish whites "remarkably crisp and aromatic," and devotes a whole section of his famous wine atlas to them. U.S. critic Robert Finigan says he likes a white from the famous Riscal winery even better than its famous red. Yet Robert Parker, most influential of all U.S. wine critics, has called them in his *Buyer's Guide*, "neutral" at best and at worst "boring . . . . like lemon-water." Parker should update his Guide after an updated tasting. I've never much agreed with him anyway. For a vivid critique of his opinions and methods, see *Robert Parker: Anatomie d'un Mythe*. Written by his former assistant and tasting coordinator in France, it is available only in French for fear of lawsuits, but the title alone gives you a strong hint as to its content.

A Fact-Finding Mission

My wife and I often visit what is reputed to be the best Spanish restaurant in the United States, called the Taberna del Alabardero (translated roughly as the "Beefeaters' Tavern"). A reliable friend first recommended it both for food and wines; boy was he right—on both counts. I had looked forward to it mostly for the red wines, then the food, but never for the whites, which were to be the pleasant surprise. But at first I was not so sure. When the waiter asked if I would like a cocktail, I asked instead for the wine list. He asked in turn if I wanted red or white. Wondering if perhaps they had two lists, I said "white." Instead of a list, he brought me a large glass of unnamed white.

"What kind of joint is this?" I thought. Unconfrontational, I tried it. It was delicious, crisp, and flavorful. Spaniards will hate this, but it reminded me more in style of a Portuguese white than a Spanish one. Demanding the label, I saw it was a Rueda from Martinsancho. It went superbly well with a typical Spanish garlic soup.

It was followed by a glass of white Rioja, one of the best, which could not hold a candle to it. Going back to a Rueda, I tried the one from Grinon, which was even better. The waiter showed more interest when I showed a preference for what he had chosen for me and began to explain it, saying it was then fairly new to the United States and not that common even in Spain ten years ago.

Ancient Rueda New and Improved

These were real finds. Made on the high, windy, dry plains of ancient Castille, these Rueda wine were among Spain's most famous in the seventeenth century when the capital was nearby. For many years, however, they were forgotten. Probably it was because they were made like poor sherry, heavy in alcohol, over-aged in old oak barrels, and not at all to U.S. tastes.

Then about ten years ago, to help sagging sales, French wine guru Emile Peynaud of Bordeaux was brought in to advise. And advise he did. Rueda wines are now clean, crisp, and truly refreshing. They also have enough body to withstand heavier dishes, such as a huge plate of fried squid (must have been two pounds) I washed down with a couple of glasses.

Made from the Verdejo grape, supposed to be the same one the makes the Madeira called Verdelho, these Ruedas are some remarkably good wines for this price. Thus far mostly unknown in the United States, they deserve more recognition, as does the Alabardero, which is located at 1176 I Street, Washington, D.C., just three or four blocks from the White House.

Since this was written, the hottest new whites from Spain are the bone-dry whites called Albarino from the old Gallic province of Galicia, just across the river from Portugal, and somewhat reminiscent of Vinho Verde.

Sea Air Cools Temecula Valley

Wine writers are sometimes as jaded and spoiled as voters, always seeking new experiences rather than proven quantities. Feeling that wanderlust, last month I explored the little-known wineries of the Temecula Valley between Los Angeles and San Diego, a little to the east.

Temecula, locals told me, is the American Indian word for Land of Rising Mist. It accurately describes the valley, where hot desert air over Palm Springs to the east pulls in cool sea air from the Pacific near San Juan Capistrano, just twenty-two miles west as the wind blows.

The sea air creates not only the mist, but also a uniquely cool microclimate friendly to winemaking. Hillside vineyards in Temecula often reach 2,500 feet above sea level. The rolling, windswept vineyards look much like those of the Rhone Valley in deep southern France and produce some really fine wines.

Temecula, the town, is on the west side of the valley, which was formerly the vast 98,000-acre cattle ranch known for centuries as Rancho California. Temecula, the valley, now has more than 3,200 acres of vineyards, most of them planted in the finest vinifera grape varietals, and nearly a dozen wineries. Rancho California survives mainly as a name for an expensive-looking subdivision in the Spanish style.

The largest and clearly dominant winery in the valley is Callaway, named for Eli (pronounced ee-lee) Callaway, who in his earlier incarnation as president of Burlington Mills claims to have "brought pantyhose to the world." With expert help from the staff of the famed enology school at Cal-Davis, Callaway and viticulturist John Moramarco first planted 150 acres of vines in 1969.

The new vineyards re-established the south coast as a serious vineyard area for the first time in more than a century. New to the business, for a few years Callaway made a large line of wines and sold only to restaurants. Later, judging both quality and market trends, he pulled up all his red wine vines and replanted in whites his entire 320 acres of vineyards. In 1981 Callaway was sold to Hiram Walker, the distillers.

Surprisingly, this new concern did not become conservative, but even more innovative. Its other winery, J. J. Moreau of Burgundy, had long specialized in fine Chardonnays made without any oak aging whatsoever, contrary to both French and California standard practice. To enhance flavor, Moreau leaves the Chardonnay unoaked and on its lees in both France and California.

The very first Callaway Chardonnay, named Calla-Lees to make sure no one missed the point, was produced in this way. It had a beautifully intense Chardonnay character and was for years the best-selling south coast wine—and deserved to be.

Callaway's experiments did not end in the cellar. Faced with erosion problems in its deep granitic soils, Callaway allowed natural grasses to grow between the vines rather than plowing. Besides slowing erosion, the grass unexpectedly cut down on chinch bugs, leaf hoppers and other varmints by hosting natural predators like lady bugs and "good" wasps.

But it is with the vines themselves that Callaway is still most unusual and daring. Temecula having never suffered the disastrous phylloxera lice that wiped out most European and California vineyards in the nineteenth century, Callaway still grows all its vinifera grapes on their own rootstocks, which are not resistant to phylloxera.

Nearly every other winery in the world now grafts its grapes onto resistant American roots, but not Callaway. We wish them luck. Europeans have always presumed that natural, ungrafted rootstocks made better wines, but were too risky. Perhaps now we'll find out.

Tasting the Callaway whites in the modern tasting room after a tour of the large estate revealed excellent wines: a balanced Sauvignon Blanc with an attractive aroma; a more closed Fumé Blanc with a beautiful finish; a Riesling, which I chose to buy; and a unique late-harvest dessert wine of Chenin Blanc with a honeyed aroma more reminiscent of a Sauternes than of its cousins from the Loire Valley. It was called "Sweet Nancy" for reasons I forgot to ask. I called back and Callaway told me naming it "Nancy" after his wife was the second-biggest mistake of his life. His biggest, he said, was marrying Nancy, from whom he is now divorced.

I bought a Calla-Lees Chardonnay as well, and will again. As my daughter and I were leaving Temecula, we saw a guy driving a tiny tractor among the vines. Intrigued by its atmosphere as a small, old-fashioned family winery, we stopped our rental car at the little tasting room for one last taste. Located in an old barn, the tasting room was empty. The man on the tractor soon entered, however, and offered to let us taste all he had. His name was Joe Hart. His family was originally from Arkansas, but he had been raised in El Centro in the oven-hot Imperial Valley. Joe, who now has white hair and a big, full white beard, treated us to a surprisingly good Riesling and two fine Grenaches, one red and one an award-winning rosé. They reminded me of good Rhone wines. If you see a wine from Hart Family Winery, don't pass it by.

This advice still holds in 2013. Joe Hart became a good friend during the twenty years I was a fellow judge at the San Diego International Wine Competition under the chief judge, David Lake. Joe's wines join those of new ace winemaker Jon McPherson of the South Coast Winery and Resort, the new king of Temecula.

The Wines of Texas Are upon Us

The main problem with Texas wines (like Swiss wines) is that there are not enough of them to go around. Most Americans are still amazed to hear that Texas wines even exist. They are lightly promoted, not because they are not worth it, but mainly because there are not yet enough of them to "export" widely outside the Lone Star State.

To some, Texas sounds like a place too hot and dry to grow fine wine grapes, but higher, cooler elevations are a little like France's Rhone Valley, and more temperate than many of the wine regions of Spain and Italy. If you don't think Lubbock or Driftwood can produce good wines, just try the wines listed below.

Perhaps the best argument for the potential of Texas wines was made by Cordier of Bordeaux, a classic claret producer, which spent millions setting up vineyards and a winery in conjunction with the University of Texas. Now called Sainte Genevieve, its wines first showed particularly well at the Texas Wine Classic, which was held in June 1994 in San Antonio, and where I have served as a judge, voting and awarding medals.

Of the twenty-seven then-current Texas wineries, most entered the competition. Unfortunately, all but a handful have productions too small to ship outside the state on a commercial scale. We therefore limit our comments to wines widely available, at least by Federal Express. Several gold medals were awarded.

My first memory of a Texas wine was a Fumé Blanc of the early 1980s from Llano Estacado winery [pronounced "Yahno-ess-tah-kah-doe]. The wine was clean, fresh, true to its Sauvignon Blanc grapes, and an excellent value. At the Classic, the 1993 Johannisberg Riesling was my highest-rated wine. It compares in price with California, and 7,200 cases were produced.

A 1992 gold medal Muscat Canelli from Schoppaul Hill was a worthy dessert wine. The most accessible is silver medal winner Messina Hof, a large producer, which had 7,200 cases of 1993 Riesling and an excellent, California-quality 1993 Gewurztraminer (1,500 cases).

For those who love to wow their friends with the elite and the esoteric, little Grape Creek won a gold for its 1992 Chardonnay. There was also Fall Creek's 1993 gold medal Sauvignon Blanc. Hill Country Winery garnered gold for its Chardonnay. For a really esoteric red, look for Schoppaul Hill Red River Valley reserve Cabernet Sauvignon.

For my money, the best wines overall were presented by Sainte Genevieve, the French-founded outfit. Their vineyards are on and around Texas limestone mesas of character somewhat similar to vineyard-over-limestone areas in France. Worth looking for are the following: reserve Cabernet Sauvignon; reserve Chardonnay; nonvintage Chardonnay and Cabernet; nonvintage Sauvignon Blanc and Chenin Blanc. Quality, as it does sometimes, escalates with price.

By 2014 Texas wines had exploded both in number and quality. While presenting a seminar at the George H. W. Bush Memorial Library at Texas A&M, I had the opportunity to visit the lovely and lively Messina Hoff Winery nearby. And while judging wines over a ten-year period at the Dallas Morning News Wine Competition, I became familiar with later vintages. My current favorites are McPherson and Lewis, both of which produce modest quantities of world-class wines.

Wine in Yosemite:
The Ahwanee Hotel

The High Sierras, or at least the *low* High Sierras, have been wine country since the Gold Rush, but the rocky, waterfalled beauty of Yosemite National Park is too rugged for vineyards. On a recent visit there, while my wife and daughters rode the mountain horse trails, I sought a quiet porch, a rocker, and a good view. All these I found at the Old Ahwahnee Hotel in the heart of Yosemite Valley. Little did I imagine the wines that went with them.

Turning the corner in the venerable lobby, I stumbled upon the massive dining room. At the entrance was a display of one of the best wine lists in the U.S. Nearby, a Cruvinet machine kept America's best wines ready to serve by the glass. Also available were great half-bottles, better for both the pocketbook and the head when you're dining alone or want to taste a variety of wines.

The setting for tasting wines is spectacular. Imagine a dining room over one hundred feet long with thirty-four-foot ceilings (compare that to your dining room—I did to mine), which was nevertheless cozy in a great-hall sort of way. There are no wines served by amateur waiters: all are served by specially trained stewards, polite and useful but not stuffy or overbearing. Their chief, who has the strikingly British name of Alistair Spiers, is not pretentious either. Despite his obviously broad knowledge and sincere interest in wines, his card identifies him simply as "bar manager," and not sommelier or something more intimidating.

Tired of Napa, Sonoma, or even Monterey? Want to enjoy wine without having to admire wineries during a side-trip from San Francisco? The Ahwahnee is the answer. From November 13 to December 14, they sponsor eight events called Vintners' Holidays, each consisting of three days of wine-tasting with winemakers and wine-writers, all famous and worthy of a visit, in the Great Hall. Appropriate foods are of course served.

If you lean to food over wine, from January 3 to 25, the Ahwahnee sponsors seven Chefs' Holidays featuring guest chefs and "presenters" from Narsai David to Marcel Desaulniers of Williamsburg. Everything from cultured abalone to exotic mushrooms will be tried, with emphasis on California food predominating. That does not mean snow peas at every meal as I once thought. These Californians have come a long way in getting their food up to the level of their wines, although the wines still lead the way.

The wine list, which first attracted me to the Ahwahnee after the rocking chair and the Great Hall, is one of the best selected I've seen in the country. Never entered in any of those much-publicized contests for best wine list, it still stands apart. Greeting you at the door, as a promise of things to come, are the great new California "proprietor" wines, blends of the best varietals in the French style rather than being named solely for the grape. Leading the list are Joseph Phelps's Insignia, the Mondavi-Rothschild Opus One, Geyser Peak Reserve Alexandre, and the fine Lyeth, understatedly called just a "red wine."

Add a selection of dessert wines by the glass from Chateau d'Yquem to Quady Essencia, the finest Ports and California Muscats, plus some well-priced Burgundies like Pommards and Cortons from 1985, and you have a place to spend a week, not three days. Alas, we had to leave to catch the plane and I had only an afternoon, neither a dinner nor a night there, but I plan to return.

The special events schedule has changed, but the Ahwanee Hotel and its wine list continue to thrive in 2014.

The Dark Side of France

Over seventy percent of the wine drunk by Americans last year was white. The rest was mostly red or pink. But some of the old "black" wine of earlier centuries is still around, and it is not that hard to find.

Black Pinot: Did you ever notice that the great grape of Burgundy (and recently California) is a Pinot *Noir,* and not a Pinot *Rouge*? It is a black grape not a red. So are most of the other grapes now called "red." Their juice is filtered and refined to make it less viscous and opaque; this makes the wine keep better and it looks more attractive, but it may just lose something in character. The old black wines had character in the extreme.

Wine for the Liver: The fad for red wines over deeper black ones began before Shakespeare when the first wine-writer in the English-language, William Turner in 1568, said light red wines were better for the liver than those made deeper in color. Today we know he was wrong, of course, but it's too late to change most people's habits. Black wines thrive in France, Italy, and Argentina, and exist in California, but so far are little exported.

Cahors: One of the better wines of France, and among the least known, although it is available in America, is Cahors (pronounced "cah-or"). Named for a hill town some one hundred miles southeast of Bordeaux, the wines of Cahors date from Roman times. Unlike most Roman wines, however, they were made from native grapes found in Gaul by the Romans. The primary grape of Cahors is the Malbec, a deep purple variety also blended into Bordeaux for the past 150 years to give color to its wines.

My first recollections of the black wines of Cahors are from the early '70s when I worked in a wine store in Georgetown with a young Frenchman who had been farmed out there by his Bordeaux wine-making family to learn the American market. When I asked him what French wine he liked best, he did not reply Chateau Lafite or Chambertin. His favorite was Cahors.

Boot Camp Wine: My friend had once been on a boot camp march in the mountains of southwestern France. After fifteen miles or so in the heat, his sergeant let the men stop at a farmhouse. The farmer offered them some wine. Black like ink, the wine was startlingly aromatic and complex, my friend said. To test his memory we grabbed a bottle from the shelf, opened it and tasted. Remarkable flavor, but a color like nothing I'd ever seen. It was opaque, black. Well, very deep purple anyway. The wine was Cahors, from Georges Vigoroux, the very same one my friend had tasted, and there it was in Washington, D.C. Since then I've tasted Vigoroux Cahors in Memphis, Atlanta, and all over America, and I don't believe I've yet seen it cost over ten dollars.

For years I wished someone in California would make a black Malbec wine like Cahors. I knew it was the main wine-making grape of the major red wine consuming nation of the western hemisphere: Argentina, one of whose best producers is Bodegas Lopez of Mendoza province. I knew that one Malbec had even, in 1974, placed next to Robert Mondavi Cabernet as the best "American" red at an international tasting. But where was Malbec when I needed it?

Geyser Peak: What I like most about the American wine scene is the constant search for novelty. At Geyser Peak, one of the most renowned operations in Sonoma County, experiments with the "blending" grapes of Bordeaux, Merlot, and Cabernet Franc recently expanded to take in Malbec. In 1985 they first tried a wine made entirely from their Malbec "blending" grapes, and it was one of my favorite California reds in several years: rich, soft, chewy, and like a 1982 Bordeaux in its depth of fruit. If you look for Cahors and can't find Vigoroux, try Chateau de Chambert or Clos de Gamot. There is also a Cahors co-op, called Cotes d'Olt; their wines need more aging. In my experience, the older they are, the better—up to a point, say ten years old. After that they tend to fade.

When I wrote the above column in 1989, little did I suspect the explosion of wine exports from Argentina in the new century. There are now over a hundred Malbecs on the market. Oddly, with time, my own tastes (perhaps due to some of their hundred-dollar-plus price tags) have turned to other Argentine wines, especially their Tempranillos borrowed from Spain and their fine, clean Chardonnays, which I much prefer to their traditional Torrontes, a dry white muscat which shares ancestry with the Terrantez wines of the island of Madeira. For a comprehensive, lucid overview of the new Argentine wines, I highly recommend the book Vino Argentino *by Laura Catena (see bibliography).*

Gallo just acquired Alamos winery of the Mendoza region at the foot of the Andes. Gallo, in acquiring Alamos, discontinued my favorite Alamos varietal, Bonarda, a rich red I prefer to Malbec. Gallo now blends it with Malbec into its generic Argentine "Red Blend" at ten dollars. Other wineries like Zolo and Dante Robino continue to make Bonarda unblended, however. The Bonarda was once believed to be an Italian grape from the northwestern Piedmont region, but DNA testing has recently revealed it to be a French grape, Charbonneau, little grown since the nineteenth century but due for a big revival.

In a similar revival across the high Andes in Chile, ampelographers (specialists in the DNA of grapevines) also discovered recently that what the Chileans had been marketing, innocently, as "Merlot" turns out to be an old, eighteenth-century Bordeaux grape named Carmenère, long thought to be extinct. New bottlings of Carmenère are growing rapidly and well worth trying. Carmenère is softer than Cabernet and with beautiful aromas; those tired of "the usual" would do well to try a Carmenère or three.

Never Heard of Chenin Blanc?
You've Got Company

Languishing dusty and almost forgotten on the shelves of Washington wine shops are some of the best white wines of France. Once the preferred summer drink of French kings, these wines are no longer fashionable and often sell for less than Blue Nun Liebfraumilch.

I am speaking of the fine white wines of the Loire Valley of western France, which in the United States have ceded pride of place to such upstarts as cheap Chardonnay from Languedoc. In fact it is unlikely that most American wine-drinkers would recognize the name of any Loire white wine except Vouvray, which has become better known in the past few years. The Loire whites discussed here are those made solely from the Chenin Blanc grape. Their cousins such as Sancerre and Muscadet are wines of a very different character, from different grapes.

For lovers of fine Loire whites, the present obscurity of Chenin Blanc is an ideal situation because with currency devaluations and rising prices, these summer wines are among the least expensive on the market. But with even the worst wines of Bordeaux and Burgundy selling for museum-piece prices, it is unlikely that the Loire whites will be left alone much longer. Americans may also come to know the Chenin Blancs of the Loire by way of California, where thousands of acres of that grape are planted. Most are still made into anonymous jug wines, but a handful of wineries have begun to produce some pretty good white wines, my favorite being the dry Chenin Blanc of Dry Creek Winery.

The origins of the Chenin Blanc grape are obscure. Its name comes from a Loire Valley manor house, the Mont Chenin, where it was first grown. It is a rather large, greenish grape which looks as if it would be tart, and it is. The curious thing is that it is also slightly sweet, especially when allowed to ripen well into the fall. It is at its best when grown along a one hundred-mile stretch of chalky limestone hillsides bordering the downstream portions of the Loire River and its tributaries.

The Chenin Blanc aroma is strong but not heavy, and freshly fruity. In character its wines most resemble those other excellent wines for summer, the German Moselles and the Portugese Vinhos Verdes. Like them, it is not bone dry, but usually has a slight underlying sweetness balanced by a pleasantly thirst-quenching acidity, which gives the wine its famous "bite."

Another name for the Chenin Blanc grape, used interchangeably, is Pineau de la Loire, and in California when made into a dry white wine it used to be erroneously called the White Pinot, perhaps because the two "pee-nohs" are pronounced identically.

The Chenin Blanc is grown in very few places in France outside the Loire Valley. The exception is Bergerac, home of Cyrano, which is some sixty miles east of Bordeaux in southwest France. There a tart golden wine of passable quality called simply Bergerac is made, partly from Chenin Blanc. A little Chenin Blanc goes into a nearby dessert wine known as Monbazillac, which is popular in France as the poor man's Sauternes. They are fair values, but can't match their Loire brethren.

Typical of Chenin Blanc wines is the agreeable Vouvray, which often strikes those tasting it for the first time as sprightly, refreshing, and cheerful. The French say it leaves the mouth "at ease." The appropriate motto of the town of Vouvray is: "I gladden hearts." Although it appears light and delicate, Vouvray is a sturdy wine, and if from a sunny year will be rather high in alcohol and bear aging unusually well for a white wine. Though most are meant to be drunk young, the summer following harvest, I have tasted thirty-year-old Vouvrays that were excellent and had lost almost nothing in taste or color. Vouvray's appearance is usually shiny and viscous because of its high natural glycerine content; its color varies from almost clear to light gold.

Today most Vouvrays are not the product of a single vineyard or grower, but are blends put together by shippers. Some of the most respected and reliable of these are Monmousseau, Ackerman-Laurance, and Frederick Wildman. A few growers still produce their own Vouvrays bottled on the estate. These are often the best and slightly expensive—if you can find them. Vouvray is also interesting because it is one of the most varied and unpredictable of wines. In the sunniest summer it produces a wine with so much natural sugar that it becomes slightly sparkling naturally, without any help from the vintner. This wine is the most prized by Vouvray addicts, but rare here in the U.S.

In average years, Vouvray makes a wine of the *demi-sec* (half dry) order, its natural acidity well balanced by slight sweetness like German Moselle. This wine may well be the finest summer drinking possible, either by itself after a long hot day, or with a light, cold lunch. In poor years, Vouvray makes a wine of tremendous acidity that is sometimes virtually undrinkable. In those years it is most often blended with some wine of other years, sugar added, and the Champagne method used to produce a Mousseux (sparkling wine) which is considered by many the finest in France outside Champagne itself.

With prices of good Champagne still rising, the excellent Vouvray Mousseux from Monmousseau available here is rapidly becoming better known, although nowhere near as popular as it is in France. One deterrent may be that it is not made bone dry, and current wine snobbism insists (in aggravated cases) that all wine be dry. A malicious Englishman once told me that what most American wine snobs really want is a sweet wine in a bottle that says "very dry."

Probably the finest bottle of inexpensive Vouvray now on the market is that of the Père Diard, a jolly-looking priest who owns a piece of the outstanding Vallee Coquette vineyard and who puts his picture on the label to show the drinker how content he'll be after finishing the Père's bottle. Also fine is the Chateau Moncontour, the favorite wine of the great Loire Valley novelist Honore de Balzac.

West of Vouvray, along the banks of the little river Layon, are the famed Coteaux du Layon, where fine Chenin Blanc dessert wines are made. These wines, the favorites of the Renaissance poet Rabelais, are lighter, more flowery and less cloying than Sauternes. They have a taste of wild honey that goes perfectly with a summer dessert of fresh fruit, especially peaches or strawberries. Also available at a few stores are some fine old vintages, virtually unavailable in Paris, from the best Layon growths: Bonnezeaux, Quart de Chaume, and the full-bodied Chateau de Fesle. These begin high and go up with a vengeance.

Still farther toward the Atlantic, on the banks of the Loire itself, is the Coteaux de la Loire, whose wines are the driest and most elegant of all

Chenin Blancs. In finesse they are second only to the finer white wines of Burgundy and have great "breed." Clustered near the town of Savennières are the two finest vineyards: La Coulee-de-Serrant and La Roche aux Moines. Since these wines are noticeably the driest of all the Loire whites discussed, they are best when aged for at least three or four years so that the natural volatile acidity of the Chenin Blanc grape can soften. The wines of Savennières are my number one favorite with oysters on the half-shell.

Of the California wines made from the Chenin Blanc, some of the best *demi-secs* are as follows: Chappellet, which is very good and most resembles a Loire white; Mayacamas, which is similar; and Robert Mondavi, which has a delightful slight sparkle. Drier and good in their own way, although totally unlike the French Chenin Blancs, are Louis Martini, Souverain and Charles Krug White Pinot (nonvintage).

How to Say It

Wines made from the Chenin Blanc grape are often given unpronounceable names, even in California. One reason few Americans drink them is they don't want to seem foolish in wine stores by mispronouncing the names, and not one wine-seller in ten can pronounce these names any better than the customer. If in doubt as to pronunciation, just take a shot at it. If the seller doesn't understand you, write it on a piece of paper.

Here is a rough-and-ready layman's phonetic guide to some of the names in this article:

Bonnezaux — bun-uh-zoh
Chenin Blanc — shuh-nah blaw (Californians often pronounce it shen-nun blahnk)
Coteaux du Layon — cut-oh dew lie-aw
Coulee de Serrant — koo-lay duh ser-aw
Loire — lwahr
Monbazillac — maw-bah-zee-yak
Monmousseau — maw-moo-soh
Pineau — pee-no
Pinot — pee-no (not "pee-nut")
Quart de Chaume — car duh shome
Roche aux Moines — rush oh mwahn
Savennières — sa-ven-yair

The Wines of Chateau Biltmore

To those who believe the South cannot make fine wine, I say this: taste the wines from the Biltmore Estate in North Carolina, especially the bubbly they call Methode Champenoise (Champagne Method).

Before the twin scourges of Civil War and Prohibition took their toll, Carolina was a leading wine-producing state. Since then, moonshine has been quietly favored by many locals—and some of it wasn't half bad, tasting sort of like scotch with cider added.

But the old mountains have something much better and much more legal: real wine, made in a real estate at a real imitation French chateau. Called the Biltmore, it was "built" in the 1890s by the grandson of the original Commodore Vanderbilt on 125,000 acres.

Designed in the style of the ruggedly beautiful Blois, a sixteenth-century castle in France's Loire Valley, the Chateau Biltmore has 250 rooms in its 90,000 square feet. It overlooks the Blue Ridge Mountains and the French Broad River in a spectacularly beautiful area near Asheville.

In 1971, grandson William A. V. Cecil (rich people always seem to have two middle names) decided to plant vineyards and, if they succeeded, a winery. The vineyards so thrived that in 1977 Cecil hired Philippe Jourdain to come from Carcassonne in French Provence to be winemaster on a trial basis. In 1978, he pressed his first wines and in 1979 sold his first bottle. It was so well received that Jourdain became official winemaster.

With a difficult climate of rainy spells and late frosts, the Blue Ridge Mountains proved what the Frenchman already knew from the six generations of winemakers in his family: It is harder to grow quality grapes than it is to make quality wine. Then Steve Sorensen, a graduate of the University of California-Davis, the Harvard of U.S. wine-making schools, was hired as vineyard manager. They soon were grafting fine European vinifera grapes onto hardy American rootstocks. The results are pretty impressive.

To me the only thing that really matters about wine is the taste. No matter what its name is or who its grandfather was, if the taste is not there, then nothing else is either. The viniferas—including Cabernets and Chardonnays labeled Chateau Biltmore—retail for twelve to eighteen dollars per bottle and are generally worth it. Blends, called Biltmore Estate wines, go for seven to ten dollars per bottle. The sleepers are the bubblies: one is a blend of Pinot Noir and Chardonnay; the other is a pure Chardonnay. Both are produced in individual bottles rather than in tanks.

At fifteen to twenty dollars per bottle, the Biltmore bubblies are steals, among the best in the eastern United States and comparing favorably with what Spanish producers are making in California.

In 2009 I revisited with my family the Chateau Biltmore as a consultant to assist Mr. Cecil and his family in renovating and restocking the classic old wine cellar built by his ancestor, the great gourmet and wine-traveler George Washington Vanderbilt, who built the spectacular castle. They put us up in a special guest house on the grounds (which you can still rent) complete with a chef/butler. I compiled quite a cellar list from Mr. Vanderbilt's letters, journals, and daily menus. Sadly, modern building codes do not allow visits to the cellars, but they are well stocked, and in the beautiful restaurants, you can order some of his favorite wines. The estate, which was designed and laid out by Frederick Law Olmsted, who designed Central Park in New York, is a wonderful visit at any season. Some of their own wines, including Pinot Noirs and Chenin Blancs, are made partly from imported California grapes and well worth trying. Let me sum it up this way: After Paris, the number one destination on my bucket list is the Chateau Biltmore. Hope I make it.

Irish Wines in Bordeaux

On St. Patrick's Day, peering down into a mug of green beer, I thought of how much the Irish have contributed to the world of fine wine, and of how little we think about their contributions. Perhaps drinking green beer makes one more ruminative.

If Port is the Englishman's wine, and Madeira is now dominated by Scottish families, then red Bordeaux (claret) deserves to be known as the Irish wine rather than whiskey.

Beginning in the seventeenth century and especially during the unhappy reign of the revolutionary Oliver Cromwell, the Irish flocked to Bordeaux. There was even an Irish brigade in the French army. Through these contacts, the Bordeaux wine trade with Ireland became so brisk that by 1740 Ireland imported *four times* as much Bordeaux wine as England.

By 1787, when Thomas Jefferson visited Bordeaux as American Minister, half the wine merchants he named as the best were Irish. They included families still dominant today: the Johnstons and the Bartons, whose name is still perpetuated by chateaux bearing that name. Even today, two of the greatest Bordeaux wine chateaux, Leoville-Barton and Langoa-Barton in the village of St. Julien, are still owned by Bartons. In every good wine store in America you can find wines shipped by B&G, which stands for Barton and Guestier. With the current emphasis on sobriety and moderation, perhaps the Irish will become as well known for wine as whiskey, although that may yet take a while.

Two other classified growth Bordeaux chateaux also bear a familiar Irish name: Lynch-Bages and Lynch-Moussas, both from the village of Pauillac, same as Lafite and Latour. These somewhat lighter, early-maturing wines are among my favorites for relatively less expensive claret—and as Irish as you can get.

One Irishman from Galway, Mr. Kirwan, was lucky enough to have the classified growth Chateau Kirwan named for him. He was unlucky, however, losing his head to the guillotine during the Revolution, as did so many others. The worst insult of all was the later francophiling of his name, phonetically, into Quirouen, a name still often seen in Bordeaux. Only the classified-growth chateau itself, whose wines have shown a real turn for the better recently, remains Kirwan.

The best-known Irish wine writer, the late Maurice Healy, once wrote a short treatise called *Irish Wine*, which I read as part of the Sette of Odd Volumes in the Library of Congress, but have never found elsewhere. It was privately printed in 1926, if that is of any help finding it on the Internet.

One theory of Healy's that has never been either proved or conclusively disproved is that the great Chateau Haut-Brion of the Graves region of Bordeaux was originally called O'Brien. Pronounced in French, it does sound almost identical. Stranger things have happened, especially in French chateaux.

One chateau that fooled me was Talbot, which turns out to be English rather than Irish. The Margaux called Boyd-Cantenac is Irish though, and the Dillon family is still strong in the Bordeaux wine trade, as are the Lawtons, although you would not know it from hearing the French pronounce their names.

For more on Irish wine, I suggest the best-written old books on the wine trade in Bordeaux: *The Winemasters* by Nicholas Faith and *The Wines of Bordeaux* by Edmund Penning-Rowsell, both readily available. Harder to find but worth seeking out is the inimitable *Stay Me with Flagons* by Maurice Healy, the most Irish-spirited wine book of all time.

Wines from Bulgaria

The wines of Bulgaria made their debut in Washington in 1974 at a press tasting held in the residence of the Bulgarian ambassador. Five Bulgarian wines tasted there became available in wine stores in the District, Virginia, and Maryland within weeks.

Three were reds: Cabernet, Gamza, and Mavrud. Two were whites: Hemus and Rikat. All were nonvintage blends, priced at the low end of the market. As with other Communist bloc wines, there will be a single price level for the whole line.

To most Americans, Bulgaria is about as remote and exotic as Madagascar. Of its wines, the only one I had ever tasted before was Tamianka, a Muscatel dessert wine. I somehow always had the vague idea, probably for political reasons, that Bulgarian wines were generally like most Russian wines: heavy, sweet, and high in alcohol. That notion proved to be an error.

Good but brief treatments of Bulgarian wines may be found in Alexis Lichine's *Encyclopedia of Wines and Spirits* and Hugh Johnson's *World Atlas of Wines*, each of which devotes two well-written and informative pages to the subject.

Americans and Bulgarian wine-drinkers have an immediate common ground: we have both suffered Prohibition. Yet the Bulgars suffered far worse than we. While our "noble experiment" in intolerance lasted only a few years, the Bulgarians went without wine for nearly five hundred years, from the fourteenth to the nineteenth century while their country was ruled by the teetotaling Mohammedan Turks. Irony of ironies, the Turks, who have loosened up considerably, now make and export to the United States several wines to compete with those of Bulgaria. In spite of the Turkish occupation, Bulgaria has a long and interesting wine history. In fact one of the places where wine is first recorded as having been made, Thrace, is now partly in Bulgaria along the border with Greece.

By the beginning of World War II, Bulgaria had become the sixth largest exporter of wines in the world, with over ten percent of its crop going to France of all places. After hard times during and after the war, when Bulgaria was obliged to ship its grapes to other countries for winemaking, in 1947 it nationalized its peasant wine-growers into communes and began using modern equipment brought from France. The Bulgarians also planted many acres of "foreign" wine grapes like Cabernets and Rieslings, which were better known abroad and easier to export than their own native varietals like Gamza and Mavrud. As with former Yugoslavia and Romania, the Bulgarians save their best wines for export abroad, hoping to create a good market and obtain hard currency to help their balance of payments.

In Bulgaria, as in France and Italy, the main table drink is not water but red wine. Bulgarians generally drink wines of the local countryside and only a few, such as Gamza, have nationwide renown. In Bulgaria's northern areas the wines are light and dry, like those imported into Washington. In the south and on the "Bulgarian Riviera" along the Black Sea coast, the wines are heavier and sweeter. Popular in many areas are wines of the Muscat grape, there called Misket, but these were not thought to be suitable for the American taste, probably rightly so. Lots of beer is also drunk in Bulgaria, which gives Bulgarians another common ground with Americans.

Taking the whites first, Hemus is extremely light in color, almost clear. Its flowery, fruity nose promises a sweeter and heavier-tasting wine than the delicate Rikat. The finish is short. Although described on the label as semi-dry, it is actually less sweet than this would usually suggest because it is so extremely light. Hemus is pronounced "hay-moos," and is the Bulgarian word for "Balkans," which is the Turkish word for "mountains". It reminded me of a Gewurztraminer.

The Rikat ("ree-kaht") is also flowery and delicate, but more acidic than the Hemus, and to my taste has a less distinctive character. Both wines resemble each other more than either resembles any other white wine I have tasted. Our hosts said that the best way to drink them is slightly chilled with a *chopska salata*, a Bulgarian salad of feta cheese, red tomatoes, and peppers, dressed with oil and vinegar. Such tangy salads are said to bring out and enhance the delicate character of these two whites. I somehow doubt it, but they should know.

Of the reds, the heaviest was the Cabernet, a blend of Cabernet Franc and Cabernet Sauvignon, which was somewhat darker in color than most Bordeaux and had a strong, fruity nose. The bottle at the tasting seemed ready to drink but not markedly Cabernet in varietal character. It finished fairly full if without distinction and left a nice chewy taste in the mouth.

A second bottle, which was given to me to take home, proved to be extremely young, acidic, and hard, decidedly too young to drink with pleasure. Yet after being open overnight, the second half of the bottle was fruity and drinkable the next evening.

These wines had just completed a long ocean journey and like all wines usually take weeks, even months, to settle down into their true characters. So it would be inappropriate to make snap judgments on their ultimate qualities at this early point.

My personal favorite of the reds was the Gamza, the most widely grown red wine grape in Bulgaria, which is medium-bodied, has a good ruby color, and was pleasantly smooth. Its grape taste is decidedly exotic and will no doubt strike American palates at first as rather foreign. It is said to descend from the Hungarian Kadarka grape, but the taste was totally unfamiliar to me. It has some finesse.

The third red tasted was the Mavrud ("mah-vrood"), which at the tasting showed little nose, medium color, and a rather neutral character. As noted earlier, these wines have just traveled, so may not be showing their true characters, for wine books describe Mavrud as an extremely dark, heavy wine used for strengthening weak wines.

Curious to get an early reading of public reaction to Bulgarian wines in Washington, I asked a half-dozen friends to blind-taste a Hemus, a Gamza, and a Cabernet left from the tasting. Most of them took the Hemus for a somewhat unusual California white, like a light, dry Riesling. The reds they thought were *sui generis*, and could only guess exotics like South Africa. Most liked the white better, but the Gamza went over fairly well, especially if inexpensive. In fact the main rivals for Bulgarian wines on the Washington market today will probably be the wines of other Eastern European countries.

Probably the crucial element in the success of Bulgarian wines in Washington will be price. If they can remain at the levels of their Eastern European brethren from Hungary and Romania, they may do pretty well.

If they get up to French or even U.S. prices, they begin taking on pretty formidable competition.

A related and equally crucial point will be public reaction to the fact that these wines are deliberately standardized and mass-produced. Each bottle is intended to be just like the last without variations for vineyards or vintages. The success of Bull's Blood seems to support the theory that many Americans prefer reliability and uniformity over individuality in wines, as long as the wine is basically good.

Yet that is only true at a certain price level. Once the prices pass jug-wine levels the American wine-drinker, like his European counterpart, begins to expect the nuances of individual character, rather than merely a safe but standardized product. My guess is that, as wine *détente* continues, Bulgarian wines must walk on the sunny side of this line if they are to be successful.

As devoted wine-drinkers will note, few Bulgarian wines have had any impact on the U.S. market. There is apparently just too much competition here, and the Bulgarians have a ready market for their wines among the newly affluent Russians.

All Is Ducky at the Peabody

The second annual Beaujolais celebration was held this November at the Peabody Hotel in Memphis. The celebration was in two parts: a buffet lunch with Nouveau Beaujolais at one o'clock and a seated dinner with Nouveau Beaujolais at seven o'clock. Both were in the elegant, marbled confines of the Chez Philippe restaurant overlooking the timeless Peabody lobby, that pre-eminent Deep South institution. The true test of any institution is that it transcends and outlives the people it serves—or which serve it. Generations may come and go, but the institution will remain. So it has been with the Peabody. Since its Phoenix-like reopening in 1981, the Peabody has already outlived most of its supervisory staff, only two of whom remain.

Just since the last Beaujolais Day it has a new general manager to replace the irreplaceable Transylvanian, Csaba Ajan, a new maitre d', and a new pastry chef. Even my favorite captain, John Harris, has made like the Baltimore Colts and moved to—of all places—Indianapolis. Since last year the Peabody has also added a third restaurant, a combination New York deli/Viennese pastry shop called the Cafe Expresso. The marriage of those two wonderful institutions is not as unnatural as it sounds and is somehow held together by some beautiful Italian wall and floor tiles. The staff insists that they really do know how to spell "espresso," but deliberately misspelled the name to call attention to the speed of its service, which aims at making it a sort of downtown galloping gourmet carryout.

Presiding over the Cafe Expresso is a large brass duck, the symbol of the Peabody since the 1930s and perhaps America's least-boring corporate logo. The duck in question perches atop a large brass Russian samovar, which was originally crowned by an eagle. But at the Peabody even that noble bird had to yield pride of place to the ubiquitous duck.

It might fairly be said that the Peabody has given a whole new level of meaning to the term ducks *unlimited.* It displays not only its famed fountain full of live ducks, but now offers for sale in its gift shop duck lampshades, duck shoe horns, and even duck-billed wine decanters. Perhaps in honor of its recent emphasis on fine wines, the Peabody also has duck wine glasses and corkscrews. Having recently strained my back, I even bought myself a black Peabody cane with a brass duck head for a handle.

Alas, not every Peabody tradition is unscathed. At the supposedly stately march across the red carpet from elevator to fountain, one of the four female mallards outflanked the greenhead drake and started racing him for the fountain, a gross violation of tradition. As the poor fellow tried to recover, another liberated female also tried to pass him, forcing him to fight a rearguard action with his bottom that looked like something from the old American Bandstand dance hour. The poor, beleaguered drake never caught up and the female took the gold. It probably has been happening for years, and we just never noticed it before.

As if Chez Philippe and Cafe Expresso were not enough, you can also overeat in style at the Peabody Bar, called Mallards, referred to in press releases as a third "food outlet." Once I was an outspoken foe of all such jargon. But recently a friend explained that all professions worth their salt develop jargon to fit their specialties, and that what seem to be needlessly obscure words to most of us are actually useful and even necessary parts of the job.

Armed with that new insight into modern life, I approached John Voegler, one of the few returning lettermen from last year's Peabody squad. I had been told by the youthful P.R. director that Voegler was in charge of the Peabody's "F and B side." She had to explain to me what that was too. Being now a dedicated F&B man, and no longer anti-jargon, I asked Food and Beverage czar Voegler about the continuing lack of duck meat on menus of the Peabody "food outlets."

After all, many of these restaurants' most avid patrons are also avid duck hunters and duck eaters. The original Peabody ducks themselves were live decoys placed in the lobby fountain by an enthusiastic duck hunter on one particularly convivial evening in the 1930s. So, why no canards on the menus? "You don't eat your symbol," was his authoritative reply. Never bandy words with an F&B man.

Returning Peabody chef Jose Gutierrez, the Bocuse-trained Frenchman with the Spanish name, has really hit his stride this year at the Chez Philippe and is developing a menu that showcases his talents. He has come up with a centerpiece series of classic dishes, which, whether by design or not, comes close to the duck theme: both the luncheon and dinner featured goose.

Gutierrez could, of course, be accused of a sort of reverse nepotism, a regular eat-your-cousin motif just as an attention-grabber, but I don't think so because the goose dishes were the best things on our table, not mere gimmicks. Goose is a traditional dish in France, even if not seen much in American restaurants nowadays.

At the buffet luncheon we had the inevitable *foie gras*, the only goose dish often seen most places. Its full name, which sounds more lah-dee-dah in French and less appetizing in English, is *paté de foie gras*, or "fat liver paste." Its complete full name in French is never used because it produces an unintended pun. In English it would be "fat goose liver paste." Try selling that for twenty dollars a pound.

In French it comes out *foie gras d'oie*, pronounced like "fwah grah dwah," which sounds ridiculous except perhaps after several glasses of Beaujolas and sung (as we did) to the tune of *Frere Jacques, Frere Jacques, Fwah-grah-dwah, Fwah-grah-dwah.* But enough of that.

An extremely fine terrine of goose, a sort of upper-level paté made with typical French thrift from all parts of the goose except the breast and the liver, was served with Nouveau Beaujolais. Another goose terrine, this one encased in a pastry crust, was the perfect accompaniment for the light, tart, pleasantly cool Beaujolais.

The goose honored the Beaujolais, the Beaujolais honored the goose, and our grateful company of wine writers and serious eaters honored both jointly. It was with real regret that we adjourned for an afternoon nap to prepare for the evening's dinner, when the rest of Jose's goose would be cooked, so to speak.

The best dish of the evening was, in fact, the goose breast in red currant sauce. This bird, a domesticated variety flown in fresh from the wilds of Chicago, had more of the texture and color of fine pork than wild fowl. It was not dry. Like the best French food, it seemed mild, even bland at first, and then got better with each bite. To say it was delicious with the tangy currants is a gross understatement. So good was it that we ordered up a bottle of 1975 Bordeaux Chateau Ducru-Beaucaillou to keep the Beaujolais company.

The occasion became festive to the point of exuberance, but never got out of hand. New maitre d' Jean-Pierre Enguehard, a veteran of the Air

France–owned Meridien of New Orleans, is a native of Normandy and can trace his ancestry back to the twelfth-century Norsemen who gave the province its name. His reputation having preceded him, Enguehard did not even have to unsheathe his Viking sword to keep us in line. It is true that we fell on the dinner like Nebraska linebackers on a fumble, but when closing time came, we adjourned discreetly to the lobby to continue the party. After all, it was supposed to be a celebration.

Cool Reds for Summer

"A wine's first duty is to be red," says the French proverb. Until a decade ago, the same was true in America. Today the opposite is true: seventy-five percent of the wine now drunk in America is white, not red.

Why? Some speculate that because white wines are normally drunk chilled, and most Americans are used to cold beverages like soft drinks and iced tea, white wines are naturals here.

Also, Europeans drink nearly all their wines with meals, while Americans drink at least half their wines without food, either at "happy hours" after work or at cocktail parties. At those times chilled white wines show better than the heavier reds, which are made to drink with foods, not alone.

Perhaps more practical factors are also at work. An Ole Miss co-ed recently rejected a particularly deep and dark Chateauneuf I offered her, fearing the red wine might stain her lovely white teeth (they *were* pretty lovely). And some hostesses, like my wife, don't want people drinking red wine over their white couches or rugs.

Whatever its origin, the white wine fad has caused nervous California wineries to shift gears. They even make white wines from their red grapes now. You can now get (or preferably avoid) white Pinot Noir, white Cabernet Sauvignon, and that worst abomination, white Zinfandel, whose production should be made a misdemeanor.

The one red wine that has thrived during the white wine fad is Beaujolais. Traditionally drunk cool if not chilled, red Beaujolais sales have exploded during the white wine craze. Even in more traditional France, Beaujolais is the single most popular red wine in the country. It is not hard to understand why. Beaujolais is a light, pleasant, unpretentious wine that is easy to drink and does not require serious analysis. Too many people now take wines much too seriously. Beaujolais is not subject to that type of abuse and is prospering from its simplicity.

The current favorite, young Nouveau Beaujolais, is mostly a post—

World War II phenomenon. Thus it is at least one wine on which the French do not have their usual head start of centuries. The Gamay family of grapes, which is used to make Nouveau Beaujolais in both France and California, is the subject of some dispute. The Gamay has more clones than Michael Jackson, not all of the same quality. Several centuries ago, when one of its low-quality cousins was overused in a blend, the Duke of Burgundy outlawed all Gamays. Calling them "disloyal plants," he ordered them all uprooted. Now only the finest are used, the ones called "black Gamays with white juice."

As usual, it was the irrepressible John Grisanti, a regular pied piper of wine, who introduced the best American Nouveaus Beaujolais to the South. On November 11, he hosted a dinner for wine lovers at his new American Harvest restaurant in Germantown, a Memphis suburb. The featured attraction of the evening was the Nouveau Gamay from the Charles F. Shaw winery of Napa Valley. Last year's version of this wine, made by Ric Forman, one of California's most renowned young winemakers, received rave reviews in California. Despite its promise, the affair had drawbacks. It was "black tie," a euphemism to me for "rent a tuxedo." When I put on a tux, I usually expect a somewhat stuffy evening. Fortunately, I am sometimes wrong, as was the case this time. As I approached the restaurant, the scene of several memorable evenings when it was the old Swiss Manor, I looked forward to seeing John Grisanti, one of those rare souls who can make everyone feel at ease with wine and enjoy themselves, no matter how wary they may be of the very idea of a wine-tasting.

Charles Shaw was there in person, and was not wearing those extra-shiny shoes they always give you with rented tuxedos. His tux itself was extra-fine, no doubt hand-tailored in Paris when he was a banker there after his graduation from West Point and Stanford. It was in Paris that Shaw met Beaujolais and decided to return and make a similar wine in America. From there also, I concluded, came the unusual gold studs in his shirt. They, too, looked handmade and expensive. I was slightly intimidated.

More reassuring were his eminently human glasses and his balding head—no contact lenses or toupees there. His Nouveau Gamay proved similar: authentic, unpretentious, light, and easy-drinking, with a particularly pleasant aroma of fresh Gamay fruit and a nice balance of acidity. It had a body Mickey Spillane would have had some choice comments on.

Winemaker Ric Forman was as low-key as Shaw, calling his commentaries on the wines we tasted "singing for his supper," rather than trying to give a learned dissertation. He even admitted a classic Freudian slip he made at a similar dinner in Dallas. When he tried to say the winemaking process for Nouveau Beaujolais, called "carbonic maceration," it came out instead as a considerably more risqué phrase, carbonic mast--------.

Of the other wines tasted, I enjoyed most a unique Pinot Noir from Jim Clendenen of Au Bon Climat winery of Santa Barbara County. It was reminiscent of those red Burgundies the French rarely make anymore and that we can no longer afford.

The best dish of the evening was undoubtedly the main course, a mesquite-grilled rib eye of veal, which complimented both the Shaw Gamay and the Pinot Noir of Au Bon Climat. Why do California wineries always have foreign names you can't pronounce? Is Arroyo Seco really that much more appealing than Dry Creek? Maybe so.

The sauce for the veal, a mix of Gamay and cranberry, was Shaw's idea, which Grisanti followed. It would be a good addition year round.

The wine world continues to turn in mysterious ways. The wealthy Charles F. Shaw became overextended financially and ended up bankrupt. Voracious wine entrepreneur Fred Franzia bought his unsold wine as well as his name and used them to produce some of California's best really cheap wine, corrupting Shaw's brand to the now-famous two-dollar "Two-Buck Chuck." It reminded me of the old Snoopy cartoons where Peppermint Patty kept calling Charlie Brown "Chuck." As Charlie Brown said, "How humiliating."

In New Orleans
the Cajun Tide Ebbs as French
and Italian Wines Flow

For years Creole and Cajun foods have swept the country. People still write me to ask what to drink with blackened redfish. At last the wave finally seems to be receding. The other week a friend asked me to recommend a couple of non-Creole restaurants in New Orleans with wines to match. Why avoid Creole? "Too spicy. I want French or Italian foods that bring out the best in wines," was the reply. Maybe Creole food is a little spicy, but French food in the French Quarter?

One problem with finding French food in the United States is all the phony imitations. Too many joints named Chez Pierre or Chez Louis are not run by French chefs. The first trick is to find a legitimate French restaurant. If you do, the wine list will probably be no problem—except perhaps for the prices. One good bet in a dozen or so cities is the Meridien Hotel chain, where we got lucky. The Meridien New Orleans is right on Canal Street, which separates the French Quarter from the old "American" section, now called the Garden District. Its restaurant, called Henri, is five-star sensational, yet I had never eaten in it before.

French in the French Quarter

Modeled on Haeberlin's great Auberge de l'Ill in Alsace, the menu, décor, and wine list are all chosen by Mr. Haeberlin himself, who even painted the watercolor on the menu. Chefs from his kitchen in Alsace man his New Orleans outpost year-round.

Painfully familiar as I am with the prices of French restaurants in the United States, I usually try them at lunch first—they are so much cheaper then. Henri was reasonable, just $16.95 for the fixed price lunch with fresh fruit, fresh soup, fresh salad of the day, and selections of cheeses and pastries. You can also have an appetizer of truffle wrapped in foie gras if you have fifty-one dollars handy. For wines, Henri is equally simple. There are Bordeaux for several hundred dollars, but in Alsatian restaurants, do as Alsatians do: Order a glass of Riesling before dinner, then a bottle of Hugel Pinot Gris with dinner—it is superb with the fresh Gulf fish.

For Italian, Take a Drive

French food properly prepared is really very light, and my friends wanted Italian one night—something substantial. So we took a drive. The best real Italian place in New Orleans is not in the city at all. Like the Cajuns and many of the restaurants, Andrea's Restaurant has moved to the suburbs, to Metairie, until now best known to me when I lived in New Orleans as something you pass through between real life and the airport.

The Andrea menu has a map right on the front, because finding it can be a challenge. I found it in Tom Fitzmorris's *Guide to New Orleans Restaurants*, which has replaced the *Underground Gourmet* as my local favorite. Andrea's is one of just seven restaurants he gives five stars, rating it above Brennan's. What to order at Andrea's? Fresh pompano should never be passed up. For appetizers you can have smaller helpings of their pasta entrees, of which their linguine with pesto was among the best of my life. But the greatest dish of the night was a simple-sounding veal cutlet Valdostana, a long, curved, juicy, delicious monster equal to any I've tasted anywhere, from the beautiful but obscure French part of northern Italy called Val d'Aosta.

To order wine in Italian restaurants, a good rule is to choose one of Thomas Jefferson's favorites from his visit there in 1787. In this case it was white Pomino and red Castello di Ama Chianti. How to remember these wines? These were so good I asked the waiter to soak the labels off for me, which he did gladly, as any really good restaurant will do. When dry, I keep them in big albums like treasured family photos, taking some out to carry in my pocket for assistance when dining in fine restaurants with fine wine lists.

A Deep South Winemaking School Thrives—For a While

Later this month *[September 1983]*, the students and professors at the school for winemakers at Mississippi State University will begin this year's grape harvest at the vineyards on campus. They will carry the ripe grapes to the winery near the dairy barn off U.S. Highway 82, crush them and ferment them into wine, then fill and cork the bottles and apply labels reading: "Mississippi State University Cabernet Sauvignon (or) Johannisberg Riesling, *for evaluation only*, not for sale."

Eat your heart out Ole Miss: Since 1980 Mississippi State has had wine to go with its cheese.

It is no homemade bathtub stuff either, but quality wine from the world's finest grape varieties, grown and vinified right on campus. The very existence of the school will come as a great surprise to most people in the U.S., as it did to me. But even more surprising than the school's existence is the quality of its operation. The $500,000 facility is perhaps the finest in the Southeast and one of the finest for its size in the country. Officially called the A.B. McKay Food and Enology Laboratory, it is part of the land-grant university's College of Agriculture, and is located on the premises of its Agricultural Experiment Station, just like U.C. Davis, the Harvard of U.S. wine schools. The offices and laboratory are housed in a large, white, chalet-style building fronted with brown half-timbers. It sits on a hill about a half-mile off U.S. 82 and is just visible next to the dairy barn.

Access to the chalet is by a white limestone road past vivid reminders that grape growing is a kind of farming. A split-rail fence leads to an Italian arbor covered with familiar Muscadine vines.

Below the Swiss-looking balconies of the chalet are several acres of neatly tended vineyards. On my first visit there this past winter, I was wary and not too optimistic, expecting maybe some improved strains of Muscadines, or at most some French-American hybrids.

Thanks to the lab's director, Dr. Boris Stojanovic, I found to my amazement a thriving experimental vineyard of not only Muscadines and hybrids but the purest and finest European vinifera vines: Cabernet Sauvignon, Chardonnay, Johannisberg Riesling, Pinot Noir, Chenin Blanc, and several others.

Although still less than five years old, the vines are thriving and for the past two years have produced plenty of healthy grapes for making representative wines. The wines made from them have so far had the typical varietal character of each grape type, the goal of all good winemakers. Nor does the vineyard slight French-American hybrids, having Seyval Blanc, Vidal Blanc, Baco Noir, Marechal Foch, and others, plus three each of the most-improved strains of native southeastern Muscadines, including Magnolia and Carlos.

Inside the chalet are spotless crushers, stemmers, fermenting vats, corking machines, tasting cubicles, and all the usual paraphernalia of a modern winery. There is one special touch: a vinoteca or "library" of bottles of all the wines made at Mississippi State, to be used by students for comparing vintages and varietals. One machine, painted a decidedly familiar red and blue, was said by a student to be nicknamed "Colonel Rebel" because it never functioned reliably. The professors stoutly denied any official recognition of such a satirical name and called the Ole Miss Rebel color scheme "mere coincidence."

Most notable of all the equipment is a centrifuge, a sophisticated modern machine that uses centrifugal force rather than traditional crushing to remove juice. It was used last year by the Rushing Winery at Merigold on some of its Muscadines to produce a lighter-flavored wine.

One of the school's most useful byproducts to date has been a book, *Commercial Winemaking*, a readable and practical five-hundred-page tome written by the school's cellar-master, Dr. Richard Vine, who also selects the wines for American Airlines flights and has his own international wine judging competition, the Indy International.

A Mississippi State graduate in Agricultural Economics, Vine was the winemaker at both Taylor Cellars in upstate New York and Warner Vineyards in Michigan. Vine, an experienced and respected winemaker and teacher with a national reputation, has taught several popular classes in wine appreciation at the University Center in Jackson (and later at Purdue University).

If anyone had doubts about the success of Mississippi State's enology school or its national standing, those doubts should now be removed. The Vinifera Society of Virginia has just given its highest award, the Monteith Trophy, to Mississippi State for making the most significant contributions to vinifera winemaking of any institution east of the Mississippi River during the past year.

As is well known, winemaking and especially grape-growing are risky enterprises. In the 1980s, the vines at Mississippi State were struck by Pierce's Disease, a deadly malady most prevalent in humid climates with warm winters, like that of Mississippi. The promising vines all died and the enology school, sadly, closed.

A Mouse-Jump
for White Burgundy

During a recent visit to Washington, an old friend invited me to dinner at one of the city's most luxurious restaurants: Mr. K's *[It is now, alas, closed]*. The place is a sybaritic enclave full of priceless Chinese vases and gold-plated cutlery. I assumed it was plated; if it had been solid gold I would have been afraid to eat with it. Expense apparently being not much of an object, we began with shark fin soup, a delicacy which too many Chinese places require you to order at least a day in advance, even as a main course. From there we proceeded through delicacy to sublimity.

As often happens on such occasions because I write this wine column, it fell to me to order the wine. That task is not as enviable as it sounds. Wines are living things, as unique and unpredictable as human beings, and subject to the same whims and inconsistencies for which human beings are so well known. The higher the expectations, the greater the letdown if the wine is less than extraordinary.

What to do in such a spot? After some nervous bumbling disguised as careful consideration of the wine list, I asked myself what Thomas Jefferson, America's greatest wine expert, would have done in such a case. There was some precedent. Once, returning home after five years as American Minister in France, Jefferson had to decide what wines to bring back. Everyone expected some really great ones based on the enthusiastic letters he'd written from Paris about French wines. But he could only bring back a few cases on the boat, and most of those were promised to that other great wine lover, George Washington. In the end, Jefferson chose four cases of his favorite white Meursault Burgundy, as the best white wine of France that was still relatively affordable to Americans.

The best way to pronounce Meursault is to combine the familiar biblical word "myrrh" with "sew" as in sewing. Pronounced thus to a French wine steward, he will sneer, but will still bring you the right wine.

Not even the French know for sure what Meursault means, but they know good wine has been made there for more than nine hundred years. The great French writer Albert Camus named one of his most famous characters "Meursault," a choice I never quite understood. I kept thinking of him as a glass of wine. Some French scholars say the name comes from a mur (wall) once fortified against "assault" by the Romans. Much more popular is the theory that Roman soldiers named the town "mouse-jump" in old French after the tiny creek which still runs through it and is almost narrow enough for a really motivated mouse to jump across.

Whatever the origins of the name, Meursault is a superb wine. It is said that one French bishop would celebrate communion only with Meursault, saying to use a lesser wine would have slighted his Creator. Meursault is made from one hundred percent Chardonnay grapes in the best domains. Its color is light golden, its aroma a combination of ripe peaches and toasted almonds, and its aftertaste something to write home about, wherever you live.

Meursault, while expensive, is not nearly as rare as its competitor Montrachet, which costs as much as a small car because of its scarcity. More than 170,000 cases of fine Meursault are made each year, which keeps prices to about one-fourth those of Montrachet, just as in Jefferson's time. As whites go, Meursault is relatively hardy and ages well. Older bottles are often not marked up with inflation, so good prices are sometimes available. I have drunk several bottles of my birth year, 1942, all from the collection of the famous Dr. Barolet.

The bottle we drank at Mr. K's was of the year 1984, good enough in Burgundy. It was from the vineyards of a Mr. Boillot-Buthiau, a name no one should have to pronounce. The label is distinctive and easy to recognize, however, bearing a large, multicolored map of all the Meursault vineyards from Goutte d'Or (Drop of Gold) to the aptly named Charmes. Like most reasonable restaurant wine prices, its markup is "only" one hundred percent, a relative bargain for this place, especially in light of the complexity and finesse of the wine.

But you can't spend every night at Mr. K's, and not every bottle can be

Meursault. Just as in professional football, replacements must be found, so some California Chardonnay backups are here suggested. There are old standbys such as Beringer, BV, and newly improved Sebastiani. For fifty percent more there are Raymond, Monticello's Jefferson Ranch, and the fine but little-known Gundlach-Bundschu of Napa. Still too expensive? You could try less expensive Chateau Souverain or Fetzer. All give Chardonnay character, and from there, Meursault is just a mouse-jump away.

Red Wines Flow
When Chill Winds Blow

When winter winds are upon us, cold-weather wines are in order. A cold white wine is a chilling prospect in January, which requires red wines, and robust ones at that.

A good place to start for winter wines is the Rhone region of France, which produces some of the most rugged and warming of red wines. Its own climate is part of the reason. The chilling winter mistral wind that sweeps down the Rhone Valley from the Swiss glaciers high above it has given natives a taste for something substantial. And the long, hot summers on the Rhone have produced solid wines to meet the need.

The best wines of the Rhone are made mainly from the Syrah grape, said to be the Shiraz of Persia, brought to the Rhone from the Middle East by the crusader Chevalier de Sterimberg, for which a fine Rhone Hermitage is still named. He is also featured on the label. Legend has it that the knight became a hermit on a crest overlooking the river. The Rhone's best red wine still comes from there, and is named Hermitage in his honor. Hermitage reds to look for are those of Guigal, Chave, Delas, Jaboulet, and Chapoutier, the last two being easiest to find. These wines take a while to age.

Welcome to America

One of the happiest developments in American winemaking has been experimentation with recent Rhone grapes in California. Joseph Phelps Vineyard of Napa has made fine Syrahs since the 1970s, but only in the '80s did others start to catch on. Now there is keen competition to produce the best red Syrah here. In addition to Phelps, whose 1986 Syrah called "Mistral" was terrific, Qupe winery of Santa Barbara and McDowell Valley and Kendall-Jackson wineries of Mendocino County have made a series of good Syrah vintages recently.

For finesse in red wines, I've always liked Bordeaux, Burgundies, and Riojas from Spain. For sheer power, however, it is hard to beat Italy. The heartiest of the hearty is Barolo, a deep, dark, slow-aging wine from the Piedmont or foothill region of the northwest around Alba. Made from the Nebbiolo grape, said by its admirers to smell of tar and roses (in the best sense, I suppose), old Barolos are worth waiting for. The 1952s are good now, for example. If you don't have time to wait, try its lighter cousin, Barbaresco, which is drinkable a little younger. Better yet, try some of the first successful U.S. attempts with the tricky Nebbiolo grape, again from Santa Barbara, this time from Au Bon Climat winery, a small but lingering outfit that has had outstanding success not only with Pinot Noir and Chardonnay, but even with Nebbiolo.

Italy's other great red grape, the Sangiovese, makes not only Chianti, but also the highest-flyer of rich Italian reds: Brunello of Montalcino. This wine can really warm a cold winter night. It can also scorch your pocketbook, demand having driven prices to overheated levels. Best and most expensive is from Biondi-Santi.

Not much Sangiovese is so far grown in the United States. Richard Peterson, in conjunction with Italian Sangiovese experts from Antinori, planted a considerable vineyard on Diamond Mountain above Napa Valley, but their project for making great Sangiovese stalled. As of this writing, the best U.S. Sangiovese I've tasted came from Mosby Winery of Santa Barbara, a hotbed for successful experiments with new grapes. The most unusual U.S. Sangiovese is made in small amounts at Monticello in honor of Thomas Jefferson's love of the grape, which he imported to the U.S. and tried unsuccessfully to grow several times.

For heavy-duty winter wines, nothing surpasses vintage Port, the so-called Englishman's wine. With their climate, they need it. Producers to look for are: Fonseca, Graham, Taylor, Quinta do Naval, and Dow. Some of the names are even English. Vintages I've found especially warming are 1985, 1977, and 1963.

The Great Old Reds of Italy

This past week we had our first taste of autumn temperatures. In such weather one's fancy turns to thoughts of red wine. Young men may have other ideas—young women, too—but old wine columnists feel different tugs.

Vino Nobile: For years I have studied the hundreds of letters written by Thomas Jefferson about wine. Despite his reputation for being a great lover of Bordeaux, my impression is still that if Jefferson could have chosen only three wines, one of them would have been an Italian red: Montepulciano. Known traditionally by the over-lengthy name of Vino Nobile di Montepulciano, this robust red wine deserves to be called "noble," even if such a title sounds a little stuffy nowadays. As in France or California, even when you have the basic name of a good wine, or even an idea of a good vintage, the crux of choice is the producer. In Montepulciano the best to my taste are Avignonesi, especially for their 1982, 1983, and 1985. On the same level for the same vintages, is more of a newcomer to my personal experience: Fattoria del Cerro.

Brunello: If it is possible to re-create Thomas Jefferson's taste in Italian reds from his letters and account books, it seems to have been for wines made from the Sangiovese or Sangioveto grapes which, in his time, were hard to distinguish. Today the most famous and by far the most expensive of them is Brunello, which Jefferson never mentioned by name but is made at Montalcino, which *was* familiar to him. Fortunately, not all Brunellos are totally expensive. There is a fine one that recently blew my Italian brother-in-law's socks off when I served it to him blind. It is called La Chiesa di Santa Restituta, and it was worth twice what it was going for when I tasted it in July.

Carmignano: We do know for certain which Italian wine Jefferson liked second-best after Montepulciano because he wrote of it and ordered it: Carmignano. Until just a few years ago, this fine red was not even bottled under its own name. Most was called, as it still can be legally, just Chianti. Best of the Carmignanos to my taste is Villa Cappezzana. These wines have a finesse that will surprise you if you're expecting old-time Chianti.

Chianti: Speaking of which, Jefferson did mention Chianti by name occasionally, not because he only liked it occasionally, but because it was not called by that name so often back then. Most referred to it as Jefferson did as simply "red wine of Florence." But if Jefferson had to pick just one Chianti today, my guess is he would choose Monsanto, especially the Il Poggio. It has nothing to do with chemical companies.

Le Pergole Torte: Such discussions whet the palate and make one speculate on which noble Italian red the third president would prefer of today's choices. Although he never heard this name, from tasting what he did talk about and the tastes he preferred—richness, ripeness, and a certain "silkiness" on the palate as he called it, joined by a slight "astringency" (he truly was ahead of his time)—my pick would be Le Pergole Torte. A good Pergole has all Jefferson's favorite notes and is made from one hundred percent Sangiovese, whose name is old Italian for "Jove's Blood." As Shakespeare's Falstaff used to say about wine, "S'blood!" Jefferson probably would too if he tried an old Pergole Riserva.

The Great New Reds of Italy

For the past twenty years I have followed the evolution of the "new" red wines of Italy: aged in oak, fermented to mature younger, and often with some French Cabernet Sauvignon (grown in Italy) in the blend. How are they doing now? Very well indeed.

At first the new blends, like all new ideas, were met with howls of outrage and indignation by Italian traditionalists. As with most reformers, the leaders of the new movement were called revolutionaries by the old guard. The rest of the wine world, however, especially the American press and to some extent the French, were impressed.

Tignanello: The first of the new reds I remember was Tignanello, the brand name given to what was actually Chianti from Santa Christina made by Antinori. Even though the blend was more than eighty percent Sangiovese, the classic Chianti grape, legally it could not use that name because of the "foreign" Cabernet grape in the blend. The Tignanello was a revelation; it tasted wonderful, far fresher, and less casky than most Italian reds of that day, too many of which were oxidized before they really matured due to antiquated cellar practices.

Sassicaia: Soon thereafter, in the early '70s, I tasted something even more revolutionary: a pure Cabernet from Italy. Like Tignanello, the new Sassicaia was made in the ancient heartland of the Etruscans, which we call Tuscany. That airy, picturesque country has been renowned for wine since the times of the great Italian painters of the Renaissance. Michelangelo is said to have swapped his shirt for a Tuscan wine. Changing how they were made, even when the result tasted good, was like tampering with Mother Nature. But the taste of Sassicaia was too successful; its sales grew.

Torre Quarto: Actually Sassicaia had been made since the 1950s but just not marketed or publicized. As interest in the new wines grew, another wine, supposedly solidly Italian, was found to be of foreign origin as well. Torre Quarto, from the Apulia region, was actually made from seventy-five percent Malbec grapes, again originally from Bordeaux and not Italian at all. A member of the famous French Rochefoucauld family brought it to Italy in 1847.

The innovator, or culprit if you will, the Antinori family, has nevertheless continued to make mainly traditional Italian wines, including their greatest Chianti, the Riserva di Marchese. Being traditional themselves, the Antinoris have begun consolidating the gains from their experiments with "new" wines. In 1982, the Sassicaia estate went back to the control of its owner, the Marchese Incisa, who now bottles and markets it. Tignanello was by then too popular and profitable to change, but its character was so dominated by the Cabernet that it no longer seemed Italian. Then came Peppoli.

Peppoli: This spring the Antinoris launched their compromise: a wine made totally from traditional Italian grapes, (more than ninety percent Sangiovese in fact) with no Cabernet at all, and with a notably Italian taste. Called Peppoli after the fourteenth century estate where it is produced, it was just released this spring and fulfills my every request of an Italian red. It is rich and full, but ready to drink; it is deeper-colored than most Chianti, but aromatic rather than tannic as its color would suggest.

The only Peppoli vintage yet on the market is the 1985. With Tignanellos going for thirty dollars and Sassicaia for forty, Peppoli is a bargain at sixteen, costing less than Antinori's own Marchese Chianti reserve at twenty dollars plus. Peppoli appears to have a brilliant future. Even if not, its present alone is reason enough to justify it. I recommend it highly.

In the year 2014, as this book is written, my opinion of the Peppoli has not changed. It is still an outstanding value and still highly recommended. Since I've retired from writing my syndicated columns and no longer receive those coveted free samples of Tignanello and Sassicaia, they now are out of my price range. But the lower end of Antinori Chiantis are still affordable, and I plan to drink them weekly till I die.

America Conquers Pinot Noir, the Holy Grail of Wine

The Holy Grail for U.S. winemakers—always sought, never attainable—has long been the Pinot Noir. Pronounced "peeno nwar," this fickle grape makes all the great red wines of France's Burgundy region. But almost nowhere else has anyone had much success in producing a great Pinot Noir—until now.

After generations of failures, winemakers in the U.S., especially Oregon and certain cool regions of California, have finally tamed this Scarlett O'Hara of grapes. During a series of tastings over the past several months, involving over one hundred Pinots, real resemblances to Burgundy have begun to emerge. There are even several I can recommend.

In Oregon the vintages to look for are 1983 and 1985. In California you're on your own, but 1985 is probably most consistent. U.S. Pinot Noir success began in Paris when a Pinot from 1975 Eyrie Vineyards of Oregon "beat" French Burgundies at a blind tasting called The Judgment of Paris by the press. Most startled were the judges, who were all French. Since then, Oregon Pinots have been so hot that California wineries, some over one thousand miles away, have imported Oregon grapes for their Pinots. Is that sane?

Perhaps. American winemakers, after several bankruptcies and many broken hearts, learned that Pinot Noir does well only in a few cool, isolated microclimates. When you find some good Pinot grapes, you'd better buy them. Most Cabernet Sauvignon vineyards in Napa Valley, for example, make rather poor Pinot Noir, overripe and tasting like jam. Only in the foggy hill country called Carneros, at the extreme south end of Napa County, is good Napa Pinot Noir now made.

Wines to look for from Carneros are: Acacia, Saintsbury, and Carneros Creek among Pinot specialists. Among traditional, well-distributed Napa wineries, only BV and Mondavi have done really well with Pinot Noir, but Monticello is coming on.

My other favorite Pinot Noirs have come from wildly varied locations throughout California.

In Santa Barbara County there are Sanford, Au Bon Climat, Austin, and Qupe. At San Luis Obispo there is Edna Valley. In Marin County, Kalin Cellars makes an excellent Pinot. Good Pinot now comes from high above Monterey County, especially from Chalone. In nearby San Benito County there is Calera, which may well be the best of all, especially the wines from the Jensen and Selleck vineyards.

Of Oregon Pinot Noirs, the best are considered to be Eyrie, Rex Hill, Adelsheim, Amity, Adams, and Yamhill Valley. Also good, but uneven from my tastings, are Sokol Blosser, Tualatin, Ponzi, Arterberry, and Knudsen Erath (Where do they get these names?). Next to microclimates, the biggest element in improving Pinot Noirs in the U.S. has been selection of good strains, called "clones" in wine-jargon. Pinot Noir, the oldest-known wine grape of Europe, is also the most unstable, mutating early and often. The French say there are over one thousand clones of it around.

Some of the earliest clones in California were brought to the Santa Cruz Mountains south of San Francisco in the mid-nineteenth century, where they have evolved to suit the soils and local microclimates. Whether soils, climates, or what, some of my favorite Pinot Noirs have recently come from Santa Cruz, including David Bruce, Bonny Doon, Santa Cruz Mountains, and Mount Eden.

Saving the worst till last, the problem with great Pinots in the late 1980s is price. Most of these wines go for twelve to eighteen dollars. Still, that beats your fifty dollar red Burgundies. And there is one, equal to just about any of them, for ten. It is called La Crema and is produced at Petaluma in Sonoma County, where good Clos DuBois Pinot Noirs are also made. The 1985 "California" La Crema, which owns no vineyards and buys all its grapes, may be the sleeper of the whole lot. If not exactly the Holy Grail, it is a mighty fine bottle of wine.

Looking back on this column from this year, 2014, nearly thirty years later, I was pleasantly surprised at how consistent Pinot producers have been. It was at a 1985 Napa Valley Wine Auction luncheon that Michael Mon-

davi, then president of the family-owned Robert Mondavi winery, told me that they had finally found wine's Holy Grail, and he was right. Although prices have now skyrocketed, I recently found a very delicate, drinkable, everyday Pinot Noir called Coastal Vines. At six dollars retail, it is my personal answer to my lifelong search for good, affordable Pinot.

While we're on Pinots, the whites should not be overlooked. Until a few years ago they were almost totally ignored, the fruitless, super-acidic Pinot Grigios of Italy were selling for almost nothing and the lovely Pinot Gris of France were almost unobtainable here in the U.S. Then suddenly, like most trends, the big one arrived and Grigio was everywhere, softened for American tastes and rivaling Chardonnay in popularity at jug wine buffets. Then, ever so slowly, Pinot Gris began to appear, especially from Oregon wineries like King Estate. Last night I had a lovely one from the Pulenta Winery of Mendoza, Argentina. Like its more famous cousin Pinot Noir, it appears the noble Pinot Gris has finally arrived.

A Friend Comes through with Spanish Treasure

It pays to have friends. A few months ago my Lebanese friend Issam Loutfi, an Ole Miss engineering graduate, asked what it would take for me to keep a protective eye on his beautiful daughter Leila, a freshman in our college town. "Nothing," I said, and I meant it—at first. But he insisted, stressing that his new Paris-based profession took him to all the best wine regions of the world with astonishing regularity. He asked if there was not some wine somewhere in the world that I truly wanted to taste for the first time.

There was one, of course, a rare red wine of Spain called Vega Sicilia, which Winston Churchill once allegedly called the finest "unknown claret" he had ever tasted. Vega Sicilia was, so I had heard, a cross between the best Bordeaux and best unbrandied Port. But why did it have an Italian name if it was a Spanish wine? And why was it so incredibly expensive? My friend said that the guy who later sold it to him said it was like buying a yacht: If you have to ask the price, you can't afford it.

It Only Sounds Italian

Bookish research, the last resort of the truly dry, revealed that Vega Sicilia is located in old Castille, some 130 miles northwest of Madrid, twenty five miles east of Valladolid, on the road to Zaragosa, if that means anything. From my old Spanish hitchhiking memories, that is in the true boonies— sheep country, wild, dry, and exotic. On the south side of the river Duero, which becomes the famous Douro across the border in Portugal, where all true Port is produced, this winery is unique.

First of all, Sicilia has nothing to do with Sicily, referring instead to Saint Cecilia; the Vega referring to the *old* hillsides where the vineyards are located. The vineyards have been there since at least 1864 and are not the product of French flight from Bordeaux, as once rumored, but are uniquely Spanish. Oddly, the owners now live in Venezuela, which gives a sort of New World appeal to a very old-fashioned wine.

One day, from the blue, my friend's daughter arrived with a package, well wrapped, as if of special value. Inside was a 1962 Vega Sicilia "Unico," their top wine. The price was expressed in pesetas too numerous to mention in a family newspaper. After sitting on it for a couple of months, one evening I uncorked it secretly, decanted it into an old carafe, and let some friends taste it without telling them what it was. Their guesses were instructive.

Mystery Wine Wins High Marks

Some said it was either a really expensive old Bordeaux, or an unusually fine, very old wine from Australia. The most perceptive said it tasted like a Spanish Rioja that had died and gone to heaven.

To me, the only one knowing what it was, it recalled somewhat an unbrandied Port, but softer and much more subtle. If it was like anything, it was like a big Rioja about forty years old, smooth beyond belief, ruby in color, not a bit over-old, and in great balance. Without knowing its identity beforehand, I don't believe I would ever have guessed it.

All true wine lovers search constantly for great values, those really special wines that cost no more than the most ordinary, and I try to find and recommend just such wines as often as possible.

Once in a while, however, you have to take the plunge for something special and walk on the wild side. When that time comes for you, if Vega Sicilia falls in your path, don't pass it up. If you can't afford it, drink old Riojas from Cune, Heredia or Murrieta, but if you can spring for it, old Vega Sicilia is still one of the ultimate red wines.

CHAPTER THREE

Tips for Enjoying Good Wine

Finding a Good Wine Shop
Old Wine Books to Savor
Be Assertive with Annoying Waiters
Serving Wine Is Not Brain Surgery
Problem Corks
What's That Floating in My Glass?
Resveratrol for a Healthy Heart
Judging Wines
Detective Sonny Crockett Called His Favorite Wine D.P.
These Gizmos Do All but Drink Your Wine for You
Those Maligned Muscats
Sauternes and Foie Gras
Wine as Dessert
Bottle Builders
Half-Bottles and Marbles: Solutions for Leftover Wines
To Decant or Not to Decant
Wine Yeasts, Wild and Tame
The Big Chill
Best Beer? Czech It Out
Nebbiolo: As "Brisk" as Champagne, as "Silky" as Madeira
Swiss Wines for Winter
Friends of the Oyster
Bad Wine? Don't Pour It Out
Cabernet Franc, A New Star?
A Dark Horse Grape: Petit Verdot
Hi Yo, Mourvèdre, Away

"Sour Wine" Has Added Zing Since Biblical Times
Sulfites Suffice
Tannin in Wine: It's How It Feels
The Trick to Drinking Champagne
Wine Words: Not So Confusing after All

Finding a Good Wine Shop

Several readers have asked for advice on how to buy wine in a wine store without being ripped off or made to look like a fool. This is a legitimate question and a problem for nearly everyone who enters a wine shop.

In truth, unless you've actually tasted the particular wine from the particular year and winery that you are considering, there is no way to know for sure that you will like the wine inside the bottle you're considering. There are lots of totally incompetent wine clerks, and even some who will sell you their worst wine just to get rid of it. To protect yourself from their tender mercies, there are defenses.

First of all, insist on shopping in a store that looks like a good wine store. This sounds rudimentary, but many people still think they are likely to get great bargains at liquor stores whose salespeople "don't know what they have." If they don't know that, and you see some fine bottle with a shockingly low price tag, don't think it's a bargain. It's probably been on that overheated shelf with its cork drying out for years, ever since that yellowing price tag was first slapped on it.

After you've picked a reliable store, usually based on tips from knowledgeable friends who shop there already, it's important before going in to have some idea of what you want to buy, for what occasion, and how much you are willing to spend. Even knowledgeable clerks have limits on their time, and if you don't know if you want to drink it with a T-bone steak or a chocolate cake, they probably can't help you.

If, on the other hand, you know you want something to go with steak, any good clerk probably has tasted a few of the store's better reds, at various price levels, and can recommend a good one for your pocket that he knows personally. California Cabernets and Zinfandels are among the best buys nowadays, as are Riojas from Spain for slightly less. If it's fish you're having, tell them that and whether it will be grilled with a sauce, poached, or how it will be served. A good white like a Chardonnay is excellent, and there should be someone in the store personally familiar with several of the wineries and vintage years offered.

One of the best ways to be sure you get a wine you will like is to soak off the labels of the ones you like best after you drink them. A dose of hot water in the old lavatory will often do the trick. Then keep the label until you go back to the store and show it to the clerk. This practice avoids those embarrassing moments I used to experience as a clerk when the customer would say, "Well, it was in kind of a green bottle, and . . ." Next best is jotting down what appears to be pertinent on the label, although on some labels, especially Germans, the writings are in indecipherable Gothic script and unintelligible anyway. Better to soak the labels or just keep the bottle itself and carry it in with you.

Once you've found a couple of good stores, to choose between them I usually look at several factors: What discounts do they give? Can you mix cases and get a discount or do you have to buy a whole case of one wine? A good way to find new wines is to buy a case of twelve different wines, then return and buy more of only those you really liked. I also like stores that keep at least some good wines in their coolers; sometimes you have no time to chill a wine before dinner.

Another good sign about a wine store is if they have their own tasting club and classes. If so, their clerks and buyers are usually more interested in the subject. A good selection of wine books for sale is also a good sign. Really great stores like Sherry-Lehmann and Morrell's in New York, Martin's in New Orleans, or Buster's in Memphis now normally have e-mail lists for specials, although it is very rare for a store to have a complete list of their regular stock because it changes too often.

I try to get on these e-mail lists, even if I can't get to those stores, because the wines they have can often be found at your local store. If you are on the mailing lists of several stores, which are free, you know better what to ask for at your own store.

Old Wine Books to Savor

Readers from across the United States have taken the trouble to write and ask for a list of the best old, out-of-print wine books, the more esoteric the better. I am happy to oblige. Even though a modest flood of new books seems to flow out of the tap every fall to give for Christmas, there are some really timeless classics out there worth buying and holding forever.

Leading the list are superb wine-histories like *Gods, Men and Wine*, published in 1966 by William Younger. It is unsurpassed for stories and anecdotes, and has 516 of the most interesting pages about wine ever written. For the history of *ancient* wines there is *Dionysus* by Edward Hyams, which is superbly illustrated. Even older and remarkably detailed is *The History and Description of Modern Wines* by Cyrus Redding. Almost anything by the late André Simon is good, and his old multi-volume series from McGraw-Hill, *Wines of the World*, has recently been condensed into one large volume.

If you seek something short but stunning, try Egyptologist Leonard Lesko's forty-seven-page-volume *King Tut's Wine Cellar*. It has great illustrations from ancient tomb paintings and even has quotes about what vintages ancient Egyptians preferred. It is available from one of my favorite old sources, The Wine Appreciation Guild in San Francisco, phone (415) 566-3532.

Available only from libraries on loan is André Simon's *Wine in Shakespeare's Days and Shakespeare's Plays*, a fascinating study of all wine references in Shakespeare and how the Bard's moods evolved from the "happy, wine-drinking days" of Queen Elizabeth I in his comedies to the "morbid, spirit-drinking nights" of King James in his tragedies. Xerox it if you can. I did at the Library of Congress. It is unique.

The first wine book ever printed was by Italian physician Arnauldus. He described the medieval wines that he prescribed as a remedy for melancholy as: "eyebright, colder than crystal, green as buffalo horn, strong as a monastery, subtle as Paris logic, and going down impetuously, like thunder." Where are those wines when we need them today?

For serious lovers of French wines, the dean of the Bordeaux wine world, maxi-consultant to half the great chateaux in Bordeaux, Emile Peynaud, has written a little book now translated into excellent English: *Knowing and Making Wine*. Unique and uniquely beautiful in its illustrations is *Yquem* by Richard Olney.

Patrick Forbes, an Englishman, wrote *the book* on Champagne in 1982. Many lavishly illustrated editions on Champagne have come out since, but to my taste none equals Forbes's. You'll know it by the cover. It pictures a porcelain wine-cup molded for Louis XVI from one of Marie Antoinette's ample breasts. It was that sort of decadence that brought on the French Revolution, but it still makes good reading now.

The best wine-scandal history is *The Winemasters* by Nicholas Faith, also a good history of claret in general. Still the classic of classics on the wines of Bordeaux is Edmund Penning-Rowsell's tome of that name, another readable oldie rich in esoterica.

Some think he is a grumpy snob, but for my money the first popular English wine-writer, George Saintsbury, a professor of French literature at the University of Edinburgh, is still hard to beat. His 1933 *Notes On a Cellar-Book* is a sincere hymn to the pleasures of wine, written poignantly after his liver failed and his doctor ordered him never to drink another drop. A typical quote is: "I have known *senior* hocks and *senatorial* ports." Those were the good old days. Saintsbury's friends and protégés also wrote an incomparable series of sequels, all of them worth keeping: *The Romance of Wine* by H. Warner Allen; *Stay Me with Flagons* by Maurice Healy; *In Search of Wine* by Colonel C.W. Berry; and *Wayward Tendrils of the Vine* by Ian Campbell. These books all have a light-hearted, eccentric atmosphere vaguely reminiscent of Dickens's *Pickwick Papers*.

Does anyone today still write like these guys? Yes: Hugh Johnson in his Encyclopedias and Wine Atlases and Gerald Asher of the now defunct and much lamented *Gourmet Magazine*, whose essays are collected in several books. There is also Frank Prial of the *New York Times*, whose pieces are collected in several more volumes, all good reading even today.

Perhaps the best of all wine memoirs since the venerable George Saintsbury is Hugh Johnson's A Life Uncorked, *not exactly an oldie, but it
reads like one and goes back many years in its recollections. For label-
collecting fanatics like me (I have twenty photo albums full of old labels
to thumb through on quiet evenings), there is the lavishly illustrated* Sotheby's Guide to Classic Wines and Their Labels *by English Master of
Wine David Molyneux-Berry with hundreds of full-color reproductions
on large pages.*

*Last, and far from least, along with my fellow L.A. Fair and other
international wine judges, I always rely on the definitive* Oxford Companion to Wine *edited by Jancis Robinson, which came out in 1994 and
is updated regularly. There. That should keep all those readers of wine
books busy at least until next year.*

Be Assertive
with Annoying Waiters

In the world of sports, intimidation of the opponent is often critical to success. This idea has now moved to the more manicured playing fields of wine. For generations now, some waiters have tried to intimidate customers by handing them corks to sniff, labels to decipher, and other provocations.

Now the tables seem to be turning, so to speak, and customers are counterattacking.

The other night I overheard a dissatisfied customer make an incompetent waiter pronounce the entire wine list, then corrected him when he got Pouilly-Fuissé wrong. Brutal. The French can hardly pronounce that word right themselves. She could have just ordered it by its bin number like everyone else, but we wine drinkers are in no mood to be conciliatory, and are demanding more competent and less arrogant service when it comes to wines.

This new vinous vigilantism first came to my attention in a column by the late Russell Baker, that bitter but usually passive enemy of pretension and snobbery. Baker was in one of those horrible, pseudo-French restaurants in New York where pure chance often seems to land him. Presented with a wine cork to sniff, Baker assertively told the waiter to take it back to the kitchen, chop it fine, and sprinkle it over his salad.

This confrontation seemed like an isolated incident until a similar thing happened to columnist Calvin Trillin of the *New Yorker*. Trillin, if you haven't seen him on TV, is a mild-mannered, balding, former Midwesterner who now inhabits Greenwich Village. His numerous books focus mainly on his overwhelming love of food. He wrote recently on his quest for the best cheeseburger in Paris, but his specialties are dim sum and barbecue.

Despite his preference for American food, Trillin had never been known for verbal violence toward uppity or incompetent wine waiters. Nevertheless, he claims that once when he was presented with a cork to sniff by a waiter in a posh restaurant, he first eyed it appraisingly, then ate it, smacking appreciatively and gratefully at the astonished waiter. Don't try this at home.

Is all this hostility necessary? I think maybe it is. The reason the French and Chinese have such great food and attentive service is that they constantly demand it. The incompetent snobbery that too often passes for service in American restaurants has gone on long enough. We need waiters who know what they are talking about and who do not get their jollies by intimidating the paying customers. Please understand me: I do not advocate eating the cork they tender you. That victimizes us, not them. Just curl your lip a little while squeezing it, toss it aside as if unworthy, then lean in and swirl and sniff the partly filled glass you are about to taste.

Cork-sniffing is, after all, a useless affectation. If the cork feels sound, then it will not likely have spoiled the wine. Even a broken, crumbly cork does not mean a bad wine. Superlatively fine old wines often have corks so old they come apart during extraction from the bottle. The real test of a wine is in sniffing the wine, not the cork. When the waiter pours you out a splash, swirl it around, taking care not to dampen any onlookers, then sniff it well before tasting. The aroma will tell you quickly, even if you have no technical knowledge of wine, whether it smells good, and if it does, nine times out of ten it will taste just as good. You do not even have to put it in your mouth if it's really bad.

Never let the glares of a supercilious waiter intimidate you. Take a few seconds to really taste it, and ponder what it tastes like right *after* you swallow it. The waiter is being paid to *wait* for you to be satisfied. If the wine is vinegary, make him taste a glass of it too, and make him tell you what he thinks. If he disagrees, call the captain or the next person up the line until you receive satisfaction.

One last point. Despite the sexual revolution and the obvious fact that women now buy as much wine as men, most waiters still tender the wine to the man for tasting. If you disagree with this or would like her informed opinion, just pass her the glass without explanation. If she nods her approval, you've not only improved both of your evenings, you've gotten one up on the waiter, with whom you may have to contend on other issues later. He is probably insecure about his own wine knowledge anyway, and this will put him more under your control. And, who knows, maybe you'll get lucky and he'll bring her the check, too.

Serving Wine
Is Not Brain Surgery

The other night, at what passes for a reasonably good restaurant, my wife and I ordered a simple bottle of white wine. The waitress, when confronted with opening it, stammered and admitted she had never opened a bottle of wine before, it being her first night on the job. Bypassing the chance to berate the owner for not training her in such an obvious skill, we opened it for her.

Talking to friends later, it became apparent that even those who have enjoyed wine for years are still sometimes apprehensive about opening wine in restaurants—*in front of* everybody and all. Are you really supposed to sniff the cork? What if there is something floating in your wine? Should you ask for an ice bucket if a red wine is too warm? How do you check the label if it's covered by a white napkin?

It is apparently time to reassure people that opening a bottle of wine is not that complicated. Despite the aura of ritual, all you're doing is getting a piece of oak bark (the cork) out of the neck of a glass bottle. If necessary, you could cut the neck off the bottle with a sword like one French expert does or snap the neck off using red-hot Port tongs. But those are extreme measures. With most bottles all you need is a good corkscrew with a lever. The simplest and handiest, called a waiter's corkscrew, has a small knife blade encased in the handle. You use it first to cut off the outer covering, called the capsule, which protects the cork. You cut the capsule off parallel to the table with a circular motion right around the little lip just below the top.

After you have neatly removed the capsule, you wipe the top off with a clean napkin or paper towel so no mold or other foreign goop living under there falls into the wine after you pull the cork. Then you stick the point of the screw (or gimlet) into the center of the cork. With a twist of

189

the wrist you bore right in, straight down, until the screw has just about disappeared.

Next, you place the lever on the top edge of the bottle, and holding it on with one hand so it won't slip off (it's so embarrassing if you drop the bottle), you pry the cork out. A slight pop still gives me a cheap thrill, even when more mature onlookers scorn me for doing it.

Then you pour out a couple of tablespoonfuls into your own glass first, never anyone else's—that way you get any stray pieces of the cork. Deftly dipping out with your finger any pieces of cork that have fallen in, you swirl the wine slightly, sniff it without showing off, and taste it. So much has been made of cork-sniffers that I try to do it as quickly and unobtrusively as possible. If it's bad, you'll usually smell it from a foot away anyway. If the wine is okay, as it usually is, pour for your tablemates next, filling your own glass last. You should fill the glasses no more than two-thirds full.

When deciding on an ice bucket, it is useful to consider the fact that in America, most white wines are drunk too cold and most red wines too warm. The "room" temperature long accepted as proper for reds comes from *English* rooms, which are usually sixty-five degrees or cooler, as compared to our seventy plus, which is too warm for wine. Although it grosses out some waiters, many whites need to sit out on the table for a few minutes to get less icy, while many reds could stand a quick dash in the ice bucket to drop their temperature five or ten degrees. Whichever course you choose, don't let the waiter intimidate you. You paid for the wine and you should drink it at the temperature you like. He works for you, and not the other way around.

Problem Corks

A lot of things can go wrong when you try to drink a quiet glass of wine after work.

The cork can break off while you're screwing it out, or it can slide down into the wine as you're trying to put the corkscrew into it. I've even broken a piece of the neck off a few bottles while trying to pull old, hard, dry corks. What do you do when this happens?

You don't have to throw the whole bottle away just because the cork falls into it. Except in rare cases, corks won't hurt wines in the short term. The easiest thing to do is to ignore it and drink the wine. The only problem may be that every time you try to pour it, the cork will come up into the neck, shutting down the pour. Then when you shift it a little, the wine all comes rushing out at once, drenching the tablecloth and your clothes instead of your palate.

If this happens, just pour the wine over the sink into a decanter, or even an ice tea pitcher will do. If you insist on using the same bottle, for about ten dollars most wine supply stores sell cork retrievers for the purpose. They work like a fishhook. My experience has been that these things are more trouble than they're worth, but bobbing for corks can at least be a new experience once.

A trickier problem is breaking the neck, or even a small piece of it, off the bottle. You never know for sure that none of it fell into the wine. Here you need a simpler, handier tool—an ordinary paper towel—to use as a filter while pouring the wine off into a clean bottle or decanter. My advice is to take it into another room where no one can see you. Some people are squeamish about broken glass and keep staring so intently into their wine looking for bits of glass that it bugs me. Some would say you need a coffee filter, but that's only when you have sediment that needs filtering from a wine; paper towels will handle all glass bits.

Recently a friend called with multiple problems: He had pushed a cork down into his bottle trying to get the corkscrew in, then chipped glass into the wine while trying to get the cork out. But those were not enough. He also wanted to know if wine was bad for two other reasons: it had dark-brown gook on the top of the cork and little crystals that looked like salt on the bottom and in the neck of the bottle. Ruined? Not at all.

The brown stuff is usually dried wine that seeped out when the bottle got too hot in shipping and storage. Some delicate wines may be ruined in this way, especially whites, but usually not, and it is not uncommon. Just wipe it dry with a damp sponge or towel and go on. The shiny salt-looking things are tartrate crystals precipitated during the winemaking process or from the bottle's getting very cold. Winemakers do this sort of thing on purpose as a method of filtering in steel tanks. Just reach in with your little finger and lift them out and go on. You can rinse them off the bottom of the cork by putting it under running water and rubbing them with your thumb before replacing the cork.

My friend's bottle seemed to have had an unusually harsh childhood, but he reported it tasted excellent once he used the right Boy Scout first aid. He also admitted learning that there is more to this business of drinking wine than opening your mouth and pouring it down.

Satisfied with my free advice, he asked next what to do with very old bottles of fine red wine whose corks have begun to come apart. The answer: top up and re-cork. If you have several identical bottles, use a little of one to raise the level of the ones you intend to keep. Then shove in a new cork, preferably after putting in a shot of nitrogen from one of those ten-dollar pressurized cans like Private Preserve like they do on bottling lines in wineries. Then drink what's left of your other bottle.

With wine there's always a solution.

What's That Floating in My Glass?

Several things are known to float around in wine: small pieces of cork, tiny crystals, and clouds of dark substances collectively called "sediment." Several readers have asked what they are and whether they are harmful to wine or health.

First of all, they are not harmful to health. They can be, on the other hand, injurious to the taste of wine, depending on which ones they are and their concentration.

Tartrate Crystals: These shiny little particles, usually the size of grains of sugar but sometimes as big as rock salt, occur naturally in wine. They precipitate from tartaric acid, the most prevalent natural acid in wine. Normally they are removed before bottling by chilling them to make them stick to the sides of the tank before the wine is drawn off and bottled.

If you have bottles with tartrate crystals, you can remove them by chilling the bottle upside down. They will adhere to the cork, and when you pull it, they disappear with it. Since they can be a bit acidic, this process is worthwhile if there are too many of them for your taste, but a few very firm ones won't hurt anything.

Sediment: This is the name for solids floating in a wine bottle or sitting on the bottom. They are fine particles, if you are lucky, of grape pulp, skin, yeast, and stems. If you are less lucky, leaves and even bug parts may be in question. Sediment is best dealt with by leaving your bottle upright for a couple of days till the sediment falls to the bottom, which it will. Then you can carefully pour the wine out into a clean decanter. Lacking the decanter, any clear glass vessel will do, say an ice tea pitcher.

Trying to lay bottles on their sides in those fancy wine baskets or cradles has seldom worked well for me. They tend to mix the sediment with the wine much worse than if you used the simpler stand-up method. If you have no time for standing it up, but want to drink it right away, the best way to filter wines at the last minute is with a coffee filter. Next best is a simple paper towel.

Lees: Sediment found in barrels before wines are bottled is usually called *lees* in English and *lies* (pronounced the same way) in French. Lees are removed by filtering, or by fining, which is dropping a magnet-like substance into the barrel to attract floating solids. Egg whites are the traditional substance. After the fining agent pulls the solids together and falls to the bottom of the barrel, the tainted wine at the bottom is drawn off and only the "clean" wine remains. This process, called "racking" is often performed monthly for some of the denser wines.

Wine "Sur Lies": Not all lees are bad. In Champagne, the wine is left on the lees to absorb the flavor and aroma of the yeast in the lees for several months. Muscadet, the great white seafood wine of western France, also uses this process and even brags about it on labels. Lately American wineries, notably Callaway in California and Chateau Biltmore in North Carolina, are making Chardonnays "on the lees" to enrich the flavors, then removing them before bottling.

Crust: One other sort of sediment is actually sought after. Some dessert wines like Port and Setubal of Portugal are often totally unfiltered and throw such heavy sediment that they totally encrust the insides of their bottles. If you want to drink them without the crust, you can shake them vigorously to loosen it, let it fall to the bottom, wait a day, then decant them. Or you can do it the old-fashioned way: do the same shaking, set the bottle upside down for a few days to let the crust stick to the cork, then break the whole neck off the bottle with heated Port tongs, a really colorful way to open a bottle.

Personally I've always liked good Port crust. Some think I'm crazy, but I like to let the sediment sink to the bottom, drink the wine, then slosh around the crusty, spicy sediment and spread it on bread. It is uniquely delicious. It's not as crazy as it sounds. Really.

Resveratrol for a Healthy Heart

I once wrote a column about the recent finding that red wine can reduce heart disease. Then CBS's *60 Minutes* did a long segment on the same subject. Called *The French Paradox*, it stressed how the French have two-thirds fewer heart attacks than Americans, even though they eat much more fat and hardly exercise at all.

In the first month after that program, sales of Cabernet Sauvignon, the most popular American red wine, went up twenty-two percent. At Robert Mondavi, sales of their Napa Cabernet increased seventy-eight percent. In the three months after the *60 Minutes* segment, sales of all red wines in the United States increased fifteen percent. Beyond the raw selling power of television, what does this mean?

First of all, there is a dramatic shift in wine color patterns. For the past twenty years, white wine had grown constantly in sales while reds had slowly dropped. Some say this was due to the "chill factor," i.e., Americans like their beverages cold, and white wines are usually drunk colder than reds.

The new trend is easier to understand. Americans are now turning to red wines because it is only in reds that resveratrol, the presumed heart-saving chemical, resides. Well known to Chinese herbal doctors for centuries, resveratrol is found only in grape skins. Red wines are fermented on the skins, causing not only their red pigments but also their resveratrol to dissolve into the wine.

White wine, on the other hand, is usually made with minimum skin contact to keep it from being too acidic. Most whites don't have skin contact beyond the few minutes they are being pressed, so have much less resveratrol.

In Burgundy, winemakers keep submerging Pinot skins into their juice, unwittingly getting more resveratrol as well. In Bordeaux, especially at both the old-style wineries and ultra-modern ones who imitate them, skin contact can last three weeks or even a month. Perhaps the old French winemaker saying, "A wine's first duty is to be red," had more folk wisdom than even the French realized.

Another side-effect of the *60 Minutes* segment has been a flood of reader mail asking which reds have the most resveratrol, which has become a sort of liquid oat bran for clogged artery sufferers.

No in-depth scientific studies have appeared on this issue yet, but your best bets would be wines of deep red color like darker Bordeaux, Burgundies, California Cabernets and Zinfandels of the dark persuasion, and heavy-duty Rhone grapes, such as Syrah. Wine tip: For inexpensive reds rich in resveratrol, try Sangre de Toro from Torres, near the site of the Summer Olympics at Barcelona. In U.S. wines, try BV Cabernets. They ferment their wines warmer than most, to remove "off" aromas, and in the process keep lots of heart-saving resveratrol.

There is, of course, another way to ingest plenty of resveratrol. Since it is contained in grape skins you do not have to drink wine at all. Just eat the grapes. That method is both cheaper and more practical than buying those resveratrol pills they now sell.

Judging Wines

A veteran wine-taster once observed that in judging wines, "One peek at the label is worth years of experience." Barring such help, how do you go about evaluating a wine? This past fall I got the chance to compare some of the better techniques in action as a judge at the Atlanta International Wine Festival.

One of the world's largest tastings, the 1986 Atlanta event attracted 1,621 wines from all major wine-producing countries. The wines were evaluated "blind" by panels of judges over eleven evenings of tastings. My panel, six of us, was assigned to taste in a single evening thirty-eight young Chardonnays with retail prices from ten to fifteen dollars.

Seated at a white tablecloth under good lighting, we followed the classic wine-tasting progression: swirl, sniff, sip, and spit. Swirling the wine causes its "legs" to stream down the inside of the glass, revealing its weight or "body" (this is all so personal). Swirling also causes aeration of the wine, supposedly releasing its volatile esters and other elements into the air in what is called "breathing."

Speeding up aeration of wine allows tasters to judge its aroma and bouquet, known in wine jargon as "getting the nose." Authorities differ on how you best get a nose. Famed wine auctioneer Michael Broadbent recommends "a vigorous sniffing." Heavyweight enologist Maynard Amerine of Cal-Davis, the Oxford of wine-making schools, prefers a "light inhale," so you don't suffer "olfactory fatigue" (tired nostrils). Those at my table seemed to use both methods, sniffing more vigorously only those bouquets they really liked.

Nearly every wine was visually correct, and we differed little in our views of their appearance. But in getting the nose we parted company. From too many years of living in France, I cannot stop making that gargling sound the French tasters make. It is wonderfully revealing of the wine, though, and only moderately hard to learn without choking. You hold a small mouthful of wine, then inhale vigorously over your tongue, creating a sort of mist of wine in the back of your mouth.

You then close your mouth and breathe out quickly through your nose without swallowing. This causes the mist to go up the back of your nasal passages, where your most sensitive olfactory nerve endings are. The taste of wine being roughly seventy-five percent smell (that's why you can't "taste" anything when you have a cold), this exercise is probably the most important part of any tasting. Those at my table had the drill down pat, but some used it too sparingly in my opinion.

The downside of this important practice is the noise it makes, which my wife describes as "gurgling." My daughters love it, and call it "making the wine noise." Less charitable friends, at whose tables I have demonstrated it, liken it to a drowning sound or to a horse trying to drink and eat oats at the same time. Unfortunately, once you get the hang of it, you tend to do it whenever you taste a wine.

Our panel really parted company in the last stages of the tasting, splitting neatly into two groups known in the trade as "dry-bucket" and "wet-bucket" tasters. We each had beside us on the floor our own genuine plastic spittoon bucket with about two inches of lentil-sized rocks in the bottom to prevent splashing. Other competitions where I've judged use sawdust or wood shavings. Since we were to evaluate thirty-eight wines in about two hours, I knew I had to join the wet-bucket brigade if I intended to complete the tasting without bursting into song.

The only bad after-effect of the Atlanta tasting was the next morning, when my tongue was so red and swelled up from being doused in acidic young wines that all I wanted to soak it in was milk.

Detective Sonny Crockett Called His Favorite Wine D.P.

Our fast-paced world is a natural for abbreviations and acronyms. From BMWs to IRAs, we speak increasingly in letters instead of words. It is much the same in the otherwise old-fashioned and elaborate world of wines. And for most of us this is a good thing.

BV and DRC: When you want a good California Cabernet Sauvignon, it is a lot easier to ask for a BV than to pucker up and try to pronounce Beaulieu Vineyards, which goes something like "boh-lee-ooh." The same applies when, after a long day, you want a fine Burgundy but can't possibly say, "Domaine de la Romanee-Conti." Nowadays all you need to say is, "Let me have an '85 DRC, please."

D.P.: Sonny Crockett of TV's old *Miami Vice* cop show *[now on cable]* was a trend-setter when, while working some lavish undercover scene, he told a waiter to "take my friend a bottle of D.P." If he'd tried to pronounce Dom Pérignon, the wonderfully expensive Champagne he'd ordered, which sounds roughly like "daw-pay-reen-yaw," he would probably have blown his cover with his tongue.

M.D.: Some wine abbreviations lead more complicated lives. The marketing people at Mogen David, realizing their old name had a stodgy, sweet-wine image, tried to upscale it by naming one of their wines MD/20-20. To their surprise, everyone was soon calling it Mad Dog, a classic example of folk wisdom seeing through ad agency glitz. Sales are up, mostly from the nasty-macho image of the unofficial name. Mad Dog definitely does not go with quiche.

AC-DC: There are pitfalls in abbreviation of course. The initials A.C. on a French label do not refer to air conditioning, but the legally controlled region of origin or *Appellation d'Origine Controllée.* Italian labels usually have similar lettering, preceded by a D, which means basically the same thing. Abbreviated, you get DOC, or DOCG if it has a special official guarantee of quality. But it gets really tricky where the label says, elaborately, that it has NO guarantees. *Appellation d'Origine SIMPLE* means no guarantees at all, but looks at first glance to mean the opposite.

BATF: If you find label violations, you can report them to another abbreviation, the BATF, short for Bureau of Alcohol, Tobacco, and Firearms, successor to the old revenuers of the Snuffy Smith moonshine era. They are to wine-labelers what the KGB is to dissidents.

The Heartbreak of Metrics: To pre-metric people like me, the true heartbreak of a wine label is the content description. A perfectly normal-sized wine bottle now has "750 mls." (milliliters). Why they needed to call it 750 thousandths of a liter instead of just three-fourths is beyond me. So watch out when a clerk asks if you'd like a "375." He is talking about an ordinary half-bottle (half of a 750) and not trying to sell you a large handgun.

TBAs: Still on the practical side, when someone asks if you like TBAs, he is not inquiring about unannounced TV movies. Trockenbeerenausleses are German dessert wines made from dried, individually picked, ultra-ripe grapes. The French have dessert wines somewhat similar in character called VDNs, which stands for *Vins Doux Naturels* (naturally sweet wines).

The Ph.D. of pH: I've always had trouble remembering which letters to capitalize in Ph.D., and whether to put periods and spaces. Now, to complicate matters, winemakers have started to add the pH, or acid balance, of their wines to their wine labels. The chemistry of wine is no easy subject, and you almost need a Ph.D. to figure out pH. In my experience winemakers concerned too much with pH on their labels couldn't leave their wine alone and probably added acidity of an artificial kind. You don't have to read that stuff if you don't want to.

WINOS: One of my favorite wine acronyms came from a wine club in California—where else? Founded in the living room of the late wine journalist Jerry Mead in 1969, no doubt at the end rather than the beginning of an evening, the club was called W.I.N.O.S. The letters stood for Wine Investigation for Novices and Oenophiles. They even published a highly informative newsletter of their proceedings, which showed you don't have to be stuffy to enjoy good wine.

Following their lead, some friends and I now have a club we call OWLS— The Oxford Wine Lovers' Society—here in Oxford, Mississippi.

These Gizmos Do All but Drink Your Wine for You

From all sides we are bombarded with offers of new wine gizmos, without which we as wine-drinkers supposedly could hardly survive. Referred to as "accessories for the discriminating," these items do everything but drink your wine for you. They can also cost you in the high five figures if you like temperature-controlled wine vaults.

My taste in wine gadgets runs more toward under ten dollars, or at most under twenty-five. The kind of thing I usually look for is something to chill my wine quickly when I get home and want a good white but have nothing cold. My latest foray into the world of wine gizmos was last week, when I finally bought one of those things that cuts what the French call the "capsule," and Americans often call the wrapper, from the top of the bottle. As you have probably noticed, if you leave too much of this wrapper on an old bottle, the moldy stuff under it can seep into the wine when you pour it.

Thus I thought the Screwpull Foil-Cutter might be good. It was. The foil-cutter looks like a small pair of jaws with a row of teeth around the inside. Sharp little blades cut around the top of the bottle, neatly lifting off the top of the sealing capsule. It works great. Of course, you can still just cut the capsule neatly off with a sharp knife, as I always did before.

My next endeavor, entered with little hope of practical success, also worked well. Knowing that my wife has a sense of temperature much better developed than mine, and can tell when both white and red wines are not at just the right temperature, I bought a wine thermometer.

When I got home, it became apparent that you did not stick this one down the wine's throat, so to speak, but wrapped it around its body. It looked sort of like a wrist radio from "Star Trek." The Wine Thermometer, which identifies itself as "liquid crystal," whatever that is, slipped onto my first medium-cold Chardonnay like a sleeve. A digital dial immediately began to light up. I had expected to have to read an elusive line of vertical mercury as if my mother were taking my temperature during an attack of measles. You don't anymore. The Wine Thermometer prints it out for you in big digital numbers, legible to even the most nearsighted.

The best unexpected side benefit of the Wine Thermometer was that my daughters love it. They compete to see who can go check my latest wine in the fridge and read the numbers and bring back the news. It has also allowed me to experiment with varying temperatures for wines. I've learned that I like my California Chardonnays colder than my white French Burgundies from the same grape.

So far, I haven't felt the need for any thousand dollar wine tapestries, nor any five thousand dollar wine vaults, nor any expensive crystal "wine-duck" decanters, even though Thomas Jefferson bought several eighteenth-century equivalents. Jefferson was a great wine connoisseur, but he also died bankrupt. I'm sticking with the simple twenty-dollar glass duck, in which you can easily see the wine. I still cut my capsules off by hand, pull my corks manually, and chill most of my wines ahead of time. But right now I'm watching the digital numbers go down on that good Chardonnay I put in to chill just eight minutes ago. Maybe these gizmos can be our friends after all.

Those Maligned Muscats

Rich, heavy, high-alcohol red wines, thanks largely to uber-guru Robert Parker, are right now terribly in. Sweet wines are pretty much out, as are most Portuguese wines except Port, which is staging a comeback.

Such fads and fashions in wine drinking usually begin for arbitrary reasons: transportation problems, wars, personal tastes of famous people, and often have little to do with the relative qualities of the wines. Once they catch on, some last a few months, while others persist for generations.

Like politicians and deodorants, wines also suffer from image problems, the most dramatic current example being the wines made from the Muscat grape. Once universally considered among the world's finest, and still very popular in Mediterranean countries, Muscats today are the lepers of the American wine world, mainly for reasons unrelated to their often excellent quality.

Vermouth and Asti Spumante are made wholly or partly from Muscat grapes but not one reveals it. Why? To avoid association with their infamous cousin, Muscatel, the wino's wine, the beverage par excellence of Skid Row. Good Muscats dare not mention their family origins for fear the specter of Muscatel will drive away their American customers. Yet this very reticence has caused people here to assume that all Muscat wines must be bad.

It was not always thus. Shakespeare praised Muscats often. Thomas Jefferson and his guests drank many a barrel of fine French, Italian, and Portuguese Muscats, most of which are still produced today in the same locations but are rarely imported here for lack of demand.

Recently, however, a slight change has appeared here. Admirers of the Muscat have begun to emerge from hiding and are cautiously praising good Muscat wines they've drunk, especially certain ones made in California. Since a hallmark of old-fashioned Americanism is support for underdogs, Muscats may even be about ready for a mild comeback.

Let it be clear that the Muscat is not related to Muscadet, a totally different grape grown in the Loire Valley of France, which produces a good, inexpensive dry white wine. Confusion of the two is common because of the similar spelling. Recently a national wine magazine featured an article in which someone wrongly described a Muscadet as having a Muscat aroma.

Nor is Muscat related at all to Muscadine, the homemade wine of generations of Southern grannies. Muscat is of the European species *vitis vinifera*, like the Cabernets and the Riesling. Muscadine is of the native North American species *vitis rotundifolia*, and closely related to the old "Carolina wine," Scuppernong.

Actually it is only in America that the ancient and honorable Muscat grape has fallen upon evil days, and even that fall was for understandable historical reasons. Here, following the lifting of Prohibition, many acres of coarser Muscat varieties grown for raisin-making in California were hastily and unwisely pressed into cheap wine, fortified with cheap brandy, and sold as Muscatel. These bad wines were and still are twenty percent alcohol, and amount to nothing but a cheap intoxicant. Their popularity on Skid Row has nearly ruined the name of all the good wines made from the Muscat grape, which has become a sort of closet varietal.

Today, with the rise of a new generation of moderate and discriminating drinkers of quality European and American wines, including good sweet wines in their place, it is past time for a revival of respect for well-made Muscats in this country, which now makes some of the best and most unusual ones in the world from finer European grape varieties.

The Muscat (pronounced "musket") family of grapes was brought to Europe from the Middle East by returning Crusaders. The name is from the Persian word meaning "strong-scented," and probably related to our word musk. It is also the name for the capital of the lovely Gulf country Oman, also named for the grapes once shipped through its Port, which is directly across the Gulf from Iran. Since it came west, growers have bred new Muscat strains and re-spelled its name to suit their own languages. In Italy it is *moscato*, in France *muscadelle* and *muscat doré*, in Spain and Portugal *moscatel*, and in Eastern Europe *muscat ottonel*.

California's best Muscat wine for now, made from an Italian strain, is the Moscato di Canelli of Charles Krug Winery in Napa Valley, which the State Department has chosen to be served at American embassies abroad. It is a wine to be chauvinistic about. It has a light straw-yellow color and an aroma that is surprising: fresh, light, and a little flowery, reminiscent of a Gewuztraminer. Most bottles have a slight sparkle that is pleasantly suited to the taste, which is not dry yet is no sweeter than a German *spatlese.* It may be served with the same dishes as a good Moselle, but my own preference is to drink it by itself, cool, as you would a good German Riesling or Portuguese *vinho verde.*

The key to the success of Moscato di Canelli is judicious blending of Moscato with milder white wines to tone down the excessive Muscat aroma and sweetness. Lack of such blending was no doubt a major cause for the current unpopularity of Muscats in the United States.

Robert Mondavi Winery also makes a very fine Muscat called Moscato d'Oro, which is nearly identical in quality and character to the Canelli except that it is a bit more golden and lacks the sparkle. As more people ask for it, its arrival across the country will be hastened, and as demand and production increase, perhaps its price will go down.

Both Louis Martini and Bargetto wineries in California produce a sparkling, semi-sweet Muscat more like Asti Spumante. Its low alcohol content (eight percent) and unstable condition cause it to lose its sparkle and freshness easily, so it must be kept refrigerated at all times. Retailers dislike carrying Moscato Amabile because it spoils easily and it does not travel all that well but it is still sometimes available and cheap.

Beaulieu Vineyards (BV) makes a dessert wine from the best French Muscat called Muscat de Frontignan. It has brandy added, like the French. Although is not much to my taste, those who like French Frontignan generally like it, which included wine lover Thomas Jefferson.

The other American Muscat of note is the Muscat Ottonel made by the winery of Dr. Konstantin Frank along Lake Keuka in New York state. Frank, a Russian of German descent, is best known for his Rieslings, which at their best are to me among the finest American white wines made. Frank's Muscat Ottonel, made from the predominant Muscat strain of Russia and eastern Europe, is fortified and strong, though not as sweet as most. It is something of an acquired taste. The best Muscat Ottonel wine now available here is the excellent Murfatlar from Romania, a light-gold, very fine dessert wine somewhat less sweet than Sauternes.

An unusual French sparkling wine and Champagne substitute is Golden Guinea, a Loire Valley Muscat made more in the Italian tradition of sparkling Muscats than the French tradition of heavy dessert wines. It is good bubbly and generally lighter than most Asti Spumantes. Although the importer had intended to label it "sparkling Muscat," Treasury representatives suggested it would be more "proper" to change the label so as not to show it was a Muscat. The front label now says Golden Guinea, but in fine print the back label still honestly proclaims it to be a Muscat.

In Spain and southern France a favorite before-dinner drink is light Spanish Moscatel served with a dish of green olives. Although sweet aperitifs are generally too heavy to be really good appetizers, this one is very pleasant outdoors on summer evenings. It is also a favorite in Portugal, Greece, and all around the Mediterranean, so it must have something going for it.

Naturally sweet Muscats were once prized as healthful tonics much like Hungarian Tokay. Today only a handful remain, but if you need a sweet wine for a maiden aunt who is a little off her elderberry, these are the thing. It is ironic to think that Falstaff once drank these Muscat wines thinking them manly and heroic.

From the island of Cyprus comes Commandaria, a Muscat first made by the crusading Knights Templar. A dark-brown dessert wine with a caramel taste, Commandaria can be pleasant on occasion with pastries. It comes in squat, dark-brown bottles. Constantia, once the most famous dessert wine of South Africa and a tremendous favorite in England, is still made by the Paarl Cooperative and can usually be found for the price of an inexpensive Port. A similar wine from Spain is the Pedro Domecq Vina No. 25, a blend of Muscat and the Pedro Ximenes grape, a vital ingredient of Oloroso Sherries and Malaga.

In 1824 Daniel Webster visited Thomas Jefferson at Monticello and noted that they drank together some fine "Samian" wine. Today Muscat of Samos is made by a growers' cooperative on that Greek island. This unique "straw wine" is so called because the grapes from which it is made are laid in the sun on straw mats after picking. The partly dried grapes make a thicker, heavier wine which when well chilled can be surprisingly good with Greek or Arab pastries, with which only a very sweet wine is drinkable.

In South America the Muscat strongly persists as well. In Argentina, Chile, and especially Peru a brandy called Pisco is produced from Muscat grapes and is a popular drink with North American travelers returning from Machu Picchu. Marketed here as Inca Pisco, bottles of it are widely available in the U.S.

By 2014 Americans have fully discovered and embraced this grape, now universally called by its Italian name "muscato," and it is one of the most popular appetizer and sipping wines of the United States—and at very popular prices.

Sauternes and Foie Gras

A few years ago the late wine guru John Grisanti of Memphis, who once had the best restaurant wine cellar in the Deep South, invited several of us to taste two great Sauternes with him. The wines were 1982 Chateau Rieussec (ree-oo-sek) and 1983 Chateau Suduiraut (sood-wee-roh), a favorite of Thomas Jefferson. Sauternes names look hard to pronounce, but they are not if you work at it. Both wines were golden, rich, and decadent enough to make decent people feel guilty. But we didn't, far from it.

Sauternes is a late-harvest wine often mistakenly served with desserts, which are too sweet and destroy its subtle flavor. Real Sauternes freaks, among whom I count myself, often drink this wine alone before dinner, as an appetizer or aperitif wine. Others drink it alone after dinner as a light liqueur. Sauternes fanatics like it best with foie gras (fwah grah). Before you think too hard about what foie gras really is, if you haven't tried a good one, let me explain. Foie gras is rich-tasting, but extremely mild. It goes best on slightly toasted bread because what it most resembles is super-fine butter.

Recent studies have shown that in Gascony in southwest France, where more foie gras is eaten than anywhere else in the world, heart disease rates are the lowest in France, whose rates are already a small fraction of ours. Why? Some say it has "good" cholesterol and copper traces, but no one really knows. Foie gras was developed by the ancient Egyptians, who fed figs to ducks to make their meat mild and tasty. In the Middle Ages the French found that hybrid ducks from non-quacking Muscovy fathers and Long Island (Pekin) mothers make the finest eating. An eight-pound hybrid, called a Moulard, (the word comes not from mallard but from the same origin as "mule") has a two-pound breast, heavy thighs, and a two-pound liver. It is mild and lean liver, at least compared to the more traditional goose liver.

The key to foie gras is freshness. For most of the history of this country, the only way you could taste fresh foie gras was to travel to France. The canned stuff is good but not the same thing. John Grisanti invited an expert to show us how foie gras goes with Sauternes. Just six years ago Ariane Daguin, a tall, witty Frenchwoman from Gascony, started the only Moulard farm in U.S history in upstate New York. It now does two thousand ducks per *week*, including not only terrific foie gras but also magret (breast) and confit (marinated thighs). Ariane is the daughter of famed chef André Daguin, who was a consultant to the famed Pyramide restaurant in the Louvre in Paris.

Ariane prepared, as we watched and tasted, foie gras both one hundred percent raw and unblended as a fresh terrine and also lightly bronzed in a frying pan. My favorite was a whipped, aerated *mousse* of pure foie gras. It costs half what the unaerated costs, is amazingly light, and complements Sauternes extraordinarily well.

The name of Daguin's company is, appropriately for Gascony, D'Artagnan, as in the three Musketeers with their southern-French muskets and swords. They also have venison, grouse, wild boar, rabbit, and pheasant. A half-pound of foie gras mousse costs forty dollars, but it goes a long way.

Ariana and D'Artagnan are still going strong despite foie gras being banned in some places like Chicago because of the way the ducks and geese are force-fed corn to produce such giant livers. For those not opposed to that process, her products are readily available by an Internet search.

Wine as Dessert

Poet Elizabeth Barrett Browning, probably trying to cheer herself up about getting old, once wrote about "the last of life, for which the first was made." Whatever the merits of that idea generally, it is certainly true for dinner: The best part of a meal for me was always dessert. Yet it used to be during dessert when U.S. wines failed to measure up to French and German wines. At last that's changing.

There are now so many good, American-made dessert wines, mainly from California, that it is hard to tell which is best, although I will have suggestions later. Probably the first good sweet wine from the United States that I appreciated at all was the Muscat of Frontignan from BV. It is still available, and for wines with brandy added, it is still probably the best.

Next came Robert Mondavi's Moscato d'Oro, a unique treat and unbeatable by itself for quiet sipping. But for really sweet foods, chocolate being the ultimate test, even the Mondavi was too light. Only true French Sauternes from Bordeaux would do. And for those with a tooth for Sauternes, the 1970s were grim times. Several of the oldest chateaux producing those great and venerable wines fell upon hard times, some were sold and some were even in bankruptcy.

Then, just as all seemed grimmest for Sauternes, which are incredibly expensive to produce, but which sell for less than most red Bordeaux, along came California. With the true spirit of independence and sheer cussedness that has always marked Sauternes-like wines, American vintners ignored the apparent lack of any market for such delicacies.

Sauternes, like a German Auslese (pronounced "owss-lay-zuh"), can be made only from grapes picked very late in the year, when shriveled and dried and gross-looking, long after all reasonable wines are already in the cask. It was such wines that a few California vintners sought to make. Several, including that pioneer Robert Mondavi, made some very fine late-harvested Sauvignon Blancs that tasted much like Sauternes.

But it was Joseph Phelps who first convinced me that late-harvest wines in the United States could be as good as those of Europe. Ironically, it was a Phelps late-harvest Riesling that brought me over. When old in the bottle and turning amber and even orange, it was ambrosial, tasting like a distinguished old apricot that had died and gone to heaven. This wine, while still distinctly American, was as good as German.

Then Phelps returned, this time with a wine from the second white grape of Bordeaux, the Semillon, which had rarely made a dry wine above mediocre for any U.S. winemaker. The 1985 Phelps, officially called Delices du Semillon (a very apt title), is the closest thing we will get to Sauternes on this side of the Atlantic in my lifetime. In fact, it is so much better than anything I had hoped for that I would swap most any good Sauternes I've got for just a half-bottle. After two tastes of the 1986, I'll say it is as good as the '85, perhaps lighter, but subtle and fine.

Stealing a half-tad from Rupert Brooke, the World War I poet, I will say that, "If I should die, say only this of me: There is some corner of Hailman that is forever Delices du Semillon." This wine does not just go with dessert. It *is* dessert.

Since this column was written, American dessert wines have continued to evolve dramatically upward. Unfortunately, their prices have followed suit. Sauternes prices, by contrast, have leveled off. Great Australian dessert wines (called "stickies" by the Aussies) have joined the fray, also at a very high level. Now is truly a golden age for lovers of dessert wines.

Bottle Builders

A reader recently asked: "Why are wines bottles so many different colors and shapes? Do the differences serve any useful purpose?" The answer is a qualified maybe—sometimes. As with so many subjects, the origins of the differences in bottles lie more with history than logic.

The Romans used wine bottles, occasionally even with corks, but not to the extent we do. During the Dark Ages and Middle Ages, however, glass-making so declined that most wines were drunk straight from the barrel. Without bottles and cork-stoppers, wines spoiled within one year, so no aged wines at all were drunk for nearly a thousand years.

The rediscovery of the corked wine bottle began in the seventeenth century. The first bottles were squat, bulbous affairs with large bottoms and small necks (like some lawyers I know), which were tougher for hard-drinking squires to knock over. Only later, when they rediscovered the use of corks to keep the air out of bottles and needed to keep the corks moist by laying the bottles on their sides, did our long "binnable" bottles come into being. The classic example of a bottle made for stacking or "laying down" is the Bordeaux bottle. It is also much easier to knock over.

The Better to See It, My Dear

Some medieval wine bottles were made of leather, while beer bottles were made of crockery well into the nineteenth century. When the switch was made to glass, people began to notice that wine in colored bottles kept longer than wine stored in clear ones. Originally, most bottles had been dark-colored to hide the flaws in wines, which were often murky and had strange things floating in them. To this day the quasi-official glasses for drinking German wines are not clear but light green, imparting proper color to those golden wines, even though no longer necessary.

Clear glass came into use for white wines only recently. It lets you know what the wine looks like without opening the bottle, but it also lets in all the light, which can spoil delicate wines quickly if left in the sun. At the other extreme are most Italian reds, such as Barolo, which are still bottled in dark brown, even blackish bottles. One of the best Spanish Champagne or cava producers, Freixenet, bottles some of its wines in totally opaque black bottles, thus giving them the ultimate protection.

One Champagne producer, Roederer, has made a fortune doing just the opposite: bottling in clear glass, exploiting the beautiful color of its classic Cristal.

Much bottle color is pure habit. In German wines, for example, Rhine wines come in medium-brown bottles while Mosels come in medium-green ones to distinguish them quickly. German wine labels are so ludicrously esoteric and obtuse, it is not a bad idea to make them identifiable by the colors of the bottles—at least in my opinion. Both Mosel and Rhine bottles are shaped the same way: so tapered they are hard to stack for aging. Germany also produces the strangest-looking wines bottles I've seen lately—pharmaceutical blue. Have you seen those bright blue bottles like chemists used to use? They're supposed to protect chemicals from light. Now there is a German winemaker called Dr. Zenzen (sounds like a bad British TV series) who sells his Rhines in chemical-blue bottles. I suppose they taste the same, but I keep expecting to smell ether and keel over.

All in all, with the stability of wine being what it is today, the color of the bottles has less practical importance. If stored properly, out of excessive light, clear glass can be as safe as dark green.

The old colored bottles are of course still useful for old-fashioned bottle trees—to keep away evil spirits, they say. With the few exceptions cited above, bottle color is otherwise mostly a matter of habit and personal taste. As for Dr. Zenzen, maybe he is like the family who all chose to wear blue denim Levis: People said they must have had "blue genes." Sorry.

Half-Bottles and Marbles: Solutions for Leftover Wines

Having too much wine has seldom been my problem, but it can happen. As one reader recently wrote: "One problem I have in experimenting with wine is that my wife doesn't drink wine, which frequently leaves me with a good portion of the bottle undrunk after a meal." Apparently unwilling to find another wife, this gentleman has "frequently rushed the consumption, with unfortunate results." Such can often be the fate of those who live, or at least dine, alone.

Fortunately, help has arrived. One aid is that great wine institution, the half-bottle, known in the metric world as "the 375," because the contents are expressed as 375-thousandths of a liter, not a simple three-eighths. Metrics notwithstanding, the major drawback to half-bottles is that there aren't enough of them. Most wineries only make a few, and most stores don't carry any. The ones you can find are usually are not the ones you want. Otherwise, no problem.

If no half-bottles are available to you, the second-best expedient is the empty half bottle for reuse. Open the full bottle, then fill a well-washed half bottle (fill it all the way to the cork to exclude air) and drink what you have left in the full one. Because all good wines are living things, excluding air is the key to wine preservation. When combined with oxygen, their volatile components turn to acetic acid, or vinegar. Surprisingly, people drank wine for many centuries without knowing exactly what created it (fermentation), or what spoiled it (acetification). A Frenchman, Louis Pasteur, finally discovered the secret in the last century.

In Pasteur's honor, sort of, cheap jug wines are now pasteurized, that is parboiled to death so that no living element is left to combine with oxygen and spoil the wine. Fine wines, meant to develop and improve in the bottle, are allowed to live, but they retain the tendency to spoil overnight. Killing wine in order to save it has never seemed like a very good choice, so it's best to choose quality over quantity every time.

Another option is a pressured nitrogen machine. Attached to a partially empty wine bottle, it keeps out oxygen, and thereby spoilage, by filling the space between the cork and the wine with inert nitrogen. However unappetizing that sounds, it works fairly well. Until recently, the machine, at two thousand dollars, was too expensive for anyone but high-end restaurants. Modern science, with help from expiring patents, has made the home nitrogen-filled bottle possible. While still not cheap, if unfinished bottles are a serious problem at your house, an eighty-dollar model may be a good investment. Think of it as what you waste by leaving four bottles of good Burgundy unfinished. Called the Vintage Keeper, this machine is available from The Wine Enthusiast.

One final idea is as old as the Greeks. Keep a set of small marbles in a plastic mesh sack like you buy oranges in. Then, like the smart crow in Aesop's fable, drop the little marbles into your partially empty wine bottle until its level is up to the cork. The next evening, when you pour wine into your glass, fishing out the occasional marble that falls in with it, your wine is still unspoiled—usually. The marbles can then be washed in the sack and reused.

To Decant or Not to Decant

I always try to give my wife Christmas gifts that I will also enjoy my-self. Champagne and chocolates are good examples. Another relative success has been wine decanters. Before the mass-produced bottle was perfected, most wines were served in decanters. Some decanters were made dark brown and green to hide the things floating in the wine or its lack of proper color. Nowadays most wines look pretty good, so why do we still need decanters? The answer is: for several reasons.

One reason to decant wine is that it looks good in crystal or clear cut glass. Decanting lets you show off what you paid for. The practical reason for decanting is to remove the often-bitter sediment from old wines. To do this, stand the bottle (usually red wine) upright for a day or three before opening. Obviously this requires people who think ahead. Then, disturbing the wine as little as possible, uncork and pour it into the carafe, preferably above a candle or light bulb, stopping just before you reach the cloudy-looking sediment in the bottom of the bottle. They sell expensive cradles and baskets for pouring wine from its side, but I have never found these to work too well; most serious wine people con-sider them useless pretensions.

Decanters for Whites? White wines, usually filtered, rarely have sedi-ment, so why decant them? One reason, again, is just to look at them. If that seems lightweight, there is the pragmatic reason: to chill them and keep them chilled. If you are like me and forget in the morning to chill a white for that evening, there are decanters, glorified pitchers actually, which have ice cylinders in the center for keeping wine cold while it sits on your table. You don't have to run to the fridge for re-fills, and your white doesn't get watery. If you think that is frivolous, I note that Thomas Jefferson often used just such chillers. Monticello still has some of his.

Bargains: My favorite bargain decanter is one I found years ago at Antoine's restaurant in New Orleans; most of the best restaurants there still use them as water jugs. It is clear cut glass and looks much like the same items you see on fancy restaurant tables in Paris. It costs a mere ten dollars but looks like a hundred. The old restaurant supply house Loubat on Carrollton Street has them.

Offsets: Another reason for decanting wine is to let it "breathe," i.e. for its volatile esters to combine with oxygen, thus in theory "freeing" its bouquet. I actually believe that idea, as do most other experienced winetasters. To breathe best, the wine must be exposed to the most air possible. For this a broad, wide-bottomed decanter with a broad mouth is advisable. For a "mere" $150 you can get a lop-sided "offset" decanter called a Crystal Magnum. Not worth it.

Wine Ducks: More offbeat, and also ancient, is the so-called "wine-duck," so named by Thomas Jefferson's grandchildren because the thing looks like a duck. It neither quacks nor waddles, but does have a long neck and a bill-like opening. Technically, it is a modern re-creation of an ancient Greek askos, or wine skin, which Jefferson had copied in silver at Nimes while he was on tour in France. They used to cost several hundred dollars, but there is now an Italian version available in lead crystal with a silver-plated bill for seventy-nine dollars.

Our own wine duck pleased not only my children, but also my wife, who usually thinks wine gadgets are wasteful. It is an outstanding decanter. Jefferson occasionally let his grandchildren keep their jams and jellies in his, but old Bordeaux is much better.

Wine Yeasts, Wild and Tame

Humans made and enjoyed wine for thousands of years without knowing what caused grapes to ferment. Only in the nineteenth century did Frenchman Louis Pasteur discover that it was wild yeasts on the grapes that converted their sugar to alcohol. Pasteur also found that if you boil wine it kills the yeasts, thus "pasteurizing" it against further fermentation. Since then we've learned a lot about different yeasts and how they work, but we could stand to learn more.

Yeasts are probably one of the most underrated elements in fine wine, sometimes having as much to do with a wine's taste and aroma as either the land where the grapes were grown or the barrels they were aged in. If you get the wrong yeast, a wine can be sickeningly foamy, smell funny, be sweet and fizzy, or can re-ferment in the bottle and get cloudy and funny-tasting after you take it home.

Yeasts are one-celled, asexual plants. The best yeasts are well behaved, working feverishly till all grape sugar is absorbed, then dying. Others are not so cooperative, hanging around after fermentation ends and giving off bad tastes and smells to wines. Worst are the yeasts that die too soon, causing a "stuck" fermentation where partly fermented wine tastes bad and spoils quickly.

In modern winemaking there are two basic types of yeasts: wild and cultured. There is no such thing as "artificial" yeast. The cultured ones are natural, just cultivated to multiply outside their own areas. Most cultured yeasts still come from Europe, especially France and Germany. For some reason, the natural yeasts of Europe, like the grapes, seem to make better wines. But like the grapes, once transplanted to America they make wines in our climates just as good as, if not better than, in Europe.

For reasons not yet wholly understood, some vineyards in California now produce better wild yeasts than in the past, and many wineries are experimenting successfully with them. But they are tricky. Different wild yeasts existing together can give wines greater complexity, but can also clash. One group of yeasts can predominate in hot, dry years and another in cool, wet years, giving wines of very different character. Wild yeast tastes are seldom consistent from year to year.

One wine, Port, receives a special yeast treatment to soften its natural harshness, being dosed with grape brandy before fermentation ends to kill the yeast before the wine gets too dry. Other wines like Chardonnay are often left for months on the expired yeast cells among the "lees" in the bottom of the barrel, which some say makes wine creamy, spicy, and more complex in flavor.

Cultured yeasts are usually put into a vat of grapes dry, allowing the juice to activate them.

Some U.S. wineries use "liquid starter," yeasts already multiplying in small amounts of wine. These so-called "hot" starts are less often "stuck," but old-timers say the faster you ferment a white wine, the less subtle it is, so cooling tanks are used to slow white wine fermentation. For reds, on the other hand, many winemakers claim a warmer fermentation "burns off" unwanted smells, so they are fermented much warmer.

You may soon be reading more wine labels which describe the yeasts used, whether wild or domesticated, with names taken from famous wine sites like Champagne or Montrachet from France, or Steinberg from Germany. Those words on a wine label are not esoteric wine snobbery, but evidence of a winemaker seeking the cutting edge, trying yet another way to make wines more varied and enjoyable.

The Big Chill

The temperature at which you should drink wine is partly a matter of opinion, but it will greatly affect how much you enjoy it. If you don't believe me, try drinking warm beer. Or serve it to someone expecting cold beer. (On the other hand, the English actually *like* warm beer.)

Tradition says white wines should be served colder than reds. And with wines, tradition usually counts for something even if we no longer recall where it came from. The best teacher, of course, is experience, but experience can be harsh. Drinking warm whites and cold reds is sort of a vinous boot camp: good to have behind you, but nothing to repeat.

Wine books' descriptions of ideal serving temperatures are tricky to understand. "Room" temperature in the United States is more like seventy degrees, while in France—and especially in England, where most of these rules were first written down—it is more like sixty-two degrees.

Thus, most red wines—especially in summer—are served too warm in the United States. Wine that is too warm tastes more tannic, astringent, and alcoholic than wine that is cooler. Putting your red bottle in the refrigerator for ten to fifteen minutes can help.

A Calculating Mind

Trying to convert Celsius temperatures into Fahrenheit is a great source of bafflement for me. Unfortunately, too many wine guides are written in Celsius, and even when I can remember the formula, I hate doing the math. So here's a rough but handy guide to temperatures that are about right for typical white and red wines.

For white wines, use thirteen degrees Celsius and fifty-five degrees Fahrenheit. Just remember the bad luck number thirteen and the fifty-five mile speed limit. Serve red wines at eighteen degrees Celsius and sixty-five degrees Fahrenheit. That's eighteen, just like the age at which you once were allowed to buy beer, and sixty-five, as in . . . Come to think of it, it might be easier to just do the math.

Some practical tips: If your Champagne is warm and your guests are arriving, it is faster to chill it in ice-cold water than nestled in ice cubes. For some reason, wines—unlike beer—don't take well to being served in iced glasses. Besides, that's just not generally done, although Thomas Jefferson and the other Founding Fathers used to do it. They even had specially made wineglass chillers.

To test a wine's temperature, use a clip-on thermometer, which costs less than ten dollars at most wine supply stores or online. Wine thermometers are nearly always in Fahrenheit in the U.S., and they generally have easy-to-read digital faces.

Another rule of thumb: Burgundies taste better a little cooler than Bordeaux, and they say sweet wines can be chilled more safely than dry ones. It is neither a sin nor a misdemeanor to chill reds, but normally only the lightest and youngest are chilled much below sixty-five degrees.

My favorite fast cooler is a gadget called Winechiller, a sort of metal coil device hidden in a black plastic box filled with ice cubes. You pour the wine in warm at one end, wait thirty seconds, and pour it out cold via a spigot at the other.

A silver ice bucket is okay, but it looks better when it isn't sweating. To prevent this, wrap it in a clean white towel—but that of course hides your expensive silver. It's better to use a simple black steel ice bucket that is shaped like an upside-down top hat. It's much cheaper, but looks spiffy enough to go with Champagne.

When all is said and done, wine temperature is a matter of personal taste informed by experience, and most people's experience says that you chill whites, not reds. The differences are not radical, but a small change in temperature can mean a large change in taste. You might say wine temperature is just a matter of degree.

Best Beer? Czech It Out

The weather in August is often too hot for words—or wine. At such times even wine columnists turn to beer. My favorite for many years has been the great Pilsener Urquell from the Czech Republic. It was my first choice at a blind tasting of fifty top beers at the *Washington Post* when I wrote the wine column there, and it has been ever since. For the record, the overall favorite of the other dozen tasters was Beck's from Germany, a tad lighter, drier, and more "modern."

If you don't think the Czechs make fine beer, check it out with the Germans who import more Pilsener Urquell than any other beer. I also read somewhere, and believe it, that for a German restaurant to get four stars in a local guide it has to serve Pilsener Urquell from the cask. Even the name they use on U.S. bottles is actually German, perhaps because the Czech name is even harder to pronounce. Urquell, pronounced "irk-well," means "original source," referring to the town of Pilsen as the place where the method of making clear, light-colored beer was first discovered in the 1840s.

What is so special about this beer? First of all, it goes down more like wine than any other beer I've tasted. They don't call it the Chardonnay of beers for nothing. Like fine wines, it is made in oak vats, not stainless steel, and aged or "lagered" in oak barrels in cool, limestone cellars. Like Coors, it is made from special water—not from mountain springs, but from artesian wells. Its hops are the unanimous choice among beer experts as the best in the world. Its barley has only two rows of grains, not six, sort of like the best clones of the best wine grapes.

One thing I don't enjoy is people making too much of a fuss about describing the taste of beer as if they were tasting wine. They are not the same. Nevertheless, if you need a little of that sort of thing, the *Gourmet Guide to Beer* describes Urquell this way: "amber-golden color with a rich, expansive, fruity nose, complex on the palate, full-bodied for a pale lager, with thrilling balance and dry, woody, hoppy finish." There you have one view. I would have called it subtle and delicious.

The Czech's on Its Way

Pilsen was chartered in 1291 by the famed "good King Wenceslas," who really existed, along with one other beer-brewing town: Budweis, where the original you-know-what came from. With the fall of communism, talks began for U.S. Budweiser to drop its non-compete agreement with the Czechs so we can drink their version here also. Guinness Imports already has raised its Urquell quota for the U.S., where we drank nearly a half-million gallons of it in 1989 alone. They made forty million gallons, one-third for export, so they will be able to handle our needs.

At around a dollar a twelve-ounce bottle (it doesn't come in cans), Pilsener Urquell is one of the last affordable luxuries. The glass I just finished made me think of Prague, perhaps the most intriguing of European cities after Paris. There is nothing like a beer cellar in Prague for nostalgia.

The taste of Urquell is old-fashioned, and for my money that is good. The Czechs call it "liquid bread." Who wants beer whose self-proclaimed best quality is that it has no aftertaste? Hold the light beer and pass me a rich, full, mellow, golden, lingering . . . well, you get the idea.

Michael Jackson, the one with *two* gloves, wrote the current best seller of beer books called *The New World Guide*. He theorized that the Czechs make their beer so wine-like because they live on that invisible line across Europe between the warm, wine-drinking countries of the south and the cold, beer-drinking countries of the north. His book reproduces labels of twenty-three different recommended Czech beers, including "Dragon" and "Golden Horse." Until they arrive, my choice is Pilsener Urquell.

Nebbiolo: As "Brisk" as Champagne, as "Silky" as Madeira

During a tour of northern Italy in 1787, Thomas Jefferson tasted a new red wine and pronounced it: "very singular . . . as sweet as the silky Madeira, as astringent as Bordeaux, and as brisk as Champagne." The wine was called *nebiule*, after the grape from which it was made. Today Italians spell it *nebbiolo*, and make from it some of their best red wines, including Barolo, Gattinara, Carema, and the numerous wines from the Valtellina area in the foothills of the Alps. These wines are hearty and full of warmth and depth.

Today wines from the Nebbiolo are becoming better known in America, partly because so many French reds are priced off the market and partly because the American wine-drinking public is becoming more sophisticated and seeking new wine-drinking experiences.

Many Nebbiolos are good value, and have been popular at recent tastings in the Washington area. Unfortunately, just as the public is beginning to know and like them, wholesalers are talking about discontinuing them because they have not "caught on" well enough to sell in gross quantities. As usual, the consumer will be the loser. A wiser course would be to make available more of the moderately priced Nebbiolos and cut back on the too-expensive that customers are sensibly refusing to buy. Otherwise, local wine drinkers are about to be deprived of some very pleasant wines for no good reason.

The word *nebbiolo* comes from the Italian *nebbia*, meaning "fog." The grape was so named because at harvest time the hills on which it grows best are usually covered by heavy fog for several hours each morning. The taste of the Nebbiolo, like that of all great wine-grapes, is unique. Just as attempts to describe the taste of a Chardonnay or Cabernet Sauvignon quickly succumb to a lack of vocabulary, so it is with describing Nebbiolo. After a few general adjectives such as rich, firm, and powerful, words tend to fail. One feels like the Frenchman who wondered how he would describe the taste of a potato to someone who had never eaten one.

If there is a consensus on Nebbiolo, it is that the body is heavy like a good Rhone red, with thirteen to fifteen percent alcohol. In the mouth it is very substantial, chewy, and pungent like some Portuguese reds. Although a "dry" red wine, it also has a slight sweetness or "silkiness" like a Pinot Noir. It ages slowly and retains for several years considerable astringency, tending to draw up the mouth like young Bordeaux, but if aged enough it can be downright velvety.

The aroma of the Nebbiolo, probably its outstanding characteristic, is an unusual combination, frequently compared to a mixture of tar and violets. Those few who do not like its taste and aroma often say that it is more impressive than enjoyable.

When Jefferson described the Nebbiolo he tasted, and later imported and served at the White House, as "brisk," he meant it was slightly sparkling or bubbling. This volatile condition, in those days of stagecoach transport, caused plenty of bottle-bursting and Jeffersonian chagrin. Even today the Nebbiolo still bubbles naturally, and will foam considerably if poured out too quickly. For that reason it is generally bottled in thick, heavy, dark-brown bottles to protect it against light, heat, and jostling.

The greatest red wine of Italy, in many opinions, is the noble Barolo, a rich, long-lived Nebbiolo red made around the town of the same name a few miles west of Alba in the northern Italian region called Piedmont, or "foot-of-the-mountain." One of the most powerful wines in the world, Barolo can live and improve in bottle for several decades. It is often young at ten years, publicity saying it is ready at six years notwithstanding. I have enjoyed several fifty-year-old Barolos.

Barolo is at its best with heavy foods and rich, dark sauces. Served with such food, a well-aged Barolo can be a real surprise to those who look down their noses at Italian wines. Conversely, a too-young Barolo may draw up guests' mouths and pucker their opinions against all Italian reds.

After drinking dozens of Washington's Barolo offerings, I have the temerity to recommend a few. The best in town to my taste is the 1966

Barolo from the shipper Giacomo Borgogno. Better, but scarce, are the 1952s and 1955s from Borgogno for twice the price. The latter two are expensive but worth it to prove a point to those who doubt there are really good Italian reds. The best bargain is the 1966 Barolo from Galarey, recommended by writer-importer Frank Schoonmaker. This one unfortunately has already been "discovered" and many shops are almost at the end of their stocks. Probably the most widely distributed is the excellent and inexpensive Villadoria Barolo, the one in the burlap bag. The basic rules for Barolo-buying are to buy them as old as possible and from reliable shippers, including but not limited to Antoniolo, Bersano, Borgogno, Gaja, Galarey, Giri, Rinaldi, and Villadoria.

I have mentioned some of the more expensive Nebbiolo wines first for a reason: If you begin with an inexpensive one, chances are about fifty-fifty of getting one that is too young, and its harshness might discourage you from trying again. As with many things, a sample of excellence at the beginning often sets a good taste standard. My experience has been that there are more average Nebbiolos than good ones available, so that when you find a really good one it is wise to buy a case or two; experimenting seems riskier and less profitable with Nebbiolos than with most French reds. That may be why so many Americans drink lots of the plain, inoffensive whites of Italy like Soave and Verdicchio, and the light, simpler reds like Bardolino and Valpolicella, but never try the best, the fine old Nebbiolos.

Some twenty miles from Barolo on the other side of Alba is the town of Barbaresco, where a wine similar in taste to Barolo, but lighter, is made from the same Nebbiolo grape. Formerly Barbaresco, lighter and faster-maturing, was less expensive than Barolo, but they are now on a par. A good, typical Barbaresco is shipped by Bersano. Also good is the Borgogno Barbaresco, which can often provide a good comparison with Bersano's Barolos of the same year.

In the hierarchy of Italian Nebbiolos, only one wine seriously challenges Barolo for top honors: Gattinara. This Nebbiolo, grown in the Po Valley in Vercelli province in Piedmont, resembles other Nebbiolos but has more finesse, as hinted by its color, which is at least two shades lighter in many cases than the typical Barolo. Most good wine shops usually have at least one Gattinara on their shelves, some at pretty good prices. They are mostly in odd-shaped green bottles. A particularly good one is the 1962 Gattinara from Troglia. Another is 1964 Gattinara from Antoniolo.

From the same general region comes another Nebbiolo, Ghemme, which is light like Gattinara but a bit coarser. The 1964 Ghemme from the Ponti estates is pretty fair, especially with a little more aging. Inexpensive Nebbiolos, though they are gambles, can turn up winners. The best one I've tried recently is the 1965 Vino Nebbiolo Secco from Bersano. This is a shipper-blended wine which is pleasantly light for a Nebbiolo, while retaining its varietal character. Blends from reliable shippers labeled simply "Nebbiolo" can also be good values, their main drawback being lack of individuality. They are usually lighter and easier to drink than the more famous growths. Lovers of red Bordeaux will probably never find in any Nebbiolo a replacement for the lightness and finesse of their favorite claret. But those who like heavier reds like Chateauneuf-du-Papes and other Rhones will probably find a Nebbiolo to suit them. Others will no doubt prefer the lightest wine made from the Nebbiolo: Carema.

Often labeled Vino Carema, this fine wine is made from grapes grown on arbors or pergolas high on the cool hillsides of the Val d'Aosta region in extreme northwest Italy where French influence on winemaking is greatest. Carema wines have a certain elegance and probably will appeal more than any other Nebbiolo to French-taught palates. Generally available only in small quantities, larger supplies are rumored to be forthcoming. To date the best I have tasted by far is the Vino Carema from Luigi Ferrando.

East of Val d'Aosta in northern Italy lies ancient Lombardy, named for the "long-beards," Teutonic invaders from the north whose descendants, often blond or red-headed, now people this region. The capital of Lombardy, Milan, is a gourmet center and home of ice cream, minestrone, and gorgonzola cheese. From extreme northern Lombardy near the Swiss border, two thousand feet up the hillsides of the Alps, come the family of Nebbiolo wines known as Valtellinas.

Grown around a series of villages strung out along the valley, these wines at their best rival those of Barbaresco as good, second-rank Nebbiolos. Valtellina is now a controlled place-name under the Italian wine laws like the *appellation controlee* regions of France, but generally the words Valtellina or Valtellina Superiore are written in such tiny letters that you can read them only by placing your nose on the label. In large, readable letters will usually be given the name of the village in Valtellina where the grapes were grown, including Sassella, Grumello, Inferno, Valgella, and Fracia.

The first three villages usually produce the best wines. The lesser ones generally blend in fifteen percent or more of inferior grapes, but can still be good wines if well aged. A bargain of the Valtellinas I've tried, which is young in age but not taste, is from Pelizzati. The Fracia from Negri is young-tasting now, but the price is good and it should improve.

Generally the Valtellinas as a group seem younger and rougher than the Nebbiolos from other regions. The best value I found was a house wine blend called Riserva Della Casa from Penziatti.

To date, the Nebbiolo seems pretty much linked to Italy. California, although laced with vineyards founded by Italian families like Sebastiani, Martini, and Mondavi, has few Nebbolio vines thus far.

All things considered, Nebbiolos are difficult but rewarding wines. May your experience with it be no worse than that of Thomas Jefferson, who remarked with cautious enthusiasm after drinking his first one: "It is a pleasant wine."

Swiss Wines for Winter

As winter draws near, it reminds me of a wonderful snowy January I spent in Geneva in 1979 with some of the world's least-known fine wines. Although its vineyard area is small and eminently chilly, Switzerland makes some truly good wines. They are not seen often enough in the United States. The big problem is the Swiss franc, which has been so strong it makes most Swiss products too expensive for anyone but the Swiss to consider. Nevertheless, during cold weather, my mind always returns to those special wines with their unusual names.

Unlike German wine labels, Swiss labels are cryptic and simple, often giving no information beyond the name of the grape and the village. They are mercifully simple, not complicating your life with what date the grapes were picked, what they measured on a saccharometer or anything else, but just sit there waiting to be consumed. If you want to read up on Swiss wines, there is virtually no book accessible on the subject, the best current sources being the wine encyclopedias by Jancis Robinson and Hugh Johnson. But if you want to get inside the mind of a Swiss winemaker, which apparently is as complicated and subtle as a Swiss watch, I can recommend a truly interesting and little-known book by *New Yorker* writer John McPhee. Published in 1983 by Farrar, the book has the daunting title *La Place de La Concorde Suisse*, but don't let that stop you: the title is the only French phrase in the book, which is superb. I don't often say that about any book, as a matter of fact almost never. It originally cost only $12.95 in hardback when it appeared, and is worth pursuing in libraries and out-of-print bookstores and online.

Its theme is the Swiss character, as revealed in its Army, and its symbol, the Swiss Army knife. The main character (it is a non-fiction work but this guy can only be called a character) is Luc Massy, a reservist winemaker from the shores of Lake Geneva in the French-speaking, winemaking part of Switzerland. Massy spent time studying winemaking in California. Despite his taciturn nature, Massy tells McPhee the most useful thing he learned there: they get oak taste in their jug wines not by aging in expensive oak barrels, but by pouring cheap oak chips and dust into the wines in steel vats.

Massy makes the Swiss white wine most often seen in the United States, Chasselas, a white wine named for a grape also grown in France. The problem with the Chasselas is that it has a different name in almost every one of the Swiss cantons or provinces in which it is grown. The one to look for in the United States is Fendant, pronounced "faw-daw." For some reason it is one white wine that tastes good in cold weather— no doubt the Swiss developed it that way over several hundred years of experimenting. It is especially good with Swiss fondue, the hot, bubbly cheese dish that is its natural partner in alpine winters (or Colorado winters for that matter).

For those who must have red wines in winter, the Swiss make two good ones. Best-known is Dole, which can be found in most U.S. cities. It is a blend of the Gamay grape of Beaujolais and the Pinot Noir of Burgundy but must contain at least fifty-one percent Pinot to be labeled Dole. It is better than its French counterpart, called Passetoutgrain, and worth a try. Better still is Swiss Pinot Noir, but it is hard to find in the United States.

The best Swiss wine of all is the elusive Ermitage, a white similar to the Hermitage of France, downstream on the Rhone. Ermitage is a white wine made from the rare Roussanne grape with something of the body of a good Rhone, but with an aroma of ripe apricots and a lingering flavor unlike any other wine, probably from the granitic soils and harsh climate which produce it. The best I've tasted is from a family named d'Alleves. It is well worth a careful search.

Friends of the Oyster

That wonderful season has now begun when customers in wine stores are again asking: What wine shall I drink with oysters on the half-shell? Traditionally, oyster lovers have cited the clean, steely-dry whites of Chablis as ideal oyster wines. But considering current market prices and quality, a slight compromise in name to a lesser or Petit Chablis might be wise. Some fastidious wine-drinkers often insist that with fine oysters only a really fine white Burgundy from south of Chablis will qualify. One Bordeaux wine-grower I know, who professes to detest all Burgundies, has a secret cache in a recess of his cellar where he keeps a store of good white Burgundies to be drunk only with good and discreet friends when the oysters come in. Another Bordeaux wine-man, proprietor of a classified-growth Chateau, is more unswervingly loyal: he drinks young, light, *red* Bordeaux with his oysters.

As for white Burgundies, with Montrachets and other "name" vineyards priced almost off the market, determined Burgundy drinkers nowadays must risk their palates on lesser-known villages to find satisfaction. A good white Burgundy which is relatively reasonable for its quality is Pernand-Vergelesses. Another good Burgundy for oysters is the Bourgogne Aligoté. Made from the coarser Aligoté grape rather than the noble Chardonnay of which the finest Burgundies are made, the Aligoté (al-ee-gut-ay) is dry and acidic, a little rougher then Chardonnay, but refreshing with oysters. It is best when young. The Aligoté from Coron in Beaune is an excellent value. The Aligoté shipped from the limestone soil of the town of Chablis is always best, if it can be found.

A classic wine for oysters is made from the Muscadet grape grown around Nantes near where the Loire flows into the Atlantic. Wine historians believe that the Muscadet grape is actually a mutation of the Aligoté grape transplanted from Burgundy to the Loire several hundred years ago. In any case, the Muscadet, once considered among the lower orders of French wines, has recently become downright respectable, especially with oysters. The best has the specific geographic appellation Muscadet de Sevre et Maine, but several labeled just "Muscadet" are good enough at their current bargain basement prices.

This wine is best drunk young, in all its tartness, because with age the rather coarse grape taste becomes more pronounced. Currently there are far too many Muscadets on wine store shelves here that are past their prime. The older wines are often soft and flabby and lack the necessary youthful acidity. One company has capitalized on the current fashion for Muscadet with oysters and come up with a wine called L'Huitriere, which is French for "the oyster one." The bottle is complete with a useful phonetic spelling of the name, "loo-ee-tree-air," and a label shaped and colored like an oyster. It is somewhat softer than most Muscadets. It often does even better with fish and crustacea dishes than with oysters, for which I prefer a wine with more bite.

Those whose tastes run to Bordeaux have long preferred the dry whites of the Graves region, which up until recently were often available at very reasonable prices, but even rather average white Graves have now doubled or tripled in price. If you like a leaner, more acidic wine with your oysters, the much less expensive Entre-Deux-Mers from Bordeaux is widely available and a better value for the money. One I've liked has the trade name Entre-Deux-Huitres ("between two oysters") from Bordeaux shipper Louis Bert. Toutigeac and Bonnet from the Lurton family are even better.

Also fine as oyster companions are those steely dry, slightly green wines of the upper Loire region made from the same Sauvignon Blanc grape used in the better Bordeaux whites. These wines include Sancerre, Pouilly-Fumé, Quincy, and Reuilly. My own particular favorite of this group is Quincy from Pierre Mardon. Wine Tip: Beware of confusing *Pouilly-Fumé* of the Loire with *Pouilly-Fuisse* of Burgundy. Although the latter also is suitable with oysters, the former is lighter, tarter, and quite distinctively different. If one is expecting one wine and gets the other there may be disappointment.

Beware also of confusing wines labeled simply Pouilly-sur-Loire with the best Sauvignon-made wines, which must be labeled either Pouilly-Blanc-Fumé or Blanc-Fumé-de-Pouilly. Although all are from around the same town, the bottle lacking the Blanc-Fumé designation is made from the much coarser Chasselas grape, which makes a totally different wine, less good with oysters.

For jaded palates, a more off-beat selection might be Crépy, a slightly sparkling dry white from Savoy region in Southeast France, near the Alps, which has an unusual grape taste that is very interesting with oysters.

Since many German Rieslings from the Rhine and Moselle have a slight sweetness in the aroma that makes them less suitable with oysters, the lesser-known wines of the Franken, or Franconia region, made mostly from the Sylvaner grape, are often served with oysters in Germany. Franconian wines come in an easily recognizable *bocksbeutel*, a squatty, green, mateus-shaped bottle. The Rieslings of Alsace are often preferred with oysters by Parisians because of their pleasant tartness and bite. For a truly off-beat wine with oysters a Riesling from the Moselle Valley in Luxembourg, imported by Wildman, is sometimes pleasant and inexpensive as well.

No list of oyster-wines would be complete without that cheerful, festive wine whose generosity most matches that of the oyster: Champagne. While tastes in Champagne are disputed, my own favorites run to the fuller-bodied, richer ones such as Bollinger and Veuve Clicquot, whose vintage Bruts are fine and easy to find. Price tags make these "festive occasion" bottles for most of us. More readily accessible are the nonvintage Brut Champagnes. Pol Roger Brut, favorite wine of Winston Churchill, is very good.

My own fondest memory of oysters and Champagne is of a Christmas Eve years ago in Aubervilliers, a grim, frozen, industrial wasteland in the communist suburbs of Paris. That night we drank bootleg Champagne from unlabeled bottles stacked on the floor while laughing men in blue overalls shucked scores of dozens of oysters from huge washtubs and handed them around with the Champagne, which we drank from water glasses. Everyone sat cross-legged on the floor, Arab-style among low tables covered with dozens of loaves of bread and quartered lemons. The Health Department was no doubt away having a more hygienic celebration elsewhere. Sounds of human happiness mixed freely with the squawks of opening oyster shells and the popping of Champagne corks. All things considered, it is impossible to beat Champagne with oysters.

Bad Wine? Don't Pour It Out

How often have you grabbed an unknown bottle from a wine store shelf on the way home only to discover when you got there that you hated it?

After you get home, tired from the workday and miles from the wine store, it is usually too late to take it back. If it is really spoiled, you can always return it the next day for a refund or replacement from any reputable store. But the more common problem is that the wine is not spoiled, but just wildly not to your taste. You can't take it back. What to do?

At times like these, all high-minded notions of wine as a noble gift from above can be laid aside, and you can get down to a serious art well known since the Greeks: doctoring the wine. First, and simplest, if you have nothing else in the house and there is a tornado outside, you can simply water the wine a little and ice it down. Chilling covers defects in both the aroma and taste of wine if you get it cold enough, and if you get it really cold it will deaden your palate as well.

If mere chilling is not enough to save it, you can use what the French call the "Spanish" method: add orange juice and/or lemon juice and sugar, cinnamon, or almost any flavoring, and call it Sangria, a respectable drink invented to spare slightly souring wines. If you want to be a bit more classical, you can add a few squirts of Creme de Cassis kept around for these occasions and call the stuff Kir (pronounced "keer"). Kir is actually a pretty good aperitif, thought up apparently in Burgundy by a priestly member of the French Resistance as a way to make slightly vinegared white Burgundies palatable until the war was over. There are pre-mixed Kirs around if you want to try one to find out what it is supposed to taste like. Otherwise, my recipe has always been one or two teaspoons of Cassis to each wineglass full, depending on how far gone the wine is. When you make it from cheap bubbly, it is called a "Kir Royale," my wife's favorite.

In midwinter you can make the pleasantest cold remedy known to man: hot wine. The English call this "mulled" wine, for reasons no doubt known to them, and you can find recipes for it under that name in many cookbooks. For some reason, hot wine has always tasted better to me when made with red wine rather than white. All you really need to make it is a mug to heat or microwave it in, a little sugar, and lemon juice. You will also need a bed to fall into, since hot wine makes you sleepy very quickly on a cold winter's night. It can also break a fever by making you sweat profusely, so you may have to change the bed, but hey, it's worth it to get well.

If hot wine does not sound like your dish, you can violate a cardinal rule of good cooks and cook with any wine too bad to drink. Generally it is wise to cook only with wine good enough to drink, but if you have nothing else, and the wine is not really foul or overly sweet or vinegary, you can boil it down with a stock or some meat drippings into a fairly good sauce.

If you're bored with your usual sauces, you can do what my caterer-wife does: switch the old white-meat with white-wine rule, and cook your chicken in red wine (coq au vin) or simmer your beef roast in white wine, which makes it tangier and lighter at the same time.

If your wine is too bad to save by Kir-ing or boiling, it should probably be taken back to the store. Faced with an offer to either taste the stuff themselves or just give you your money back, most store owners will spare the palate and spoil the customer.

Cabernet Franc, A New Star?

Cabernet Sauvignon is still the favorite of Americans among U.S. red wines, despite the recent rise of Pinot Noir. Most of our best Cabernet is made "pure," not blended with other grapes. It was never like that in Bordeaux, home of Cabernet. In Bordeaux at least five grape varieties normally are used together: Cabernet Sauvignon, Cabernet Franc, Merlot, Malbec, and Petit Verdot.

In the last decade, however, California winemakers have engaged their penchant for experimenting by planting, maturing, and blending the "other" Bordeaux grapes into some of their Cabernet Sauvignons. Their desire seems less to imitate Bordeaux than just to see what would happen. There is also profit. In some years and climates, Merlot and Cabernet Franc mature better than Cabernet Sauvignon does.

The main grape to benefit from these experiments so far has been the Merlot, pronounced "mare-low". Merlot was first used only for blending, but several of our best wineries, such as Rutherford Hill and Duckhorn, began bottling Merlot years ago under its own name and won many gold medals (and made a lot of money) from it. By now, more than one hundred Napa wineries are making Merlot as a solo varietal.

No such recognition has yet come to Cabernet Franc. It is mentioned and bottled under its own name, but not yet a factor in the market, even though it makes the most revered wine in Bordeaux, Chateau Cheval Blanc. Perhaps winemakers have thought Franc sounds too much like the other Cabernet, and that one Cabernet to remember is enough. Some say it has problems with diseases and ripening unevenly.

In France, Cabernet Franc has no such problems. There the word "franc" is always a compliment, meaning honest and reliable. It is, after all, the name that a prominent group of Latin-speaking Germans chose to call themselves, and they still use it to describe people or things they particularly respect—to be "frank." These thoughts mingled vaguely in my mind the other evening as I tasted a bottle of California Cabernet Franc from that established star, Geyser Peak of Sonoma County. It was made unfiltered and unfined from fourteen acres of estate-grown grapes and aged in its own separate oak barrels by one of my favorite winemakers, Aussie native Daryl Groom. The color was very frank, being deep garnet, resembling a good St. Emilion. The aroma was soft and restrained. It was the taste that was the knockout: rich, chewy, and with a lingering aftertaste of ripe fruit that I'll never forget.

Chateau Le Pez of Bordeaux, intrigued perhaps by California's practice of not blending wine grapes, recently set aside and bottled separately some barrels of Cabernet Sauvignon, Cabernet Franc, Merlot, and Malbec. After aging, the owners blind-tasted them all several times. To their surprise, they preferred the Cabernet Franc to the Cabernet Sauvignon every time. It is even said by some, from DNA studies, that Cabernet Franc is the original Cabernet and that Cabernet Sauvignon is actually just a hybrid of white Sauvignon Blanc and red Cabernet Franc. Sauvignon in French does, after all, mean a *sauvage* or "wild" grape variety.

From the California Wine Institute I learned that Cabernet Franc grapes have been planted on about one thousand acres in Napa Valley, where Cabernet Franc is still used mainly for blending. Winemaker (and friend) Mitch Cosentino has long made really good Cabernet Francs under its own name in addition to using it in his blends. One of his early ones, labeled Crystal Valley Cellars, received a score of ninety-two out of one hundred points from the *Wine Spectator*, higher than most Bordeaux chateaux for its year.

Will there finally be a rush to make Cabernet Francs as there was to make Merlots years ago? I hope so.

A Dark Horse Grape: Petit Verdot

When U.S. consumers think of red Bordeaux, or "claret" as the English call it, we think of the Cabernet Sauvignon grape. Most famous Bordeaux like Chateaux Lafite and Mouton rely heavily on Cabernet Sauvignon. But Bordeaux are never made unblended. All have Merlot, Cabernet Franc, Malbec, or some other "minority" grape in them. Most also have a little of the ancient Petit Verdot grape, which is said to predate the Cabernet by centuries.

The small, tough, nearly black Petit Verdot (pronounced "put-tee vair-doh") is hard to grow: in the early falls of Bordeaux it often fails to ripen; in spring it often drops its blossoms at the first cold snap and never develops any grapes at all. It is always the last grape to be picked.

When it does ripen, however, Petit Verdot makes a deep, dark, aromatic, concentrated, spicy wine, long-lived on the palate and in the bottle. Now, thanks to a handful of pioneering California winemakers, we at last have our own Petit Verdot. One of the finest comes from one-hundred-year-old vines in Lake County, above Napa, planted by actress Lillie Langtry. The site is the 23,000-acre Guenoc Estate, which now belongs to Renaissance man Orville Magoon. Guenoc Estate was the last land grant made in Spanish California, and named for a saint of Celtic origin.

Winegrower Magoon, a native of Hawaii, has over three thousand head of cattle, eight hundred head of wild boar and twenty-four lakes on the estate in addition to an eighty thousand case winery. Lillie Langtry's Victorian mansion has been beautifully restored and is well worth a visit. Magoon's favorite wine grape is the Petit Verdot. Both his 1987 and 1988 were deep, concentrated wines with a uniquely pleasing aroma. Most of Magoon's Petit Verdot goes into his top red 1987 Meritage (Bordeaux blend) called Langtry Red.

Another admirer of the underdog Verdot grape is winemaker Bill Dyer, formerly of Sterling, who seems to be able to do no wrong whether he makes Chardonnay, Cabernet, or Pinot Noir. His bottlings of Petit Verdot tend to be on the ripe side, unlike what the French say about how hard it is to ripen this grape. Dyer's Sterling Petit Verdots have complexity, especially in the aroma and the aftertaste.

The California wine that reminds me most of French Petit Verdot is the Meritage blend from Napa's Cain Cellars called "Cain Five," named for the five classic Bordeaux grapes which compose it: Cabernet Sauvignon, Cabernet Franc, Merlot, Malbec and Petit Verdot. As if the name was not enough, to be really sure we get the point, this wine is released each year on May 5, the fifth day of the fifth month.

Hi Yo, Mourvèdre, Away

The hottest new wines of California are made from grapes from France's Rhone Valley. The winemakers who make them are called—what can I say—the Rhone Rangers! No longer do the grapes of Bordeaux and Burgundy totally rule the field. Cabernet and Chardonnay must yield, a little, to Syrah and Roussanne.

Even Gallo has gotten into the act. Finding Zinfandel too expensive for its blush wine, it now makes "white" Grenache, from a Rhone grape. Now a better Rhone grape, the most popular red-wine grape in California during the nineteenth century is making a comeback. Named Mourvèdre, it is pronounced a little like "more better." It also is creating controversy. *Los Angeles Times* wine writer Robert Balzer says most of it is coarse and should be done away with.

Jancis Robinson, wine critic of the *London Times*, calls it, on the contrary, "good and rich with an aroma of blackberries" and "deserving more attention." *New York Times* wine writer Frank Prial agrees, saying it's "moving up fast" in France, replacing Grenache in Chateauneuf, the best seller of the whole Rhone Valley. Who is right?

At the L.A. County Fair this mystery grape recently won a coveted gold medal in the blind tastings. If people had known what it was, it might not have gotten such a fair judgment. I tasted it and liked it. It is a rich, purple, mouth-filling wine, as Robinson says, like a Petite Sirah with a better aroma.

Why is Mourvèdre subject to such controversy? Partly because it has two names. Old-timers call it "Mataro," its nineteenth-century California name. The clones of it from France, however, are called "Mourvèdre," under which name it has thrived in the Rhone Valley for more than four hundred years. Ampelographers (experts in grape origins) say that Mataro and Mourvèdre are genetically identical. How so?

Mataro comes from the town of Mataro in northern Spain near Barcelona. Mourvèdre comes from the town of Murviedro in southern

Spain near Valencia. Neither grape is now grown in either place, which makes one wonder. Are they really the same? Even if they were once the same, have they evolved until they no longer taste the same, like different Pinot Noir clones in Burgundy?

So where do you find this new old wine? In California, Mataro is still made in Contra Costa County, near San Francisco, by Cline Cellars. The current best one is made in Yolo County, near Napa, by R.H. Phillips Winery, whose 1988 Mourvèdre won the L.A. gold medal. The best wine of Nice, France, called Bellet, is Mourvèdre as well, as is Collioure of the Basque country, on the Vermillion Coast of the Western Mediterranean. Perhaps the best wine bargain of France, Tricastin, also has substantial Mourvèdre in its blend.

In Australia, Mataro is grown all over the Barossa Valley. With three thousand acres in Australia and eight thousand in France, plus California, Mourvèdre is not about to disappear as was predicted decades ago. English wine guru Hugh Johnson hopes it will replace Grenache and says it rivals Syrah for character in southern France.

Perhaps this deep-colored, aromatic, powerful red wine will make a comeback, and we will return after all to those thrilling days of yesteryear, courtesy of the new Rhone Rangers.

My very favorite new Mourvèdre is a food-friendly rosé from Cline Cellars which goes well with summer fare and is also excellent drunk by itself as an aperitif.

"Sour Wine" Has Added Zing Since Biblical Times

Several readers have written for advice on wine vinegar. Some want to know how to select a good one; others want recipes for making their own. Because vinegar is not a true "wine" for drinking, I hesitated. But this week, thinking how the French word for vinegar—*vinaigre*—literally means "sour wine," I decided it was close enough to wine to deserve a column.

Vinegar is one of the oldest food flavorings. Not only have the Chinese used acidified rice wine for thousands of years, vinegar appeared early in the Bible. In the Book of Ruth, Boaz said, "At mealtime come thou hither and eat of the bread, and dip thy morsel in the vinegar." In thirteenth-century Paris, street sellers hawked "Vinaigres bons et beaux, vinaigres de moutarde et d'ail" (with mustard and garlic). The Romans, like contemporary Italians, had their version of a cruet of wine vinegar, called the *acetabulum*, on every table.

Vinegar is another of those remarkable, naturally fermenting substances, like wine, that can add so much to dining pleasure. Like wine, vinegar can be made by the natural action of substances already growing wild in the air. With wine, wild yeasts do the work; for vinegar a wild fungus called *mycoderma aceti* does it. Wild ones tend to be too wild, however. Better results usually come with carefully domesticated fungi, just like wine yeasts.

My wife, a caterer, has a keen interest in such matters and likes the recipe for homemade wine vinegar from the *Chez Panisse* cookbook. It features a well-aged oak wine keg for the vinegar barrel, some vinegar "mother" or starter available in good wine supply shops, and some good, unpasteurized wine vinegar to add to a full-bodied dry red or white wine in the proportion of one quart of vinegar to one gallon of wine. It takes about three months to age and mellow properly.

My favorite vinegar of all time has been from Sherry, the real thing from Jerez, Spain. It is remarkably smooth and rich. Perhaps it is because the vinegar fungus lies in a thick, white blanket on top of the liquid just like the special flor yeast lies on top of sherry wine until it imparts that special nutty taste of true sherry.

More radical are the so-called "wine-balls" found in Chinese specialty stores. You just add it to rice wine and before you can say "boo," you have a potent and pungent vinegar. Oddly, if you want a less acidic vinegar, that made from cider is normally slightly less acidic than the vinegar of wine, which usually varies from four percent acidity to over seven percent. I personally prefer rice wine for cooking fish.

Those familiar with fish-and-chip joints will know beer vinegar, the common accompaniment for this English specialty. But more exotic vinegars abound. In addition to wine, beer, and cider vinegar, specialists make it from milk (not recommended), pears (pretty good), and even grain alcohol—the most neutral, if not the most pleasant, of vinegars.

Experiments show that vinegar (acetic acid, really) has neither smell nor taste of its own. It is what you make it from that gives the aroma and flavor. That classic yuppie favorite of the 1980s, raspberry vinegar, is actually more than two hundred years old, appearing in cookbooks as early as the 1790s. Personally, one of my favorites in the lean, austere style is the clear one made from real, if cheap, Champagne grapes.

One last vinegar story. In the nineteenth century, fad dieters came up with the idea that drinking vinegar would make you lose weight. Ulcers usually do that too. Brillat-Savarin, food philosopher and stylish stomach to a generation, told how his "classically plump" girlfriend, Louise, tried the diet without his knowledge, and a month later, pale and hollow-cheeked, died in his arms. Dead wine is for flavoring, not for drinking.

Sulfites Suffice

Wine is the healthiest beverage. It has been so since the time of the Greek doctor Hippocrates, and was so acclaimed by Thomas Jefferson, America's greatest wine expert to date. Yet modern bottles now carry the designation "Contains Sulfites." Is this some dangerous recent invention? Is wine less safe than before? Less healthy? Several readers have written to ask about sulfites—what they are and if they're harmful.

The word "sulfite" obviously comes from sulfur, sometimes spelled "sulphur," and has become the shorthand term for all sulfur compounds associated with food or drink. Going along with that usage, it is safe to say that some sulfite is natural in wines, since sulfur dioxide gas is normally produced when grapes ferment from the action of yeast. All wine has thus always had some "sulfites" in it for that reason.

Nor is the addition of sulfites at all new to wines. The Greek warrior Achilles fumigated his wine in the Iliad with a burning sulfur stick before toasting Zeus with a Greek red. Throughout recorded time, winemakers have sterilized barrels with sulfur to kill bacteria and microbes, long before Pasteur discovered exactly how it worked. Modern sulfites are added at different stages of the winemaking process for several purposes. The liquid form is sprayed on both vines and fresh-picked grapes to kill bacteria and microorganisms. Sulfites in all forms are added to vats before, during, and after fermentation for the same reasons and to prevent oxidation (vinegaring) and to keep the wines from turning brown and having a chemical taste. Sulfites are also added during bottling to prevent spoilage during aging.

One expert says there are no foolproof substitutes for sulfites, and goes so far as to say that without them "there would be no modern wines." So why all the fuss? The modern concern for health has at last met ancient wine tradition. People ask: If sulfites kill bacteria, what do they do to your stomach? While crucial to wine, they are, in large doses, harmful to humans. Do we give up wine then? Of course not.

The answer, as the Greeks knew, is moderation. As with fire, sex, and most good things, when carried to excess sulfites become destructive. The level of sulfites in wines is now legally controlled at about three hundred fifty parts per million. Most wines are now much below that. Just a few years ago levels three times that were not uncommon, so progress has been made, now that we have better yeasts, cooler and faster fermentations, healthier grapes, and effective filtration. Overall, modern winemakers have reduced sulfites significantly.

General rules for detecting sulfites: if the wine smells like someone just struck a sulfur match, don't buy it again. If it makes your nose tickle or tastes pasty on the tip of your tongue, the same applies. Many times, letting a wine breathe, even a white wine, will allow the free sulfur dioxide to dissipate, or "blow off," quite a bit. But if it is strong enough to make you sneeze, or deaden your sense of smell, don't buy it again.

The most reliable way to avoid over-sulfured wines is by sticking to the best wines of the best producers, those who take pains to keep sulfites down by proper winemaking. If that is too expensive, then avoid the wines agreed to be the worst offenders: cheap whites and tank-made bubblies, especially those with an overly sweet artificial taste.

Tannin in Wine: It's How It Feels

Readers wrote last week to ask: "What are tannins in wine?" and "Is there such a thing as 'soft' tannin, since tannin is an acid?" Although referred to as "tannic acid" by some writers, tannin is not really an acid at all, but an organic compound called a phenol. If that sounds too complicated, it is the puckery stuff in strong tea that makes you want to put sugar or milk in it as the English do. Tannin in nuts also makes your mouth pucker if the nuts are too green. The same goes for wines.

Tannin is natural in wines; it's present in grape skins, grape seeds, grape stems, and even in the oak barrels where wine is made and aged. Red wines have much more tannin than white wines because they are left on the skins longer during fermentation to obtain color. The color in red wines also comes from phenols in the skins, unlike "white" wines, which get their light yellow color from the juice rather than skin pigments.

The relation between tannin and color remains with wines as they age—old red wines get lighter and browner in color as they age. Tannins separate from wines and fall to the bottom of bottles just like the coloring agents do. In this sense tannins, like colors, do not really soften, they just fall out. Lost tannin is a major reason why an old red wine often tastes better than a young one.

There is some dispute among enologists and wine chemists, but most agree that some tannins start out softer than others if they are riper. All plants have tannins, but those in persimmons are a lot more biting than those in grape skins. More surprising than tannins' part in the taste of wine is their part in a wine's smell. Young wines that smell only of fruit are said to have "mere" aroma. Later, after years of bottle-aging, the fruit smell is replaced by something more subtle and mellow, much sought-after by wine lovers: bouquet. Tannins contribute greatly to bouquet, even though scientists cannot explain precisely why, at least not so I can understand it.

In addition to flavor and bouquet, tannins also give wine stability, preventing oxygen from turning it to vinegar. For this reason, when wine is low in natural tannins, some winemakers add tannins artificially. You can taste this unpleasant addition in cheap jug wines.

Among the worst sources of added tannins are chestnuts and galls from oak trees. Better winemakers never use foreign tannins in their wines. They simply leave more grape stems in the crusher from the grapes themselves, which are rich in tannins compatible with those naturally in the wine. A bad source of natural tannin is grape seeds, which can be highly bitter. Wine containing seed juice, called "press-wine," is usually cheap; as opposed to wine from lightly crushed grapes, called "free-run," which is more expensive and worth it.

If tannin is not acid, what word do you use to distinguish between acid and tannin and how they taste? Acidic wine usually is called bitter or sour like lemons; tannic wine on the other hand is called "astringent," like green nuts or strong tea. Tannin is actually best sensed not as a taste at all, but by touch, how it *feels* in your mouth. Highly tannic wines—like young red Bordeaux—actually draw up your mouth. You can also feel tannin on the surface of your tongue when a wine is over-oaked.

Like wines themselves, ripe tannins are good in moderation, but rough and harsh if used to excess. When balanced with ripe fruit from good grapes and a light acidity, tannin in wine is refreshing, however chemical it might sound from this brief description.

You did ask me.

The Trick to
Drinking Champagne

Champagne is perhaps the world's best-known wine name. Yet the wine itself remains largely a mystery. Readers often write to express befuddlement about the different types of Champagne and irritation at how little useful information Champagne labels give you.

Champagne is also tricky in having its cork wired in. Readers write about that too, asking the best way to remove corks without getting injured or shooting expensive foam all over guests and wallpaper.

The Samurai Sommelier, or Getting the Cork Out: The most dramatic method of removing a Champagne cork is often used by Robert Gourdin, U.S. director of Moët et Chandon. With a twist of the wrist, Gourdin cuts the whole neck off the bottle with an antique saber from Napoleon's time. For a modest fee, he will do this at your next party. His method is not, however, recommended for the rest of us without practice. I can do it, but I am not for rent unless it's a really good bottle, in which case call me.

Cork Wrenches, Literal and Figurative: Less dashing is the cork wrench, or "star." These little devils can be had from most wine supply stores and mail-order houses. If your cork gives you trouble, the wrench gives you more power, or cork-torque, as it were. Whatever, it definitely works.

Never Look Down: That wise old pitcher Satchell Paige always warned us to "never look back, something might be gaining on you." Wise Champagne un-corkers never lean out over a cork after unwiring it to see how it is doing. Always watch a cork from the side, out of the line of fire, with it pointed at something unbreakable, never at a window or a spouse. They will never believe your cork shot was an accident, and the law might call it "pointing and aiming."

The Discreet Pop: Purists insist on opening Champagne as silently as possible, but most humans feel cheated unless the cork gives the party at least a little pop and fizz. My compromise is to pop it just enough to dazzle the onlookers without dampening them or losing wine. Slurping the fizz off the bottle-top is another no-no except in winning locker rooms—catch it in a glass instead.

How Much to Buy: Nervous hosts are forever asking my wife, a caterer, about how much Champagne to buy for how many people. The answer varies according to the occasion. For light toasting, at three-ounce glasses per person, you would need just fifteen regular bottles for fifty people. For a jovial Champagne cocktail party, Thomas Jefferson recommended thirty-five bottles for fifty people.

Estimator Cards: One helpful item is the "estimator card," also known as a serving chart. It tells how much Champagne people should be allowed to drink on various occasions, from aperitifs to desserts. The cards also explain bottle sizes from the smallest "split," a one-quarter bottle (or .187 milliliter for the metrically literate), to the biggest, the twenty-bottle Nebuchadnezzar. My recommendation is to stick to standard-size bottles, never serving anything larger than a magnum, or two-bottle size. Lifting those babies can put you in traction—or a truss.

Wine Words: Not So Confusing after All

This is a true story. The other night, in a fine restaurant with a great wine list, I asked a new waiter for a wine recommendation. He suggested a well-known Sauvignon Blanc. For some reason I asked him to describe the wine's taste. This is what he really said: "It is a little sheltered, but not really expedient."

Of course, his spiel was gibberish, meaningless to even the most esoteric wine snob. It was like comedians who can speak doubletalk, meaningful-sounding sounds that have no meaning but seem to have some until you listen closely. It also reminded me how much wine jargon passes right over our heads. Yet the language of wine, properly used, is of much help in telling someone what you like and dislike, and may mean the difference in enjoying a meal and blowing fifty bucks on something that doesn't go with what you're eating. There follow some of the more commonly misunderstood wine-words.

Big: As used in "big body," this term means powerful in taste, body, and alcohol.

Fat: Confusingly, this term can mean nearly the opposite of "big," since it refers to overly soft wines lacking acidity, also referred to as "round-ness" as opposed to "leanness."

Botrytised: Wines that are botrytised are seen more and more often in the U.S. They are sweet, natural dessert wines, the most typical of which is French Sauternes, on whose labels this word almost never appears. Botrytis, whose name always appears on American-made wines of this type, means literally "rotted," but with what is euphemistically called "noble" rot, a sort of gray mold which shrivels ripe grapes and concentrates their flavor. Coincidentally, honey-like botrytised wines go well with their cousins, the blue cheeses.

Crackling: Describes the sound of a wine rather than its taste. A crackling wine is one which bubbles, but less so than classic Champagne. The French term for this is *pétillant*, the German term is *spritzig*, and the Italian *spumante*. Just to be French, they also have *perlant*, which means wine with just a suggestion of bubble, and *crémant*, which is much like crackling. No wonder we Americans just call it "bubbly."

Extract: Refers not to vanilla or malt as an additive, but to those remaining mostly dissolved solids from grape pulp and heavy juice which constitute the "stuff" of wine. Wine-tasters often refer to particularly "big" or overly rich wines as having lots of "extract." California wines are known for having more of it than French wines, often too much, causing tasters to call them "overly extracted."

Extra Dry: On Champagnes for the English and American markets, this means perversely the wines that are the least dry of "dry" wines, having more sugar added before bottle fermentation. A cruel deception? Perhaps, but history has shown that the wines which sell best to newcomers are sweet wines labeled "extra dry." Politicians are not the only cynics.

Hot: Not a trendy wine, but one with too much alcohol, which gives a burning sensation as you sniff and swallow it. A "hard" wine is one with too much acid.

Foxy: Does not mean a neat wine for getting girls, nor a slinky, feminine wine. Normally it means the unique aroma (some would say the uniquely bad aroma) of the native North American Labrusca grape. This is the taste so noticeably present in Welchade and so noticeably absent from Cabernet Sauvignon.

Legs: When you swirl your wine deftly around without sloshing it on yourself, those streams that run down the inside of your glass when you stop are called "legs," for reasons better-known to Frenchmen—or Frenchwomen. Examining a rich Loire white one evening, I asked the old French winemaker what he thought of its "legs." He sighed wistfully, saying, "Ah, monsieur, those are not legs, those are thighs."

Perhaps it's like the patient told the shrink after looking at the Rorschach tests: "There's nothing weird about me, doc, you're the one with the dirty pictures." So it goes in the world of wine

It's all in the eye, or the taste buds, of the beholder.

Wine Cartoons

Wine is a healthy, cheerful subject, but can get pretty fancy in the wrong hands. Puncturing wine pretensions should be a goal of any worthy wine column. My problem is that editors often remove my attempts at humor in the interest of saving inches. One way to combat this trend is to devote an entire column to wine humor.

The most famous wine cartoon of all time was by James Thurber in the *New Yorker* way back in 1937. It showed an urbane-looking host rising to describe what was in his glass as "a naive domestic Burgundy," hoping his guests would be "amused by its pretension." Ever since, *New Yorker* cartoonists have lampooned wine snobbery and ignorance. A recent favorite of mine was of a fat Roman host, lounging on his sofa watching his drunken guests frolicking wildly as he said, "You may serve the jug wine now."

Another cartoon has one taster asking the others: "I'm getting a lot of negativity in this wine—could it be French?"

There was also the Fred Sanford show where Fred offered his neighbor Grady his preferred meal: cream of leftover meatloaf with "muscatipple," Muscatel mixed with Ripple. Hagar the Horrible always tries to take his mind off food—by drinking more wine. His wife Helga once said Hagar's idea of a wine-tasting was inviting people over to watch him taste wine.

Perhaps my favorite *New Yorker* wine cartoon of all was not overtly about wine at all. Two squirrels are sitting on a branch, each tasting an acorn. One, in classic winespeak, remarks, "Nutty, yet with a hint of oak." A classic *New Yorker* yuppie once offered to "introduce you guys to a really *gifted* young Zinfandel."

The most classic wine cartoons recently have been in *Shoe*, which features "Wining with the Perfesser," an owlish barfly who writes a wine column. He delivers himself of insights like "the key to all great wine commentary is lots of wine." When he goes to his favorite bar in the woods, he often says "Unscrew me a jug of your finest." The bartender tells him they don't have a "House" wine, but do have "Mobile Home Red." In one restaurant he worries because the wine steward has pliers instead of a corkscrew.

Once, when a waiter asked what he liked about a wine, the perfesser waxed at great length on its complexities. The waiter reminded him, "It wasn't an essay question." A typical *Shoe* wine review commended a Chablis for its "Swaggering tempo, refreshingly weaselish heft, right-handed nose, and gravelly-throated finish." A wine he didn't like was described as "a swarthy-bodied red, but its runny nose and the stubble on its legs surprised me."

Winemakers themselves get as sick of winespeak as anyone. Prime example is Randall Grahm, owner of Bonny Doon Vineyards of California's Santa Cruz Mountains. A philosophy major from Beverly Hills addicted to puns, Grahm gave one of his newsletters the Kantian title "A Critique of Pure Riesling." It was allegedly Grahm who first founded the "Rhone Rangers," the California winemakers who successfully use grapes from France's Rhone Valley rather than the usual Bordeaux and Burgundy. He claimed it was "Rhonely" at the top and wrote a regular column titled Miss Rhonely Hearts. If you can get him (or his staff) to send you his monthly newsletter, it is well worth it just for the wine puns. It reminds me of one of my favorite Napa Valley restaurants, Mustards Grill, where the parking place by the front door is reserved for the person who made the best wine pun of the month.

But it was his labels that drew the most attention to Grahm. Punning on the French words *grand cru* or "great growth," he photographed his staff dressed up as pirates on a raft, put it on a label, and called the wine "Grahm Crew." Since the French call flying saucers "flying cigars," and the town of Chateauneuf once passed a laughable law forbidding them from landing in its vineyards, Grahm calls his Chateauneuf-like red blend Cigare Volant (flying). Another, heftier red modeled on the Rhone's famed Vieux Telegraphe is called Old Telegram. Its label, naturally; is an old telegram.

His young Cigare wine he threatens to name Tiperillo, noting one year's wine was "so ephemeral we haven't produced it yet." The label noted on the back that perhaps the French were not as crazy as we thought by passing a law forbidding flying saucers from landing in Chateauneuf. "Not a single one has landed yet."

Finding the World's Worst Wine

Wine writers spend most of their time looking for good wines, especially good bargain wines. Like sportswriters, we seek out superlative performances, or at least superlative efforts. But there is another side to all this. Just as pro football used to have its Bottom Ten each week in *USA Today*, the worst teams of the week, so does the World of Wine. We just don't talk about it. After all, the last time I saw a veiled reference to it in print was in an old *New Yorker* cartoon, in which two bums were leaning up against the wall in an alley. One handed the other a screw-top bottle in a brown bag, and remarked, "Not a great wine, but a good wine."

So how to judge the worst wine of the vintage? By the time-honored vinous tradition, the blind tasting. My initial plan was to invite some friends and make it an occasion, but people kept declining. My wife and daughters refused even to watch. Undaunted, I proceeded alone. After intending to taste ten wines, a good round number, my courage failed me when I really thought about it, and I bought only seven. The whole lot came in at under twenty-five dollars.

By wine-tasting tradition, whites precede reds, so I began with the famed Thunderbird. I had never noticed before whether Thunderbird was a red or a white. Being an avid label collector, I first studied the handsome Native American–looking bird and its noble motto "The American Classic." In appearance Thunderbird looks rather good, the color of a slightly overripe Chablis. Even the aroma of Thunderbird, since it was no doubt too young to have a bouquet, was not all that bad. The taste, however, was another story, and the aftertaste was a vivid reminder of how Thunderbird got its name. It went down like feathered thunder soaked in generic cough syrup.

I had to boil the glass later to get the lingering aroma out.

To cleanse my palate, I picked up what I had hoped would be the least offensive wine of the lot, something called Yosemite Road Jug, a blush wine cooler in a sort of a miniature Snuffy Smith swilling bottle. Like most coolers, it tasted like it was made from Kool-aid mix, but it was drinkable and better than many coolers. Next came "Easy Nights" from TJ Swann. I went all the way with TJ, and to my surprise it tasted very similar to the cooler; both resembled carbonated peach soda, but not as good. All those debutantes and polo players who drink coolers and look down on TJ Swann are being fooled. They are drinking essentially the same stuff.

Then came a kind of Murderer's Row of bad wines: Mad Dog 20-20, Wild Irish Rose, Red Rooster, and Night Train Limited. The Rose weighed in at twenty percent alcohol, just like vintage Port, but the resemblance stopped there. The wine was thick and sort of oozed down the side of the glass. The aroma was pure Eau de New York subway. I got the stuff in my mouth, but could not bring myself to swallow it.

But there was worse to come. The very idea of tasting Mad Dog, the *numero uno* of bad-wine jokes, had almost caused me to cancel the whole idea. But the motto on the old locker room door urged me on: "When the going gets tough, the tough get going." Tightening my palate, I strapped on the Mad Dog, whose label bills itself "Wine of the Century." Its aroma? Essence of coal oil. Taste this? I did, and it resembled what I always thought spoiled broccoli juice must be like. A potential captain of the all-loser team.

Just two more to go. Red Rooster, which one-upped Mad Dog as "Wine of the Twenty-*First* Century," was so thick it looked like it would turn to gelatin if chilled too much. The aroma was suspiciously like moonshine and not half bad. The taste of this "red grape wine" was another matter. I could just barely stand having it in my mouth, but again, I drew the line at swallowing it. After all, it's professional to spit.

Last came the Night Train Express Limited—in more ways than one. Its aroma was like an open manhole in Cairo, and as it lay there in the glass it looked like it had been out in the weather too long. But it was the taste that won it for Night Train. Truly terrible. Its thundering wheels ran over my helpless palate like a speeding freight. Without doubt that is the most unforgettably awful wine I ever tasted.

Mad Dog, eat your heart out. That moaning sound you hear is not only my palate writhing in pain. It is the sound of the Night Train's whistle as it pulls out, leaving you in second place.

The Guinness Book
of Wine Records

Some people take wine too seriously. One who does not is writer Robert Joseph, editor of the Guinness book of frivolous wine records. Of course his book is not entitled "frivolous." If it were, no one would buy it. Its official name is *The Wine Lists*, and it gives wine facts found nowhere else.

For example, the longest Champagne cork-shot of all time was 105 feet 9 inches, accomplished at Reno, Nevada on July 4, 1981. Champagne connoisseurs might consider such an event undignified for an elegant wine like Champagne, but at least Guinness has standards: challenges to the record will be considered only if the bottle is unheated and held exactly four feet above the ground. The angle of the bottle and how much you shake it beforehand are apparently optional.

Cork-popping seems only natural in Reno, where there are so many divorces to celebrate, but even in more staid Massachusetts a similar record was recently established when a local resident caught a grape in his mouth after it was thrown 270 feet 4 inches, nearly the length of a football field. The same man, in balmier Fort Lauderdale, spared his teeth and caught a grape in his hand after it had been dropped 321 feet from the top of a 31-story building.

To justify its title, the Guinness book does have lots of lists, some of them quite useful. One list tells which wines make the best investments. Another gives the "second" or cheaper bottlings of ninety-eight of the best Bordeaux chateaux. Less useful but equally interesting is a list of folk-wine health aids, including a Russian cure for bad breath: one hundred-proof vodka mixed with myrrh and red wine. Discretion is advised, since it sounds as if it could kill more than just bad breath.

Another list tells the favorite wines of famous people, allowing that Pitt liked Port, Bismarck liked Pottelsdorf, and Napoleon preferred Moët

Champagne when he could find it. He also liked Chambertin from Burgundy, but usually added water to it. Queen Victoria, being of a different mindset, never watered her wines, perhaps not wanting to look like an American tourist. But she did add whiskey to liven up her lesser clarets. Shocking.

To tell the truth, the reason I bought the book in the first place was because of a lurid statement in gold letters on the cover that promised to tell which wine was Queen Victoria's favorite aphrodisiac. After pretending to walk by without interest, I went back to the shelf and glanced through the book, hoping the aphrodisiac part could be readily located in large type in the table of contents or index. It was not, and after pawing it for a while without success, I finally had to buy the book to satisfy my curiosity.

Even after taking the book home, it was hours before I found the name of the wine, which was deviously located on page 121 under the misleading heading "Personality Choices." If it is of interest to anyone, the wine was a white Somlo from Hungary, which I do not recall ever seeing in the United States. Might a Tokay be close enough?

My disappointment over the aphrodisiac was partly assuaged by discovery of a list of the silliest and most inappropriate wine names, which included Migraine from Chablis, a Bordeaux called Chateau Le Crock, one called La Clape, the red Champagne named Bouzy (pronounced "boozy"), and concluding with the unforgettable Le Pie (pronounced "pee") from Beaujolais.

France, naturally, had the most absurd wine names. A close runner-up was the former Yugoslavia, having not only Grk and Sipon, but Ptuj, which sounds like what Garfield might say if someone served him a wine cooler with his lasagna.

Wine Lists covers the wines of every country from Albania to Zimbabwe (it recommends neither of those) in 175 pages of squinty-small print. Although written in England, it has a lot of good information on American wines and wineries. The author's origins do show through now and then, as when he asserts that Pennsylvania is a "neighboring" state to Indiana, which will no doubt come as a surprise to people in both states.

Some of the lists are egregiously unique, particularly the editor's alleged favorite list of German wines, which he punningly entitles The Brahms Wine Liszt. The publisher, who should be ashamed, is Guinness Superlatives.

The Astrology of Wine: Your House or Mine?

Do you believe in astrology? I never have, but in an effort to leave no stone unturned in helping people select wines, I have recently consulted that New Age art for advice on matching wines with people. Before trying it on strangers, however, I tried it on my wife—a Leo. For those conversant with such things, Leo is a "fire" sign and rules the fifth house—that of pleasure and the arts. Its favorite meats are said to be lamb and caviar. Is caviar considered a meat to anyone but vegetarians?

By way of matching, the best wines with lamb are red Bordeaux and the best with caviar are Champagnes. Is it a coincidence that those are among my wife's favorite wines and foods?

Testing the theory further, I checked out my own horoscope, which is somewhat more complicated, being Pisces the Fish on the "cusp" or influential rim of Aries the Ram. This odd mix of opposites of a water sign like Pisces and a fire sign like Aries sounds schizophrenic, but their tastes could complement each other—how should I know? Fortunately, Pisces does not limit itself to drinking water alone. The influence of the planet Neptune allegedly pushes it to enjoy all liquids, including wines, especially exotic and unusual ones like old Sauternes or Bonny Doon of Santa Cruz.

Aries people, by contrast, like to spend money and impress others. They're often label buyers, and again prefer Champagne. So far as I can tell, my wife and I would be forever happy together drinking expensive Champagnes. But then, who wouldn't?

I'm not making all this up. Much of it comes from a recently published book called *A Taste Of Astrology* by Lucy Ash. The book is devoted mainly to food, but each of the twelve chapters, corresponding to the twelve houses, has suggestions for wines to go with its astrological recipes.

These "Wines of the Zodiac," as it were, have such a flattering tone toward all signs that whichever one you read you would like to believe is about you. Taurus, for example, is earthy and would probably like a good Rhone red or perhaps a Petite Sirah from California. Scorpio, the sign of my second daughter, is said to be a gourmet and perfectionist who would like really fine Burgundy. The air sign Gemini, that of my first daughter, enjoys constant motion, change and excitement, especially through talking. Why does this stuff sound so believable? Such characters are said by Lucy Ash to prefer light meals with wines to match, so for Geminis I suggest a nice, inexpensive Muscadet from the Loire with fresh trout.

What Goes with Green Cheese?

It was only when I reached the chapter on Cancer, house of the subconscious, that my doubts about all this began to crystallize. Cancer, a moon sign, is said to like wine because it likes all liquids due to lunar influence. Okay so far, but would you believe they are supposed to like white wines because white is the color of the moon? White wines are actually yellow, but no matter. And do Cancers really like reds, whites, and rosés equally "because there are three phases of the moon?"

Come on.

After a diligent effort to believe in astrology as a new source for wine knowledge, careful study has convinced me that it is probably a bunch of hooey. Nevertheless, if you have trouble choosing the right wine, you can always let the stars decide and relieve the pressure. Different wines for different signs? Why not?

Thoroughbred Wines

Some people complain that wine is harder to understand because wine-folk use such strange words to describe it. Instead of smell, they talk about a wine's "nose," and rather than being from good grapes they say it has "breeding." But this habit is not confined to wine.

Doctors and used-car salesmen use jargon, too, but horse people are probably the worst of all. My wife, who is severely afflicted, thinks shoveling horse manure ("pucky" as she and President Bush call it) is a very refined activity if you call it "mucking stalls." Being bucked off on your head, as former President Reagan was, leading to brain surgery, is called "taking a little tumble."

Wine jargon pales beside this make-believe world of thoroughbred words.

Ruminating, as it were, on this subject, I noticed a remarkable number of similarities between wine jargon and horse jargon. Both can have breeding and heart or be flighty. Of course the same words can also mean very different things in the two worlds. The "legs" of a wine reveal its relative strength or body. Pigs yield tasty ham hocks, but Hock in wine means something from the Rhine Valley and has nothing to do with legs.

When a horse wins by a nose, it means that part of its anatomy, and that part alone, crossed the finish line first. When a wine wins a tasting by a nose, it means its aroma came out in first place. "Finish" is similar. Horses finish well near the finish line; wines do likewise. Wines are said to have a long finish if they linger tastefully all the way down the back stretch, if you will, hanging around with its aftertaste in your mouth in a sort of winner's circle.

Polo, once the horse-sport of kings, and now the plaything of rich land-developers and Mercedes salesmen, was once said to be best accompanied by a British concoction called Pimm's Cup.

At a recent polo match I watched, the horsemanship was excellent, chukker in and chukker out. The drink, however, was not so thorough-bred. A bucket of iced Champagne lay mostly unopened while the men drank Gatorade and the women drank wine coolers. More encouraging was a recent thoroughbred yearling auction at Lexington, Kentucky that my family and I attended, where the fine horse flesh was appreciated at a free and lavish buffet lunch featuring a sort of vinous trifecta: Robert Mondavi red, white, and rosé. This event, which I recommend to all who enjoy horses at any level, gives a whole new level of meaning to the term "thoroughbred." We want to go back—often.

Always a critical factor in breed, in both horses and wines, is strength-ening good "old" blood with an infusion of the most promising new stock. The newest serious wine hybrid of this sort is Opus One, the California Cabernet blend made jointly by the Mondavis of California and the Rothschilds of Bordeaux Chateau Mouton. The 1985 Opus One, which I've now tasted several times with different foods, has definitely hit its stride, and is a classic example of successful cross-breeding of two thoroughbred lines.

Of course you can mix these metaphors and stretch them till they snap. A horse turning the corner is good; a wine doing the same is going to vin-egar. Old wines cannot be put out to pasture like horses; salad dressing, maybe, but more likely down the sink. But there are several horse terms which might please some of the more esoteric wine-writers. Unbalanced or "unshapely" wines with no backbone of acid could be called "spav-ined." Broken-down old bottles could be called "roach-backed" or even "goose-rumped."

They should have never given me my head and let me feel my oats like this. Think I'd better stretch out and cool down with a well-bred Bur-gundy. Something like a good Bonne-Mares sounds like a good bet.

Witch Wines for Halloween

The ancient and honorable harvest festival of Halloween began over two thousand years ago among the Celts in Ireland, England, and western France. Before they became Christianized, the Celts worshipped nature deities, including a lord of death named Samhain, whose day to rule was October 31. On that day, the Celts believed that the souls of the dead returned to visit their homes, and great bonfires were lit to welcome them. What wine should one drink to honor such an occasion? My choice would be an extra-fine bubbly from Veuve Clicquot, one of France's oldest Champagne houses, or perhaps an extra-fine bubbly from Domaine Cameros, a beautiful winery in California's misty Cameros country, owned by France's Taittinger Champagne house. This American bottling has the finesse of French Champagne, for half the price, something to celebrate in itself.

France has its Celts too, mainly in Brittany. Centuries ago thousands of them immigrated to Canada, then on to Louisiana where they're now known as "Cajuns." Although few still recall the historical reasons, Cajuns celebrate Halloween with special verve. In Brittany they celebrate it with local bagpipes, seafood, and Muscadet. Some Americans now take a dim view of Halloween, seeing not harmless trick-or-treaters but an emphasis on witches, goblins, and other scary creatures like the old Saturday Night Church Lady's "Say-tun!"

Taking all this lightly, I wonder what Satan's favorite wine might be? Perhaps an Egri Bikaver, "Bull's Blood" from mysterious Hungary, suggesting Transylvanian accents and stormy nights. Or maybe a Black Malbec wine from France's southwestern Cahors region.

For contrast you could draw on our contemporary American vision of Halloween and match a black wine with an orange one, which color apparently got popular from our custom of using pumpkins for jack-o'-lanterns. The orange Muscat grape makes some excellent dessert wines, especially one called Quady Essensia from California. Come to think of it, those names would sound strange on a dark night.

The original jack-o'-lantern was made from a carved-out potato and held a flame to symbolize the soul of Irish Jack, a man so miserly and untruthful he couldn't get into either Heaven or Hell, and his trapped, burning soul allegedly wandered the earth on Halloween until Judgment Day. A good honest wine would be wasted on such a creature. He probably drank demon rum.

One Halloween tradition, bobbing for apples, is said to come from the Roman goddess Pomona, who presided over apples. While the Romans held England, apparently their apple festival became enmeshed with the Celts' Vigil of Samhain. In that event, maybe we should drink cider for Halloween, recalling that Thomas Jefferson said "cider is more like good wine than any other beverage."

Halloween comes at the right time, when leaves and grasses are turning brown and dying for winter. As the early Catholic Church recognized, it is a fitting time to honor the dead with All Souls' Day. On such occasions, rather than mourning the passing of summer, it is better to accept the coming of winter by breaking out the season's first cold-weather wines, laying aside the Chardonnays of summer.

A good choice would be vintage Port, a rich, hearty drink which can be very warming on a cold Halloween. Old vintage Port bottles even have cobwebby sediment ringing the inside of the bottle. To avoid getting the murky-looking stuff in your glass, stand the bottle up for two or three days before Halloween to let it settle to the bottom, and then pour it carefully. Otherwise, you'll have to pour it quickly or strain it through a coffee filter.

Other outstanding bottles for Halloween, both symbolically and otherwise, are the Zinfandels and dark Petite Sirahs of Sonoma County's Hop Kiln winery. Back in the 1970s, when I first visited Hop Kiln one October evening, I found an eerie scene of gnarled trees overhanging dark ponds beside giant, odd-shaped barns once used for drying beer hops. But I loved their powerful, inky-dark Zinfandels and Petite Sirahs. Their one hundred-year-old vines finally became too old to produce enough wine, so the owners sadly ripped them up. To honor the season, however, they made one last batch, which is widely distributed, and I have enjoyed it several times. Each time I tell myself it would be even better in ten years, but can never resist uncorking it. Hop Kiln Petite Sirahs are still black as a windy Halloween night, powerful as a Druid's spell, and downright primeval in their tendency to enchant wine-drinkers. If you miss them this Halloween, they will be back next year.

Red Wine with Barbeque, White with Snake

Do white wines ever go with red meats? Several people have said so lately, apparently believing that anything goes in the "me" decade of the 1980s. Of course such matches are not illegal, but one wonders if they really taste good together. Besides, the '80s are nearly over. Recently, I tried a couple to check. For contrast, I even tried some red wines with white meats.

To give the whites a fair chance, I picked a really good one, a 1987 Cuvaison Chardonnay from California's Napa Valley, a food wine for fine occasions without being extravagant. Until recently Cuvaison Chardonnay was made in the big blockbuster style of new California. Then three years ago a Swiss gentleman, described as "immensely wealthy with deep pockets down to his kneecaps," purchased it. New president Manfred Esser, hired from a Chicago marketing concern he called "a sort of Tupperware of wine," began to turn Cuvaison into more of a European wine. It sounded perfect for our experiment.

To tune up, we tasted the Chardonnay in San Francisco with a beautiful dish of sea scallops wrapped in dark wild boar bacon. Superb. But the bacon did not really qualify as "red" meat, pork being sort of white, technically. The next course was the first real test: lamb medallions with morel mushrooms. The waiters, seeing what I was doing, kept trying to snatch away my glass of Chardonnay to make me drink a red Cabernet with it, but I finally hid it under a napkin. The Chardonnay was still good, but it did not match the lamb well at all, which was much better with a fine, soft Cuvaison Cabernet, as the waiters apparently knew.

Two weeks later, in Phoenix, I again ordered the Cuvaison Chardonnay, trying it first with smoked salmon (pink), a perfect match, then with raw tartar steak of beef (dark pink), a disappointing match. With that dish a Pinot Noir red was much better.

The next course, a beautiful white stingray in drawn butter, set off the Chardonnay in a style to which it needs to become accustomed, as a client once said in one of my divorce cases. I was just about convinced that white wine never went with red meats, having tried several good whites with steaks over the years, and having never been satisfied. Perhaps a compromise, a meat that is technically red, but looks white: veal. The Cuvaison was again too delicate; its finesse faded into ordinariness where it had been just great before. With veal, apparently only the lighter reds will do.

Another night in Phoenix, at a sort of touristy-cowboy joint where there seemed to be little to lose, I tried a good but cheaper Chardonnay, Fetzer California, with some heavy, spicy barbecued beef ribs. It could not hold a candle to Fetzer's Cabernet with the same dish. A good Belvedere Discovery Chardonnay suffered the same fate.

My daughters, enjoying novelty, suggested I really go for it; try a Chardonnay with rattlesnake, alleged locally to taste "just like chicken." In my experience, everything gross is supposed to taste like chicken, and usually does because they deep-fry it in so much batter that you can't taste it anyway. The result? In all honesty, Chardonnay is not half bad with snake. We even peeled off the batter and tasted the snake "au naturel," noting in the process that rattler is a sort of white meat and fairly fine like squid. I have tasted much worse in much better surroundings.

My conclusions? Stick to traditional red/red and white/white pairings of wine and meat. Adapted to modern conditions, that means red with barbecue, white with snake. Besides, it's easier to remember that way.

Wine Goes with Everything, Even Food That's "Bad For You"

A few years ago, I did a piece on the world's worst wines. Modeled on the satirical *USA Today* football column called *The Bottom Ten*, the column featured a brown-bag, screw top blind-tasting. As I recall, Mad Dog 20-20 was narrowly defeated as the world's worst wine by something menacingly called Night Train, which ran over my palate like a speeding freight.

I do not propose to repeat the experience. But there is a funny new book on the market that made me think of a sort of sequel. Authors Chris Maynard and Bill Scheller call their creation *The Bad for You Cookbook*, and it features lots of lard, deep-frying, heavy sauces, and popcorn dripping with butter. *Bad for You*, published by Villard in paperback, is a more serious book than it looks. Much of it lampoons Puritanism, vegetarianism, small portions, and obscurantism in nouvelle U.S. food generally. These guys are funny and irreverent, but also serious eaters, even gourmets, of substantial food.

The way that Chris and Bill answer what they call the Low Fat Police is: "If it can be poached, it can be deep-fried." They also suggest carrying around a stick of butter to scare the Fat Police, sort of like a cross for vampires. Their five main food groups are potatoes, pasta, rice, garlic, and olive oil. They also suggest, for those (like me) tired of skinless chicken breasts, that "a chicken looks a lot like a small, two-legged, winged, and feathered pig, and should be cooked the same way," in a heavy mustard-cream sauce.

Another old favorite I would never give up in any case is fettuccine alfredo in heavy cream. Unless too peppered, it is one of the best dishes to set off fine Italian reds and more robust whites. Our boys bury Caesar salad in fried oysters, which sounds like a natural for a Muscadet from the Loire. Also suited to fine white wine is deep-fried squid, which can prevent you from getting out of your chair. While stranded, I recommend with it a Rueda white from Spain. Neither killer eggnogs nor Old South lard cakes require wine, but shirred eggs (three eggs with three tablespoons of heavy cream) go exceedingly well with Champagne for breakfast.

Bearnaise sauce is one of the classier "bad for you" delights, one where you use several egg yolks and throw away the whites instead of the other way around. The wine for it depends on what meat you pour it over. I prefer the ever-popular white with white, red with red. All else being equal, a well-aged Bordeaux is always both correct and good. If you seek all-purpose wines to match with unhealthy fried foods, among reds it is hard to beat those old "monster" Zinfandels that are inky, black, and chewy and have over fifteen percent alcohol.

For whites, it is hard to beat fourteen percent Chardonnays blasted with oak until they smell like a vanilla bean farm. If also put through malolactic fermentation until they smell like peaches and slide down like mineral oil, they should fill the bill. Magnums of young Champagne, liver-quivering Portuguese *vinhos verdes* that give you mouth ulcers, and too-young Ports laced with burning brandy that makes your nose purple, are all good for unhealthy treats. To top them off, find some old leaded crystal decanters and wine goblets to complete the bad health grand slam.

This Could Be the End
and I Can't Decide on a Wine

I never thought I would be around for The Big One, let alone have to choose a wine to go with it. Yet one February, while more or less minding my own business, a 5.5 earthquake hit Los Angeles while I was visiting. We watched as boulders tumbled down suburban mountains.

As we waited to see if it was over or just a "pre-shock" for a bigger quake to come, a woman asked me one question I'd never have thought of: "What wine is appropriate to drink during an earthquake?" A frivolous question for a serious moment, but it was California. And when more tremors came on I began to think about it, hesitantly at first, then in more detail. At least it took my mind off several more earth wobbles. Champagne, for example, would never do. First, there was nothing to celebrate yet, and the tremors would cause the bubbly to foam up and be wasted, or even blow its cork prematurely.

Stepping into a solid-looking wine shop in Beverly Hills, I spied an extra-solid bottle of old Portuguese red. It had a neat label made of real cork and was thick, black, flat-bottomed, and probably exceeded the tensile strengths of most building codes. But old Portuguese reds, being unfiltered, would never do in a real earthquake: their sediment would probably be shaken up by anything over a 5.0 on the Richter scale.

This thing was starting to get serious. The Big One might be here at any moment and I had not yet chosen anything appropriate to go with it. Stalling, I selected a couple of good cheeses first, thinking that once I had them, the perfect wine to accompany them would probably pop right into my head without prompting. But no, I still couldn't think of anything.

What about a white Burgundy, perhaps the best of all white wines? No? This experience was making me realize which wines really counted for me. If I was a goner, and this was indeed my last bottle, I didn't want it to be white. Funny, I'd never thought of that before. But, as the French say, "A wine's first duty is to be red." I was starting to believe them.

My eye at last fell upon a row of fine red Burgundies from the late '70s and early '80s. No time to consult Robert Parker's numerical scales as to which producers were best in which years. Should I buy something really expensive, since you can't take it with you? But what if I survived? My wife would remind me of my New Year's pledge to spend less on wine. And I could never afford to tell her the truth—that I thought the world was ending and blew it all on one last great bottle without her.

On this sobering thought, I chose a modest but sound red Burgundy from the venerable Vienot family of Nuits Saint Georges. It was from a reputedly weak vintage, 1981, but I was getting more optimistic. Maybe 5.5 was as high as this quake would go. Besides, it had no sediment. Out in the open, away from anything that might fall on me, I drank three glasses. It was light but flavorful, perfect with a hunk of Tomme cheese from the Pyrenees. Swallowing good Burgundy before the world can swallow you seemed like a fine idea. I looked for the lady who had first asked me to select an earthquake wine, but she had apparently grown impatient with my indecision and left.

I never got to tell her how well red Burgundy suited the occasion.

Acknowledgments

To thank all those who helped me in the writing of a lifetime of columns on wine, food, and travel is impossible, but here is a short list. First I thank my parents, who graciously sent me on a junior year in Paris at the Sorbonne, which they could not afford, which I then extended (and paid for) to a second glorious year of constant wine drinking.

Next came Fred Weck and the gang at the Original Wine and Cheese Shop in Washington where I spent three great years of evenings and weekends (stolen from Georgetown Law School) working as a clerk/consultant tasting and selling hundreds of wines I could never have otherwise afforded.

Then came William Rice, editor of the food section of the *Washington Post*, who reluctantly agreed to hire me as its regular wine columnist mainly because I was a former student of his favorite writer, Eudora Welty.

After three happy years with the *Post*, my friend Charles Overby took me on as the Sunday wine columnist for the Jackson, Mississippi, *Clarion-Ledger*, where he won the Pulitzer Prize for journalism (no thanks to me). Then Charles promoted me to nationally syndicated wine columnist for Gannett News Service, of which he became president, circulating my columns weekly to over a hundred daily Gannett newspapers for the next fifteen years.

When my father heard about that gig, he quickly asked me, "Did he speak to you the two sweetest words in the English language?" I asked him, "What words?" His reply: "Expense Account!" Charles did indeed speak those very words and came through on them handsomely. With the Gannett column came hundreds of letters from readers across the U.S., asking useful questions and challenging some of my more dubious opinions about wine.

Soon I was asked by Chief Judges Nathan Chroman and Dr. Robert Small to be a judge at the biggest and best international wine-judging competition, then called the L.A. County Fair, which evolved into the L.A. International Wine, Olive Oil and Wine Label Competition. Then David Lake of the San Diego Competition and Parks Redwine of the Atlanta Wine Summit followed suit. Soon I was tasting and judging massive amounts of wonderful wine at Dan Berger's Riverside Competition, Rebecca Murphy's Dallas Morning News Competition, Jerry Mead's New World, and Don Galleano's Pacific Rim, not to mention judging at Monterey, San Francisco, and in Oregon, Washington, and Torgiano, Italy.

With the columns also came invitations to junkets across the U.S. from Santa Barbara and Temecula to the Oregon Pinot Noir Festival plus trips to France, Italy, Germany, Spain and several other wine countries, the last being the newly freed Republics of Georgia and Moldova and their exotic, little-known wines.

One particularly fun invitation was from Veuve Clicquot Champagne President Mireille Guiliano (now better known as the author of the bestseller *Why French Women Don't Get Fat*) to judge for several years Cliquot's Wine Book of the Year contest. With that assignment came scores of free books on wine and food giving me a world-class library of books to consult for column subjects and fact-checking.

I am also deeply indebted once again to Charles Overby for making me a fellow in journalism for two years at the Overby Center at Ole Miss when I first retired as a prosecutor.

Other very important inputs for this book came from two of my closest friends who were invaluable in reviewing and correcting my manuscript: Dr. Robert Small, dean of the Hotel and Restaurant School at the University of California at Pomona, who with his wife Michelle is the author of the magisterial *Understanding and Appreciating Wine*; and Peter M. F. Sichel, not only author of the classic *Wines of Germany* and manager of a leading Bordeaux chateau, but the former CIA station chief in both Berlin and Hong Kong and a hero of many hazardous missions behind enemy lines in France and North Africa during World War II. His memoir, *Gentleman Spy*, should be out next year.

The publication of the book itself was ably supervised by University Press editor in chief Craig Gill, director Leila Salisbury, marketing manager Steve Yates, publicist Clint Kimberling, art director and designer John Langston, and completed by the finesse of production editor Shane

Gong Stewart. My thanks to all those whom space prevents me from calling out by name, but you know who you are and have my total gratitude.

Oxford, Mississippi
May 1, 2014

Source Notes

There are three sources for all these essays: columns in the *Washington Post* from 1972–1974, noted as WP; the Jackson *Clarion-Ledger* from 1982–1984; noted as C-L; and the Gannett News Service national syndication to one hundred daily papers from 1985–1995, noted as GNS.

Chapter One: People Who Love Good Wine

p.19   GNS, October 22, 1989.

p.21   GNS, March 3, 1985; February 18, 1990.

p.24   GNS, October 3, 1990.

p.27   GNS, July 8, 1990.

p.29   GNS, January 17, 1993.

p.31   GNS, April 22, 1984; May 6, 1984.

p.36   GNS, March 12, 1989; October 22, 1989.

p.39   GNS, January 13, 1985.

p.41   GNS, January 20, 1985.

p.43   GNS, January 27, 1985.

p.46   GNS, November 18, 1990.

p.48   GNS, May 5, 1991.

p.50   GNS July 5, 1987.

p.53   GNS, June 2, 1985.

p.56   GNS, November 24, 1985

p.58   GNS, February 3, 1991.

p.60   GNS, July 3, 1988.

p.62   GNS, January 20, 1991.

p.64   GNS, May 3, 1992.

p.66   GNS, August 6, 1989.

p.68   GNS, May 6, 1988.

p.70   GNS, September 8, 1985.

p.73   GNS, November 26, 1989.

p.77	GNS, March 4, 1984.
p.80	C-L, April 24, 1983.
p.83	C-L, December 4, 1983.
p.87	GNS, July 22, 1990.
p.89	C-L, December 4, 1983.
p.93	GNS, October 8, 1989.
p.96	GNS, April 29, 1990.
p.99	GNS, March 30, 1988.
p.102	GNS, September 1, 1991.
p.104	C-L, November 18, 1984.
p.107	GNS," February 4, 1990.
p.109	GNS, May 17, 1992.
p.111	GNS, October 7, 1990.
p.113	GNS, June 30, 1985.
p.116	GNS, October 13, 1985; October 20, 1985.
p.120	GNS, February 25, 1987.
p.122	GNS, March 1, 1992.
p.125	GNS, June 30, 1991.
p.127	GNS, January 7, 1990.
p.130	GNS, August 9, 1987.
p.133	GNS, July 24, 1994.
p.135	GNS, November 2, 1988.
p.137	GNS, September 28, 1988.
p.140	WP, August 16, 1973.
p.144	GNS, April 6, 1988.
p.146	GNS, April 2, 1989.
p.148	WP, March 17, 1974.
p.152	C-L, December 2, 1984.
p.156	C-L, December 9, 1984.
p.159	GNS, August 5, 1990.
p.161	C-L, August 7, 1983.
p.164	GNS, November 15, 1987.
p.167	GNS, January 6, 1990.
p.169	GNS, October 9, 1988.
p.171	GNS, October 16, 1988.

p.173   GNS, April 24, 1988.

p.176   GNS, July 23, 1989.

Chapter Three: Tips for Enjoying Good Wine

p.181   GNS, March 23, 1988.

p.183   GNS, 1984, 1989, 1994.

p.186   GNS, September 16, 1987.

p.189   GNS, September 13, 1991.

p.191   GNS, September 3, 1989.

p.193   GNS, August 31, 1988.

p.195   GNS, March 15, 1992.

p.197   GNS, February 25, 1987.

p.199   GNS, March 16, 1988.

p.202   GNS, April 29, 1987.

p.204   WP, January 31, 1974.

p.209   GNS, May 21, 1991.

p.211   GNS, November 13, 1988.

p.213   GNS, September 17, 1989.

p.215   GNS, June 21, 1987.

p.217   GNS, October 21, 1988.

p.219   GNS, August 10, 1993.

p.221   GNS, July 30, 1989.

p.223   GNS, September 16, 1990.

p.225   WP, March 28, 1974.

p.230   GNS, December 13, 1987.

p.232   WP, December 27, 1973.

p.235   GNS, November 12, 1989.

p.237   GNS, August 3, 1988.

p.239   GNS, July 11, 1991.

p.241   GNS, October 28, 1990.

p.243   GNS, February 17, 1991.

p.245   GNS, April 13, 1988.

p.247   GNS, June 24, 1990.

p.249   GNS, October 19, 1988.

p.251   GNS, October 5, 1988.

Chapter Four: Finding the Humor in Wine

p.255   GNS, March 23, 1988.

p.258   GNS, October 18, 1987.

p.260   GNS, May 17, 1992.

p.263   GNS, July 9, 1989.

p.265   GNS, September 24, 1989.

p.267   GNS, October 29, 1991.

p.270   GNS, July 2, 1989.

p.272   GNS, January 26, 1992.

p.274   GNS, March 11, 1990.

Bibliography

Adams, Leon. *The Wines of America*. 4th ed. New York: McGraw-Hill, 1990.

Adlum, John. *Memoir of the Cultivation of the Vine in America and the Best Mode of Making Wine*. Facsimile Reprint of 1828 Original. Hopewell, N.J.: Booknoll Reprints, 1971.

Agostini, Hanna. *Robert Parker: Anatomie d'un Mythe: Portrait Non-Autorise*. Paris: Editions Scali, 2007.

Allen, H. Warner. *The Romance of Wine*. New York: Dover, 1971.

Anderson, Burton. *The Wine Atlas of Italy: A Travellers Guide to the Vineyards*. New York: Simon & Schuster, 1990.

Asher, Gerald. *The Pleasures of Wine: Selected Essays from* Gourmet Magazine. San Francisco: Chronicle Books, 2002.

———. *Vineyard Tales: Reflections on Wine*. San Francisco: Chronicle Books, 1996.

Barr, Andrew. *Wine Snobbery: An Exposé*. New York: Simon & Schuster, 1988.

Beradze, Merab. *Georgian Dishes*. Tblisi: Georgia Tourist Bureau, 2002.

Bernstein, Leonard S. *The Official Guide to Wine Snobbery*. New York: William Morrow, 1982.

Berry, Charles Walter. *In Search of Wine: A Tour of the Vineyards of France*. London: Sidgwick & Jackson, 1987.

Besh, John. *My New Orleans: A Cookbook*. Kansas City: McNeel, 2009.

———. *My Family Table: A Passionate Plea for Home Cooking*. Kansas City: McNeel, 2011.

Bourdain, Anthony. *A Cook's Tour*. New York: Bloomsbury, 2001.

———. *Anthony Bourdain's Les Halles Cookbook*. New York: Bloomsbury, 2004.

Broadbent, Michael. *The New Great Vintage Wine Book*. New York: Knopf, 1991.

Brook, Stephen. *Bordeaux: People, Power and Politics*. London: Mitchell Beazley, 2001.

Campbell, Ian. *Wayward Tendrils of the Vine*. London: Chapman & Hall, 1947.

Catena, Laura. *Vino Argentino: An Insider's Guide to the Wines and Wine Country of Argentina*. San Francisco: Chronicle Books, 2010.

Churchill, Creighton. *The Great Wine Rivers*. New York: Macmillian, 1971.

Conaway, James. *Napa: The Story of an American Eden*. Boston: Houghton Mifflin, 1990.

———. *The Far Side of Eden: New Money, Old Land, and the Battle for Napa Valley*. Boston: Houghton Mifflin, 2002.

Cossart, Noel. *Madeira: The Island Vineyard*. London: Christie's, 1984.

Craughwell, Thomas J. *Thomas Jefferson's Crème Brûlée*. Philadelphia: Quirk, 2012.

Crowe, Allison. *The Winemaker's Answer Book*. North Adams, Mass.: Storey Publishing, 2007.

Dallas, Philip. *Italian Wines*. London: Farber, 1989.

Darlington, David. *Angels' Visits: An Inquiry into the Mystery of Zinfandel*. New York: Holt, 1991.

Duijker, Hubrecht. *The Wine Atlas of Spain*. New York: Simon & Schuster, 1992.

Echikson, William. *Noble Rot: A Bordeaux Wine Revolution*. New York: Norton, 2004.

Ensrud, Barbara. *American Vineyards*. New York: Stewart, Tabori & Chang, 1988.

Faith, Nicholas. *Burgundy and Its Wines*. New York: Sterling, 2002.

———. *The Story of Champagne*. New York: Facts-On-File, 1989.

———. *The Winemasters: The Story behind the Glory and the Scandal of Bordeaux*. New York: Harper, 1978.

Fitzmorris, Tom. *Hungry Town: A Culinary History of New Orleans*. New York: Abrams, 2010.

Friedrich, Jacqueline. *Wine and Food Guide to the Loire*. New York: Holt, 1996.

Forbes, Patrick. *Champagne: The Wine, the Land and the People*. London: Gollancz, 1982.

Gabler, James. *Wine into Words: A History and Bibliography of Wine Books in the English Language*. Baltimore: Bacchus, 1985.

Garner, Michael and Paul Merrit. *Barolo: Tar and Roses—A Study of the Wines of Alba*. San Francisco: Wine Appreciation Guild, 1990.

Georgian Wine. Tblisi: Republic of Georgia Tourism Bureau, 1989.

Healy, Maurice. *Stay Me with Flagons: A Book about Wine and Other Things.* London: Michael Joseph, 1940.

Hewett, Edward and W. F. Axton. *Convivial Dickens: The Drinks of Dickens and His Time.* Athens, Ohio: Ohio UP, 1983.

Hyams, Edward. *Dionysus: A Social History of the Wine Vine.* New York: Macmillan, 1965.

Jacquelin, Louis, and Rene Poulain. *The Wines and Vineyards of France.* London: Hamlyn, 1962.

Johnson, Hugh. *Vintage: The Story of Wine.* New York: Simon & Schuster, 1989.

———. *How to Enjoy Wine.* New York: Simon & Schuster, 1985. VHS.

———. *Vintage: The History of Wine.* Directed by Michael Gill and Christopher Ralling. Malone Gill Productions/WGBH Boston, 1989. VHS.

———. *Wine: A Life Uncorked.* Berkeley: U of California P, 2006.

Joseph, Robert. *The Wine Lists.* Enfield: Guinness Books, 1985.

Kladstrup, Don and Petie Kladstrup. *Wine and War.* New York: Broadway Books, 2001.

Kurlansky, Mark. *The Basque History of the World.* New York: Waller, 1999.

Lesko, Leonard H. *King Tut's Wine Cellar.* Berkeley: U of California P, 1977.

Liebling, A. J. *Between Meals: An Appetite for Paris.* San Francisco: North Point, 1986.

Lynch, Kermit. *Adventures on the Wine Route.* New York: Farrar, 1988.

Macchione, Mikko. *Napoleon House.* New Orleans: Vissi d'Arte, 2006.

Mayson, Richard. *The Wines and Vineyards of Portugal.* London: Octopus, 2003.

McCoy, Elin. *The Emperor of Wine: The Rise of Robert M. Parker, Jr. and the Reign of American Taste.* New York: Ecco, 2005.

McGovern, Patrick. *Ancient Wine: The Search for the Origins of Viticulture.* Princeton: Princeton UP, 2003.

McInerney, Jay. *A Hedonist in the Cellar: Adventures in Wine.* New York: Knopf, 2006.

———. *The Juice: Vinous Veritas.* New York: Knopf, 2012.

McPhee, John. *La Place de la Concorde Suisse.* New York: Farrar, 1984.

Mendelsohn, Oscar. *Drinking with Pepys.* London: Macmillian, 1963.

Ministry of Culture of Moldova. *The Wine Road in Moldova.* Chisinau: Government Ministry of Culture and Tourism, 1994.

Molyneux-Berry, David. *The Sotheby's Guide to Classic Wines and Their Labels.* New York: Ballantine, 1990.

Nossiter, Jonathan. *Liquid Memory: Why Wine Matters.* New York: Farrar, Straus, Giroux, 2006.

Olney, Richard. *Yquem.* Boston: Godine, 1986.

Osborne, Lawrence. *The Accidental Connoisseur.* New York: North Point, 2004.

Paronetto, Lamberto. *Chianti: The Story of Florence and Its Wines.* London: Wine and Spirit Publishing, 1970.

Penning-Roswell, Edmund. *The Wines of Bordeaux.* New York: Stein and Day, 1971.

———. *The Wines of Bordeaux.* 5th ed. San Francisco: Wine Appreciation Guild, 1985.

Peynaud, Emile. *Knowing and Making Wine.* New York: Wiley, 1984.

———. *The Taste of Wine.* San Francisco: Wine Appreciation Guild, 1987.

Pinney, Thomas. *A History of Wine in America: From the Beginnings to Prohibition.* Berkley: U of California P, 1989.

Pratt, James Norwood. *The Wine Bibber's Bible.* San Francisco: 101 Productions, 1981.

Prial, Frank. *Wine Talk:* New York Times *Wine Columns.* New York: New York Times Books, 1978.

Ray, Cyril. *The Wines of Italy.* New York: McGraw-Hill, 1966.

Read, Jan. *Wines of the Rioja.* London: Sotheby, 1984.

Redding, Cyrus. *The History and Description of Modern Wines.* London: Henry G. Bohn, 1851.

Reichl, Ruth, ed. *History in a Glass: Sixty Years of Wine Writing from* Gourmet Magazine. New York: Modern Library, 2006.

———. *Remembrance of Things Paris: Sixty Years of Writing from* Gourmet Magazine. New York: Modern Library, 2004.

Robinson, Jancis. *Tasting Pleasure: Confessions of a Wine Lover.* New York: Viking 1997.

———. *The Great Wine Book.* New York: Morrow, 1982.

———. *The Oxford Companion to Wine.* 3rd ed. Oxford: Oxford UP, 2006.

———. *Vines, Grapes, and Wines: The First Complete Guide to Grape Varieties.* New York: Knopf, 1986.

Rosengarten, David, and Joshua Wesson. *Red Wine with Fish.* New York: Simon & Schuster, 1989.

Saintsbury, George. *Notes on a Cellar-Book.* New York: MacMillan, 1933.

Schaefer, Dennis. *Vintage Talk: Conversations with California's New Wine-makers.* Santa Barbara: Capra, 1994.

Schoenman, Theodore, ed. *Agoston Haraszthy: The Father of California Wine.* Santa Barbara: Capra, 1979.

Shand, P. Morton. *A Book of French Wines.* London: Jonathan Cape, 1963.

Silver, Julia Flynn. *The House of Mondavi: The Rise and Fall of an American Wine Dynasty.* New York: Gotham Book, 2007.

Simon, André L. *The Commonsense of Wine.* New York: Wine and Food Society, 1966.

——. *Wine in Shakespeare's Days and Shakespeare's Plays.* London: Curwen Press, 1964.

—— *Wines of the World.* New York: McGraw-Hill, 1967.

Small, Robert and Michelle Couturier. *Beverage Basics: Understanding and Appreciating Wine, Beer, and Spirits.* Hoboken, N.J.: Wiley, 2011.

Standage, Tom. *A History of the World in 6 Glasses.* New York: Walker, 2005.

Steinberger, Michael. *Au Revoir to All That: Food, Wine, and the End of France.* New York: Bloomsbury, 2009.

——. *The Wine Savant: A Guide to the New Wine Culture.* New York: Bloomsbury, 2013.

Stevenson, Tom. *Champagne.* London: Sotheby, 1986.

Taber, George. *In Search of Bacchus: Wanderings in the Wonderful World of Wine Tourism.* New York: Scribner, 2009.

——. *Judgment of Paris: California vs. France and the Historic 1976 Paris Tasting That Revolutionized Wine.* New York: Scribner, 2006.

Toddhunter, Andrew. *A Meal Observed.* New York: Knopf, 2004.

Turner, William. *A Book of Wines.* Reprint of 1568 Original. New York: Scholars' Facsimiles, 1941.

Wells, Patricia. *The Food Lovers Guide to Paris.* New York: Workman, 2014.

Wildman, Frederick S., Jr. *A Wine Tour of France: A Convivial Travel Guide.* New York: William Morrow, 1972.

The Wines of Bordeaux: A Video Guide. Directed by Jane Crawford. Michael Broadbent, Clive Coates, Robert M. Parker, Jr., Edmund Penning-Rowsell and Jancis Robinson. Lapham Productions, 1987. VHS.

The Wines of Burgundy. Directed by Jane Crawford. Michael Broadbent, Clive Coates, Anthony Hanson, Robert Joseph, and Robert M. Parker, Jr. New York: Abbeville Press/20-20 Productions, 1991. VHS.

Yapp, Robin. *Drilling for Wine.* London: Faber, 1988.

Younger, William. *Gods, Men, and Wine.* Cleveland: Wine and Food Society, 1966.

Yoxall, H.W. *The Wines of Burgundy.* New York: Stein and Day, 1968.

Wine Blogs

Many wine lovers now get more of their news from bloggers than from books or traditional newspaper columns. These blogs are often highly opinionated and disputatious and are not for everyone, but they are now an important focus for in-depth discussion of wines. Listed below are a flight of the most followed with their bloggers in parentheses.

1. AliceFeiring.com
2. DrVino.com (Tyler Coleman)
3. newyorkcorkreport.com (Lenn Thompson and Evan Dawson)
4. 1winedude.com (Joe Roberts)
5. sfgate.com (Joe Bonne)
6. terroirist.com (David White)
7. VinCibo.com (Craig Camp)
8. vinography.com (Alder Yarrow)
9. wineanorak.com (Jamie Goode)

One of the best online wine reports, "Vpour" by *New York Times* wine columnist Eric Asimov has been discontinued for the moment. Let us hope it returns.

Index

bottle opening, 189–90, 249–50, 260

bottles: color, 213–14; size, 70–72, 200, 215

Bottom Ten (worst wines), 258–59, 272

bouquet of wine, 66, 121, 197–98, 218, 247–48, 265

Bouzy Rouge, 94, 261

brandy, 47, 81, 208, 220

Brennan's (restaurant), 77–78, 160

Broadbent, Michael, 96, 113, 197

Brunello, 168, 169

Buena Vista Winery, 31, 34–35, 73

Bulgaria, wines of, 14, 148–51

Bull's Blood, 151, 267

Bureau of Alcohol, Tobacco and Firearms (BATF), 200

Burgundy: Chateaux of, 74, 131, 195; with food, 232; grapes, 94, 137, 231; preference for, 116, 123; red, 24, 62, 158, 275; region, 97, 117–18, 173; white, 25, 143, 164–66, 203, 274

BV (Beaulieu Vineyards), 38, 74, 106, 196, 199, 206, 211

Bynum, Davis "Barefoot," 64–65

Cabernet: California, 57, 62, 181, 196, 237–38, 266; grape, 59, 125, 149, 171, 172, 205, 238; labels, 63, 86, 108, 126, 138, 271; wine, 11, 67, 104, 148, 149–50

Cabernet Franc, 237–38, 239, 240

Cabernet Sauvignon: grape, 54, 162, 171, 237, 238, 239; labels, 25, 134, 161, 173, 199, 240; wine, 25, 104, 106, 150, 156, 195

Caesar, Julius, 29, 37

Cafe Expresso, 152, 153. *See also* Peabody Hotel

Cahors (wine), 137–38

Cain Five, 25, 240

California wine: blends, 136, 138, 237–38; Cabernet, 57, 62, 181, 196, 199, 266; Chardonnay, 194, 203, 270, 271; Chenin Blanc, 143; of Lake County, 25, 239; in Los Angeles, 274–75; of Mendocino County, 112, 167; Muscat, 205, 206, 268; of Napa Valley, 111–12, 113–15, 117, 118–19, 167, 173–74, 240; Pinot, 24, 63, 137, 141, 173–75; of Sonoma County, 64, 74, 108, 138, 174, 238, 268; of Temecula Valley, 13, 45, 130–32; wine clubs, 200; winemakers of, 157, 211–12, 229, 230, 256. *See also* *individual winery names*

California Wine Institute, 238

Callaway (brand), 130–31, 194

Callaway, Eli, 130–31

Canada, wines of, 28, 73–74

Carmenère, 13–14, 139

Carmignano, 169–70

Carneros, 173

cartoons on wine, 27, 67, 255–57, 258

Cassis, 235

cava. *See* Freixenet

Cecil, William A. V., 144, 145

cellars: books on, 58, 183–85; brands, 118, 174, 238, 240, 242; construction of, 34, 77, 78–79; famous, 43–45, 96, 145; stock of, 19, 41, 62–63, 120

Celtic wine, 51, 239, 267, 268

Chablis, 36, 37, 38, 67, 232

Chambertin, 41, 138, 261

Champagne: books on, 184, 260; with food, 36, 49, 234, 263, 273; grapes, 244; producers, 48–49, 69, 74, 234, 267; region, 117, 220; sparkling, 142, 144, 207, 252; "still," 39, 93–94; tips on, 222, 249–50

Chang, Bernard, 105, 106

Charbonneau (grape), 14, 139

Chardonnay: with food, 105, 106, 108, 110, 270–71; grape, 38, 54, 93, 100, 162, 165, 232; producers, 25, 51, 65, 88, 104, 107, 166, 194, 240; wine, 37, 38, 63, 130, 134, 139, 175, 181–82, 197, 273

Charles Krug Winery, 49, 143, 206

Chasselas, 231, 234

Chastellux, Marquis de (General François Jean), 22, 23

Chateau (estate): Biltmore, 144–45, 194; d'Yquem, 15; Kirwan, 146–47; Lafite, 12; Latour, 25; Le Pez, 238; Mouton, 12; Musar, 58; Pontet-Canet, 12; St. Jean, 73

Chateau (wine): Ausone, 30; Biltmore, 145; Chevel Blanc, 237; Croizet-Bages, 20; de Saran, 94; Ducru-Beaucaillou, 154; d'Yquem, 41; Fetzer, 166; Filhot Sauternes, 106; Haut-Bages-Liberal, 20; Haut-Brion, 19, 74; Kirwan (Quirouen), 146–47; Lafite, 22, 106, 113, 239; Latour, 84; Margaux, 19, 41, 63, 124, 147; Moncontour, 142; Mouton, 239; Pontet-Canet, 20; Rausan, 22; Rieussec, 209; Souverain, 166; Suduiraut, 209

Chateauneuf, 63, 156, 256–57

Chateauneuf-du-Pape, 103, 228

Chenin Blanc, 63, 69, 122, 131, 134, 140–43

Cheval Blanc, 57, 63, 237

Chez l'Ami Jean, 61

Chez Philippe, 48–49, 83–86, 152, 153–55. *See also* Peabody Hotel

Chianti, 63, 160, 170, 171, 172

Chile, wines of, 13, 139, 208

chilling wine. *See* temperatures of wine

China, wines of, 12, 99–101, 102, 103, 244

Chroman, Nathan, 69

cider, 46–47, 268

Claiborne, Craig, 53–54

Claiborne Vineyards, 53–54

claret, 21, 23, 25, 146, 184

Cline Cellars, 242

Coastal Vines, 11, 24, 175

Cognac, 25

Commander's Palace, 57, 77

Conaway, James, 111–12

cookbooks, 10, 11, 243, 272–73

cooking with wine, 123–24, 236, 244

corks: problems with, 44, 191–92; removing, 249–50, 260; sniffing of, 187, 190; usage of, 13, 213

corkscrews, 153, 189, 202

Corley, Jay, 117–19

Coteaux Champenois, 93, 94

Coteaux du Layon, 122, 142–43

Cotes du Rhone, 49, 206

Crépy, 234

crust. *See* sediment in wine

crystals. *See* tartrate crystals

Cuvaison, 73, 270, 271
Czech Republic beers, 223–24

Daguin, Ariane, 210
Darlington, David, 11–12
decanters, 22, 153, 191, 203, 217–18, 273
decanting wine, 97, 191, 193, 194, 217
dessert wines, 13, 41, 136, 200, 211–12, 251; Constantia, 207; Chenin Blanc, 142; Jurancon, 61; Madeira, 80; Monbazillac, 141; Muscat, 133, 206–7, 267; Pacherenc de Vic Bilh, 123; Tamianka, 148; Tokay, 24, 31
doctoring wine, 235–36. *See also* spoilage
Dole, 231
Dom Pérignon (D.P.), 93–94, 199
Dom Ruinart, 94
Domaine Chandon, 74, 267
Doyle, Sir Arthur Conan, 24–25, 56
Dry Creek Winery, 40, 158
ducks, 85, 103, 105, 106, 152, 209, 210
Dyer, Bill, 240

earthquake, 274–75
Egypt, wines of, 58–59, 183
Eisenhower, Dwight David, 59
England, wines of, 47, 73, 147, 236, 244
enology schools, 13, 53, 130, 144, 161–63, 197
Entre-Deux-Mers, 38, 233
Ermitage, 231
Estrella River Winery, 104, 106

Faith, Nicholas, 112, 147, 184
fermentation: causes of, 214; process

of, 27, 28, 195, 219–20, 243, 252; results of, 81, 93, 110, 245, 247, 273
Fetzer (wine), 38, 88, 166, 271
Fetzer Winery, 51, 271
foie gras, 123, 154, 160, 209–10
Forman, Ric, 157, 158
France: black wine of, 137–39; Basque Country, 60–61, 242; Beaujolais of, 71, 156; Burgundy region, 173; cuisine of, 84–86, 88, 159–60, 209–10; Loire region, 36, 37, 140, 141, 144; Normandy, 47; Rhone Valley, 58, 130, 167, 256; Southern regions, 116, 207, 242; wine culture of, 122; wines of, 22, 37, 40, 175, 261, 267. *See also individual wine names*
Frank, Konstantin, 14, 206
Franklin, Benjamin, 19–20, 80, 116
Franzia, Fred, 11, 158
fraud, 11, 15–16, 33–34
Freixenet, 20, 74, 84, 214
Fumé Blanc, 65, 104, 105, 106, 131, 133

Galatoire's (restaurant), 77
Gallatin, Albert, 42
Galleano Winery, 13
Gallo, 69, 139, 241
Gamay, 157–58, 231
Gamza, 148, 149, 150
Gannett News Service, 3, 9, 277, 280–83
Georgia (country), 14, 97, 98
Germany: beers of, 223; regions of, 21, 234; wines of, 59, 63, 84, 200, 206, 262; wineries of, 182, 214
Gewurztraminer, 69, 109, 134, 149, 206

Jefferson, Martha, 43

Jefferson, Thomas: advice of, 3, 13, 46–47, 203, 250; cellar of, 43–45, 204, 207; favorite wines of, 26–27, 41, 122, 160, 168, 169–70, 209; health of, 42, 109; as wine expert, 19, 116–17, 164, 218, 245; writings of, 14, 21, 39, 40, 93, 225, 226, 229, 268. *See also* Monticello

Johnson, Hugh: as expert, 14, 127, 242; *How to Enjoy Wine*, 97; *A Life Uncorked*, 4, 185; *Vintage*, 97–98; *World Atlas of Wine*, 148, 184

Jordan Winery, 51, 86, 106

Joseph, Robert, 97, 260

Joseph Phelps Vineyard (Phelps Insignia), 56, 136, 167, 212

Judge Dee (character), 99, 100, 106

Juergens, John, 66–67

Jurancon, 60–61

K.C. Joe's (restaurant), 107–8

Kien, Huynh, 102–3

King Estate Winery, 175

Kir, 235–36

Koch, William "Bill," 15–16

Kublai Khan (restaurant), 104–6

Kurlansky, Mark, 61

La Crema, 110, 174

L.A. County Fair, 69

L.A. Fair International, 13, 185

La Tartine (bistro), 123

La Rotisserie du Beaujolais, 124

labels: collection of, 58, 160, 185, 224, 258; design of, 100, 142, 165, 167,

230, 256; jargon of, 24, 66–67, 81, 199–200, 220; removal of, 182

Lacryma Christi, 29

Lake, David, 132

Lake County, 25, 239

Langtry, Lillie, 25, 239

laurel wine, 103

Le Pergole Torte, 170

Lebanon, wines of, 58, 176

L'Ecluse (bistro), 124

lees, 131, 194, 220

legs of wine, 67, 197, 252, 256, 265

Lesko, Leonard, 58–59, 183

Lichine, Alexis, 96, 116, 148

Life Uncorked, A (Johnson), 4, 185

Llano Estacado winery, 133

Louie, Michelle Chao, 99, 100

Mad Dog 20-20 (MD/20-20), 199, 258–59

Madeira, 21, 22, 30, 39, 41, 80–82, 139

Madiran, 61

Malbec: grape, 14, 137, 172, 237, 238, 239, 240; wine, 138, 267

Mamertine, 29

Manseng grape, 61

Mansson, Per-Henrick, 62

Massy, Luc, 230–31

Mataro, 241–42

Matthews, Thomas, 62–63

Mavrud, 148, 149

McInerney, Jay, 4

McPhee, John, 111, 230–31

mead, 27–28

Medoc (region), 12, 96

Meilleur Pot (bistro), 124

Mendocino County, 112, 167

Meridien New Orleans. *See* Henri

Meritage, 25, 239, 240

Merlot: grape, 138, 237, 238, 239, 240; wine, 63, 65, 68, 108

metrics. *See* measuring wine

Meursault, 25, 57, 106, 164–66

microclimates, 11–12, 130, 173, 174

Mission grapes, 13–14, 32, 34

Mississippi State University, 13, 53, 161–63

Mister Greasy, 91–92

Moët et Chandon, 74, 94, 249, 260–61

Moldova, 14

Monbazillac, 141

Mondavi (brand): Cabernet, 138, 195; Chenin Blanc, 143; Moscato d'Oro, 30, 206, 211; Opus One, 136; Pinot Noir, 63, 88, 174. *See also* Robert Mondavi Winery

monks, 27–28, 78, 93

Montepulciano, 122, 169

Monticello, 39, 43, 44–45, 116, 168

Monticello West ("Monticello Cellars"), 117–19

Montrachet, 25, 41, 165, 232

Morellet, Abbe, 19

Moscato, 30, 205–6, 211. *See also* Muscat

Mosel, 5, 59, 63, 214

Moselle, wines of, 141, 142, 234

Mourvèdre, 241–42

Mousseux, 20, 142

Mr. K's (restaurant), 164–66

Mulate's (restaurant), 50–51

mulled wine, 236

Muscadet (region), 37

Muscadet: grape, 140, 205; wine, 37, 56, 86, 194, 232, 264, 272

Muscadine, 161–62, 205

Muscat: Canelli, 49, 133; grape, 100, 149, 208, 264; wine, 30, 136, 204–8, 211

Muscatel, 148, 204, 205, 255

Napa: An American Eden (Conaway), 11–12

Napa Valley, 111–12, 113–15, 117, 118–19, 173–74

Napoleon House (restaurant), 87–88

Nebbiolo, 168, 225–29

New Yorker, The, 11, 67, 230, 255, 258

New Zealand, wines of, 13, 125–26

nitrogen, 191, 216

Nobilo, 125–26

"nose" of wine. *See* bouquet of wine

Notes on a Cellar-Book (Saintsbury), 4, 184

Nouveau Beaujolais, 86, 152, 154, 156–57, 158

Nouveau Gamay, 157–58

Oregon, wines of, 24, 74, 173, 174, 175

oxidation, 171, 245

Oxymel, 28

Palladin, Jean-Louis, 48, 49

Palumbo, Daniel, 83–84, 86

Parker, Robert M., Jr., 12, 96, 127, 204

Pasteur, Louis, 215, 219, 245

Peabody Hotel, 48, 49, 83–86, 152–55

Penning-Rowsell, Edmund, 147, 184

Peppoli, 172

Pernand-Vergelesses, 232

Persian wines, 12, 59, 167

Pete's Pool Room, 89–92

Petit Verdot, 239–40

Petite Sirah, 64, 264, 268–69

Peynaud, Emile, 128, 184

pH. *See* acidity of wine

Phelps, Joseph. *See* Joseph Phelps Vineyard

Phillips, Alan, 119

Pierce's Disease, 13, 54–55, 163

Pilsner Urquell, 223–24

Pinot Blanc, 49, 62

Pinot Grigios, 175

Pinot Gris, 160, 175

Pinot Noir: Barefoot, 65; Bon Climat, 158, 168; Coastal Vines, 11, 24, 175; grape, 36, 74, 93, 94, 145, 162; Mondavi, 88; wine, 63, 110, 126, 137, 173–75

plum wine, 99, 103

Pomerol (region), 12, 96

Pomino, 160

Pommard, 84, 136

Pontchartrain Hotel, 77

Pontet-Canet, 12, 20, 25

Port wine, 25, 69, 146, 168, 268, 273

Portugal, wines of, 43, 82, 194, 204, 207, 226, 274. *See also* vinho verde

Pouilly-Fuissé, 38, 186, 233

Pouilly-Fumé, 38, 84, 233

Prial, Frank, 4, 184, 241

price of wine, 68, 150–51, 165, 172, 174

Prohibition, 13, 108, 148, 205

pronunciation,143

Pulenta Winery, 175

Puligny-Montrachet, 56, 106

Purvis, James "Pete," 90, 92

Quady Essencia, 136, 268

Quincy (brand), 38, 123, 233

Quinta do Noval, 25, 168

Rancho California, 130

Republic of Georgia. *See* Georgia

Restaurant "A," 102–3

resveratrol, 110, 195–96

Rhone (wine), 167, 196, 241–42

Rhone Rangers, 241, 242

Rib Room (restaurant), 78–79

Rice, William "Bill," 8–9

rice wine, 100, 103, 106, 243, 244

Riesling: with food, 160; grape, 125; preference for, 131, 206; producers of, 134, 161, 162, 212; wine, 34, 100, 132, 234

Rikat, 148, 149

Rioja (wine), 122, 128, 168, 177, 181

Rkatsiteli ("R-Katz"), 14

Robert Mondavi Winery, 64, 118, 174–75, 266. *See also* Mondavi

Robinson, Jancis, 3, 126, 185, 230, 241

Rodenstock, Hardy (Meinhard Goerke), 15

Roman wines, 28, 29–30, 58, 137, 165, 213, 243

rosé wines, 5, 51, 132, 166, 242

Rueda, 128, 273

rum, 28, 41, 42, 268

Russian River Valley Winegrowers, 24

Rutherford Hill, 119, 237

Sainte Genevieve (winery), 133, 134

Saintsbury (brand), 63, 173

Saintsbury, George, 4, 184, 185

Samos, wine of, 45, 207